The Wild Bl

GRAHAM COSTER was born in 1960 in Croydon, whose famous airport saw Britain's first commercial passenger flights between the wars, and where he grew up going to every Biggin Hill Air Fair since the age of six. He read English at Cambridge, a city surrounded by former Second World War bomber airfields, and within easy reach of the Imperial War Museum's aircraft collection at Duxford and the USAF's annual Air Fête at Mildenhall, both regular haunts of his while living and working in Cambridge as Assistant Editor of Granta. He is the author of one novel, *Train, Train*, and a travel book, *A Thousand Miles From Nowhere*, which was shortlisted for the 1996 Thomas Cook Award. He now lives in East London beneath the flight path to London City Airport.

The
Wild Blue Yonder

THE PICADOR BOOK OF AVIATION

Edited and introduced by
Graham Coster

PICADOR

First published 1997 by Picador

This edition published 1999 by Picador
an imprint of Macmillan Publishers Ltd
25 Eccleston Place, London SW1W 9NF
Basingstoke and Oxford
Associated companies throughout the world
www.macmillan.co.uk

ISBN 0 330 39055 4

1 3 5 7 9 8 6 4 2

A CIP catalogue record for this book is available from
the British Library.

Typeset by SetSystems Ltd, Saffron Walden
Printed and bound in Great Britain by
Mackays of Chatham plc, Chatham, Kent

Contents

Introduction ix

H. G. Wells – *Mr Butteridge's First Flight* 1

Graham Wallace – *Alcock and Brown over the Atlantic* 7

V. M. Yeates – *Rumpties* 12

Cecil Lewis – *Air Observer at Amiens* 15

W. B. Yeats – *'An Irish Airman Foresees His Death'* 24

A. Harry Griffin – *Happy Landing on Helvellyn* 25

Captain W. E. Johns – *Biggles Shoots the Falls* 28

Beryl Markham – *West With the Night* 35

Hanna Reitsch – *Flying Indoors* 42

G. L. Steer – *Guernica* 49

Stephen Spender – *'The Landscape Near An Aerodrome'* 61

Antoine de St-Exupéry – *The Elements* 63

Richard Hillary – *Of Crashes* 75

John Gillespie Magee – *'High Flight'* 76

Paul Nash – *The Personality of Planes* 77

Paul Richey – *The Battle of France* 82

Elizabeth Bowen – *Love in the Blitz* 92

Don Charlwood – *Lancaster Navigator* 97

Randall Jarrell – *'Eighth Air Force'* 107

Randall Jarrell – *'A Front'* 108

Roald Dahl – *The Battle of Athens* 109

Guy Gibson – *The Möhne Dam* 116

John Pudney – *'The Ratio'* 126

John Pudney – *'The Siege of Malta'* 127

Samuel Hynes – *Landscape; Open Cockpit; Solitude* 131

Joseph Heller – *Milo Minderbinder* 134

Martha Gellhorn – *The Black Widow* 143

Charles Berlitz – *The Bermuda Triangle* 153

Alexander Frater – *Empire Flying Boat* 159

John J. McDonald – *Howard Hughes and the Spruce Goose* 161

Chuck Yeager and Leo Janos – *Breaking the Sound Barrier* 169

Tom Wolfe – *The Right Stuff* 183

Ann and John Tusa – *The Berlin Airlift* 198

Stanley Williamson – *The Munich Air Disaster* 212

Peter George – *Dr Strangelove* 230

Nicholas Tomalin – *The General Goes Zapping Charlie Cong* 235

Frank Snepp – *The Fall of Saigon* 243

Julian Barnes – *Fear of Flying* 252

Craig Raine – '*Flying to Belfast, 1977*' 256

Brian Calvert – *Concorde at Mach 2* 258

Colonel Jim Wadkins – *Lockheed SR-71 'Blackbird':
The World's Fastest Plane* 260

V. S. Naipaul – *Little Bits of Africa on Me* 262

Bill Buford – *Turin Soccer Charter* 263

Nicholson Baker – *Ventilation Nozzles* 269

Permission acknowledgements 275

Introduction

Thanks to aeroplanes, we are never alone. We might seek out the loneliest moorland, the barrenest desert, the most isolated mountain-top – a refuge from which we can scan every horizon and, even in the late twentieth century, see not a soul, not a trace of modern mechanical civilization, hear not a murmur of human activity. But then, inevitably, the peace will be broken. It might be the thunderous flash of an RAF Tornado arrowing through a valley on low-level NATO exercises; or the reverberant boom of a Hercules transport; or it might merely be the level distant drone of an airliner, or the lawnmower buzz of a private Cessna. The air is full. Wherever we are in the world, if we want to know how far our civilization has reached the only direction to look is up.

Powered flight is almost, but not quite, as old as our century – and so is its literature. Seafaring we can read back through history to the ancient narratives of Jason and the Argonauts and Homer's *Odyssey*. When God sent floods to inundate the world, Noah built a boat. Great battles like Trafalgar were won at sea. Nineteenth-century novelists like Herman Melville and Joseph Conrad took the oceans for their landscape. Humankind has been putting to sea for as long as humankind. But aviation is different. It lacks a proper mythological context. Icarus was a birdman, not an aviator. There are no aeroplanes in Greek myth, or in the Bible, or in Shakespeare, or in the Napoleonic Wars, or in the Victorian novel. Leonardo da Vinci may have imagined helicopters – but not until the Wright brothers took off at Kittyhawk in 1903 did men manage to fly, and thus the story of aviation is also the story of the twentieth century.

It is surprising, nevertheless, how infrequently such a quantum leap in the experience of humankind has inspired the century's writers. Let us continue our roll-call: no flying in the work of James

Joyce, or D. H. Lawrence, or Malcolm Lowry, or in the poetry of
T. S. Eliot. Amongst Nobel Prizewinners for Literature, only William
Faulkner showed an interest in aviation, to the extent of purchasing
his own plane – and yet that interest is virtually absent from his
letters, and spawned only a couple of short stories and one lesser
novel, *Pylon*, about the inter-war barnstormers. The century's most
characteristic contribution to literature, it has been argued, is the
genre of the travel book – and yet there appears to be just a single
work devoted to air travel. The sea, meanwhile, continues to inspire
literary attention, with nautical travel books favoured by Jonathan
Raban, Tristan Jones and Gavin Young, and even modern Booker
Prizewinners like William Golding and Barry Unsworth attracted to
the historical seafaring romance. There are plenty of airmen in the
modern novel – from García Márquez to William Boyd; plenty of
airline flights, too – from Anne Tyler to Saul Bellow; but over-
whelmingly they are incidental, perfunctory, subsidiary, backdrop
rather than foreground. This is not to say that no one has written
well and transcendently about flying – many have, and as many as
possible are selected here – but if we are looking for aviation as the
subject of extended imaginative attention in words, then often the
best writing has been by the amateur, in both senses of the word. A
scene here, a modest memoir there: flying has crept into modern
literature at the margin, rather than been seized as a subject.

Why? Perhaps, first of all, because aviation has developed so
quickly, too fast for it ever to become a stable fact of life, for us to
put our finger on its significance before it has moved on again.
H. G. Wells' characteristically jaunty evocations of the pioneer
flyers aside, there is virtually no graphic and developed writing
about the beginnings of powered flight – but then, only a decade
after the Wright brothers managed a few precious yards off the
ground, Fokker Triplanes and SE5As were fighting air battles above
the Western Front. Thirty years later, and the first jet aircraft were
already flying. And then, within two years of a world war fought
mostly at air speeds of around 300 m.p.h., a man flew faster than
the speed of sound. Where, as recently as the seventies, aerial
bombardment meant a B-52 excreting dozens of bombs to waste a

whole Vietnamese landscape, a mere twenty years' advance sees the next major conflict, the Gulf War, redefining bombing as a stealth fighter, invisible to radar, creeping in low for the precise laser-guided elimination of a television mast. In 1939 passenger air travel meant five days in a flying boat from Southampton to Durban for just sixteen wealthy elect. In 1996 four hundred people can fly from London to Australia in twenty hours. Flying has changed too fast for us ever to get used to it – it has never become an institution. And, like the comparably swift computerization of our daily lives – just forty years from Alan Turing's research to the laptop and the Internet, a lightning revolution – the benefit of such progressive technology, indeed its whole point, is that it allows you to take it for granted. Airliners, says Paul Theroux, 'are like seven-league boots: I could be in New Zealand or Easter Island tomorrow'. Aboard the airline flight that constitutes the opening scene of Don DeLillo's novel *Players*, the cabin lights go dim for the passengers to watch the movie. 'It is as though they are realizing for the first time', writes DeLillo, 'how many systems of mechanical and electric components, what exact management of stresses, power units, consolidated thrust and energy it has taken to reduce their sensation of flight to this rudimentary tremble.' Modern flight is supposed to make the wondrous everyday: passengers on Concorde tend to be struck less by the thrill of travelling faster than a speeding bullet than by how cramped the passenger cabin is.

But there is another reason why flight itself – superficially such an obviously poetic experience – has so seldom given rise to poetry. It is an oddly compartmentalized, one-way-glassed phenomenon. For those on the ground, the plane is the unreachable, anonymous speck up in the clouds. For the aviator, the earth below is a diminished, detached, Lilliputian ant-kingdom. This exalted perspective has, of course, provided one of the commonest clichés of writing about flying: the airliner banking on its final approach before touchdown, and the pensive passenger gazing out of the window on the new country below, pregnant with destiny and secrets. But the cliché illustrates how flight tends to offer static, relativistic perspectives – contrasts, ironies – rather than dramatic

interaction. An aeroplane is never a floating home or society, as
a ship is – or at least not for long enough. A boat's voyage has a
novelistic slowness, comprehends the passage of months, even years.
A plane is aloft for merely hours.

The poetry of flying, in particular, is determined by these framed,
frozen panoramas: either the pictorial or the personal. Aviation
poems are, therefore, for the most part either landscape poetry or
metaphysical poetry. Stephen Spender's 'The Landscape Near an
Aerodrome', for example – written in the earliest days of passenger
airline flight before the anticipatory final approach had coarsened
into cliché – uses the Futuristic image of the sleek, miraculously
modern airliner juxtaposed with the backdrop of satanic mills and
glowering church as ironic criticism of this benighted, decadent
world of obsolete industry and organized religion. In Spender's
poem 'airliner' is a word that has not yet lost poetic resonance.
There it is spelt as two words, 'air liner', as though the poet was
having to find an image to connote this luxurious floating phenomenon. Not an ocean liner, but an air liner. It is the first instance
of the airliner being proposed as a positively civilizing influence.

As for the primeval urge of earthbound man to fly, any number
of texts have developed the general notion of casting off the pull of
gravity and earthly ties into vaguely mystical metaphors of self-help
and fulfilling your dreams. Even a serious novel like John Berger's
G juxtaposes the simultaneous narratives of the Italian aviator Geo
Chavez's pioneering flight across the Alps and his eponymous hero's
determined seduction of a hotel chambermaid, linking sex, aspira-
tion and courage in an extended metaphorical illustration of the
claim that 'flying is just like anything else'. But at least such
glutinous parables of spiritual flight as William Wharton's Birdy
and Richard Bach's Jonathan Livingston Seagull have left aeroplanes
out of it, and Erica Jong's Fear of Flying forgets about airliners after
the first few pages.

Those who actually fly planes to the limits of what American
military pilots have traditionally dubbed 'the wild blue yonder' –
fliers like Antoine de St-Exupéry – are more rigorous in their
metaphysics, because death is always a factor of their experiences,

simultaneous and equal with any prospect of enhanced life. John Gillespie Magee was a Canadian fighter pilot who was killed in 1942 flying a Spitfire – R. J. Mitchell's classic fighter that offered, for its time, an exhilarating manoeuvrability – and his exultant sonnet is a truly transcendent paean to high flight, and the unearthly elevation of the flier.

It is indeed the Second World War that divides our century of aviation literature in two. Until the last war, flying was primarily and essentially a *solitary* experience. It is a further reason why none of our major writers in the first half of the century thought to write in any way about this phenomenon: it was simply outside their experience. Aviators were a select, small bunch, remote as field officers in British India. The only way to travel by air in the early days was to pilot yourself. These were the only people who could report on the experience, and most of them – Cecil Lewis and Beryl Markham honourably excepted – were pragmatic, sternly unwhimsical aviators, not writers. Sir Alan Cobham's *Four Thousand Miles in a Flying Boat* is a remarkable story of the navigation of the globe in an open-cockpit biplane amphibian, taking in forced landings in African jungle and touchdowns on water where no seaplane had previously alighted – but it is a remarkably anodyne book. Charles Lindbergh's *Spirit of St Louis* is as undistinguished as literature as his transatlantic flight was epochal.

Throughout this era, from the time of Cecil Lewis's service in the Royal Flying Corps at the Somme to Antoine de St-Exupéry's disappearance on a reconnaissance flight in 1944, writing about flying was writing about being utterly alone – bereft of radio contact, before the invention of radar, in the freezing open cockpit of a flimsy contraption made out of fabric, wood and wires: it was to write about one's isolation from one's fellow men, about the peace or terror of loneliness, and about a very bald confrontation with mortality.

A great deal of the more journeyman writing about flying, and particularly that of military reminiscence, is characterized by a chin-up gruffness and gung-ho spirit, and the slightly complacent patriotism that creeps into the last line of Paul Nash's whimsical essay. Even H. E. Bates's *Stories of Flying Officer X.*, exceedingly popular in their day, and much of the earlier sections of Guy Gibson's autobiography, seem today sadly dated in their chirpy stoicism. A modern sensibility would not want the lid kept so tight on emotion and frank confusion. But the modern voice that I have tried to seek out in all the pieces in this anthology – sceptical, agnostic, inclined to doubt rather than to certainty, and to disgust at war's destructiveness rather than to glory in its epic pageantry, unrhetorical and existentially uninsulated, neither sentimental nor sententious – is there even in the early writings of the century. There is a Zen-like starkness about V. M. Yeates's hero, Tom, wrestling with an unflyable 'Rumpty' in training for the First World War, or about Beryl Markham alone above the Atlantic, faced with a suddenly empty fuel tank. Anyone who has seen *M*A*S*H** will recognize Yeates's precociously sardonic wit, while Markham's ruminations are as coolly puzzled as Joan Didion's: both pieces pit single human beings against themselves, with the assistance of thousands of feet of altitude to point the definitive, rarefied trial.

But even as St-Exupéry was flying his last mission over the Mediterranean the character of flying was changing almost to its opposite. Fighter pilots in the Second World War – the elite aristocracy of Peter Townsend, Douglas Bader and Adolf Galland – had been the knights of the sky, aquiline and even chivalrous towards their foe, aerial combat a kind of honourable jousting, and above all the preserve, still, of the individualist. With the advent of the heavy bomber, however, requiring a crew of between seven and fourteen men, from the bombardier in the nose to the tail-gunner at the rear, flying became for the first time a *group* activity, and its human experiences assumed a dramatic configuration. In all the writing about aviation there are more memoirs by erstwhile Lancaster pilots, or Flying Fortress navigators or Halifax bomb-aimers, than any other kind of reminiscence or history. Partly, of course, this is because so many men flew with Bomber Command or the American Eighth Air Force – more than 55,000 men were lost on RAF bombing missions. But it must also be because these memoirs

– including Don Charlwood's magnificent *No Moon Tonight*, one of the finest books about flying in any age – were written to commemorate people, individually treasurable comrades.

Since the end of the war the moral audit of Bomber Command's achievement has been prolonged and controversial. But while posterity has tended to mythicize by extremes, from the clean-scrubbed *Boy's Own* hero of Dambuster Guy Gibson to the firestorm that destroyed Dresden when the war was already nearly won, the extreme fortitude of the bomber crews themselves is ungainsayable – lumbering across Europe through the night for hour after icy hour, to be picked off in desperate numbers by the German night fighters and anti-aircraft batteries. Where *West with the Night*'s and St-Exupéry's disoriented, irresolute individuals are undergoing a self-inflicted, even glamorous challenge, with no consequence outside their own personal fate, the bomber squadrons' dramas are infinitely moving tales of dependency, responsibility and mutuality: where a navigator's single map-reading error, a pilot's momentary inattention or merely the random ill luck of an unexpected change in the wind can consign their every colleague to helpless death.

But this last development in aviation – the hegemony of the bomber – portended a radical modification of everyday life. In the words of Richard Eberhart's poem:

> You would think the fury of aerial bombardment
> Would rouse God to relent; the infinite spaces
> Are still silent. He looks on shock-pried faces.
> History, even, does not know what is meant.

In 1916 bombing meant Cecil Lewis leaning out of his cockpit to toss a single cookie over the side; at that time the worst horror of war – reserved for the enlisted soldier only, far away from the civilian community – was the attritional slaughter of the trenches. The Second World War, in raising aerial bombardment to infernal proportions, turned our worst horror of war into an indiscriminate threat from above, from the air – the one part of our world from which, even now out on our tranquil mountain-top, we are unable

to hide. Early in the war, when *The Heat of the Day* is set, Elizabeth
Bowen charts the fundamental shift in consciousness brought about
by the first air raids. When anyone, but anyone, could be killed in
their next waking moment, even in their own home, by an explosive
device falling suddenly out of the sky, then life, Bowen shows,
assumed a hectic, hedonistic rashness. It is an aeroplane, droning
overhead with its inevitably fateful cargo, that quite simply causes
her trysting couple to fall in love.

As the war went on, aerial bombing was to become yet more
ferocious: it was partly the fear of renewed bombardment, hinted
at in the final pages of her last novel, *Between the Acts*, that moved
Virginia Woolf to end her life. Eventually a single B-29 Superfortress
bomber, 'Enola Gay', was capable of precipitating the end of the
war and causing the deaths of up to 100,000 citizens of Hiroshima
in a single flight. And by the time of the 'box-bombing' or carpet-
bombing campaign of 'Rolling Thunder' instituted by Lyndon
Johnson in the Vietnam War – when, in its ultimate escalation,
squadrons of giant B-52s would fly in from Guam to systematically
pulverize or defoliate segments of the North Vietnamese landscape
– no one, it seems, was writing at any length about the aviation
itself. By now there was little interest in the medium, whether a
B-52 or an F-111; only in the message – the devastation visited on
the land below. In the most graphic account of the conflict, Michael
Herr's *Dispatches*, these 'Arclight' missions are accorded just a few
lines:

> From the centre of the earth there is a tremor that shakes
> everything, running up through my legs and body, shaking my
> head ... The bombs would release at 18,000 feet and the planes
> would turn and fly back to Udorn or Guam. Dawn seems to last
> until late morning, dusk falls at four. Everything I see is blown
> through smoke, everything is on fire somewhere. It doesn't
> matter that memory distorts; every image, every sound comes
> back out of smoke and the smell of things burning.

Technology has overcome nature with such awesome, overkilled
firepower that no one is interested in a B-52's flying capabilities or

the interaction of its crew. You cannot see the aeroplane for the explosions.

There is a certain irony that the plane that dropped the atom bomb, the Boeing B-29, has escaped notoriety, unlike the B-52 Stratofortress or BUFF ('Big Ugly Fat Fuck') as its crews called it. The B-52 was designed as America's first nuclear bomber – a role it plays in *Dr Strangelove*'s dystopian vision of apocalypse with a disturbingly glamorous beauty – and it joins the few models of aircraft to have achieved a genuinely demonic anthropomorphism, along with the German Stuka dive-bomber, and briefly the 'unpleasant' (meaning homicidally effective) Argentine Pucará, in the disgusted judgement of the BBC's Falklands reporter Brian Hanrahan, who counted all the Sea Harriers out and counted them all back. The design history of the B-52, however, was contiguous with Boeing's development of the 747, the famous 'jumbo jet' whose huge capacity democratically opened up the world to mass inter-continental air travel. Seen in flight, with its immensely long, drooping wings, its eight engines pouring black smoke and its ponderous, leaning quittance of the runway – a kind of black metal condor – the B-52 has an undeniably sinister charisma. But, a mere lump of metal, it stands condemned by the historical role the military strategists chose for it.

And even though the pendulum has since swung again, and aerial bombing has, since the Gulf War, been newly approved, almost admired, as a surgical, forensic method of taking out pinpointed objectives (or such is the theory), it is probably true to say that the biblical fear of destruction from the heavens remains in the psyche, a postmodernist neurosis of fragmentation and the potential for breakdown, and our abiding apprehension of apoca-lypse – Thomas Pynchon's *Gravity's Rainbow* its classic literary articulation. As long as aircraft are up in the sky above us, that sky will always seem hauntingly open.

Perhaps the B-52 has also been written out of literature because, in a banal sense, it was historically nothing new, but only an extreme refinement. What the literature of the Vietnam War does fasten on to is the aviation technology that was being used for the

first time with significance in this conflict: the military helicopter –
the Hueys that fought a kind of guerrilla war of the air against the
ground-based guerrilla forces of the Vietcong. Nicholas Tomalin's
profile of the belligerent Texas general was the source for the
memorable scene in *Apocalypse Now!* of Colonel Kilgore's helicopter
posse floating in on a low attack to the strains of Wagner's 'The
Ride of the Valkyries' like a swarm of shimmering dragonflies. If
Coppola's film rather sensationalized the phenomenon, to deliberately beautiful effect, nevertheless the helicopter 'gunship', flitting,
darting and swoopingly elusive – and offering its most gung-ho
occupants the chance of virtually hand-to-hand combat – seems to
have been selected as the aerial symbol most in character with the
strangely friable, kaleidoscopic, diminished-attention-span texture
of this war as reported by its correspondents.

The helicopter was instrumental, too, in the last rites of American
participation in Vietnam: the evacuation from Saigon as the city
was about to fall to the North. As aviation design has advanced, it
has at certain times been able to offer up its new developments at a
timely moment to enable history to happen in a hitherto unfeasible
way. It was the air that saved Berlin in 1948 during the Soviet
blockade – but so slender was the capacity of the fledgeling air
cargo fleets of that era to transport the kinds of tonnage necessary
to relieve a huge city (no C-5 Galaxys or vast Antonovs such as now
fly aid into famine zones, but rather Lancaster derivatives like the
York, or the ubiquitous parcel-van of the skies, the DC-3 Dakota),
that, in their isolation of Berlin, the Soviets seem not to have
considered the possibility at all. A couple of years earlier, even, they
would probably have been right. Likewise, it was relief from the air
that saved the American Embassy community in Saigon – but had
their imprisonment occurred in 1948 they would not have got out.
South Vietnamese pilots fleeing in their air force's planes had
jettisoned their bombs over the airport and put the runways out of
action. This time the exodus would have to be vertical, straight out
of the embassy courtyard in downtown – but by 1975 the US had
giant Chinook supply helicopters able to operate from offshore
aircraft carriers. Frank Snepp did not set out in *Decent Interval* to

address himself to the subject of helicopters, but it was the helicopter that wrote the history described in his book's final sequences.

And in the destinies of individuals in history, the aeroplane has sometimes been instrumental. Neville Chamberlain's epitaph is that single, condemnatory image of him waving that piece of paper from Adolf Hitler – from the steps of the aircraft that has been able to rush him so precipitately home. For Matthius Rust, the only access to Moscow's Red Square was by light plane – so that's how a reckless young German eager to be world famous for five minutes fetched up there. The story of Rudolf Hess's last flight, however, crash-landing his Messerschmitt Bf110 in the wilds of Scotland on a weird and still mysterious 'peace mission' to end the war, seems to have most in common with the extravagantly quixotic aviators that flit in and out of novels like Gabriel García Márquez's *One Hundred Years of Solitude* and Peter Carey's *Illywhacker*: an extraordinary attempt to influence the course of twentieth-century history by the magic-carpet approach. In neither of these novels is there any sustained, imaginative inhabitation of the aviator, but the type occurs frequently enough for us to adduce what his presence says about the magic-realist affinities of such fiction. The aeroplane, we might say, has come to function as the postmodern translation of Don Quixote's horse: the transport to romantic, capricious adventure.

It was just that magic-carpet dream that finally nailed the credibility of Gerd Heidemann, in his unmasking as the disseminator of the hoaxed Hitler diaries. His magazine paymasters, presented with his claim to have just returned from Paraguay with confirmation of the diaries' veracity from none other than Martin Bormann, enquired as to the means of his remarkably expeditious flight back to Germany. Learjet, came the reply. It was this envious appropriation of the trappings of the jet-set that did for him. Heidemann should have known his aeroplanes. A Learjet's maximum range, it was pointed out to him, would have caused it to disappear beneath the Atlantic hours offshore. Leeming and Hinkler's landing on the summit of Helvellyn, on the other hand, is certified historical fact, which affected history not at all. Their flight was means to nothing, just a wonderfully pointless end in itself.

All these escapades show aviation feeding the aspirations of would-be great men – just as it was the State Department 707 whisking Henry Kissinger around the Middle East that ought to take at least joint credit for the term 'shuttle diplomacy', a negotiating technique pushed to an exhausting and self-destructive extreme when Alexander Haig's efforts to avert the Falklands War caused him to be almost perpetually airborne between Buenos Aires, Washington and London for about a fortnight. After the assassination of John Kennedy in Dallas, Lyndon Johnson was sworn in as the new President aboard Air Force One.

But aviation has also been responsible for many of the twentieth century's most high-profile deaths. Glenn Miller, Buddy Holly, Patsy Cline, Jim Reeves, the Big Bopper, Richie Valens, Otis Redding, Stevie Ray Vaughan and several of the band Lynyrd Skynyrd – so many musicians lost in air crashes. Poland's General Sikorski, UN Secretary-General Dag Hammarskjöld, Pakistan's General Zia, Mozambique's `Samora Machel, India's Sanjay Gandhi and Prince Michael of Gloucester all died in air crashes. Orde Wingate presumed on air supply for the success of the Chindits' campaign in Burma – 'the only thing we didn't supply was the mud', recalled one Dakota pilot subsequently – but Wingate himself later died in a plane crash. So did sportsmen like the boxer Rocky Marciano, racing driver Graham Hill and most of Manchester United's adored 'Busby Babes' football team. Somehow we remember the manner of all these deaths, as we don't the deaths of, say, Albert Camus, Eddie Cochran and Marc Bolan in road accidents. We imagine the last moments, the fog, the ice, the engine failure. We remember a death by air as part of that individual's life: not an end, a punctuation, but an ending, a process – which is why all deaths in air crashes appear untimely, even supernaturally fated, as though their victims had been marked out.

The Australian war reporter Chester Wilmot and the Mexican novelist Jorge Ibarguengoitia aside, I cannot think of a notable writer who met their death in an aircraft. But almost all these high-profile fatalities were in private planes, light planes or helicopters, and writers mostly have neither the money to indulge their use or the peripatetic schedules that require it. The story of the Munich air disaster in which so many of the Busby Babes died is a very rare enactment of what characterizes our common premonition of aerial disaster: the crowded airliner falling out of the sky: another Lockerbie. It is the image with which Salman Rushdie begins *The Satanic Verses*. In *Staring at the Sun* Julian Barnes ruminates, half gravely, half flippantly, on the reasons behind that fear of flying so many people suffer from. Arthur Hailey's *Airport*, on the other hand, helpfully sets out for the benefit of the airport-novel reader a conscientiously researched digest of all the reasons why a bomb exploding in an airliner won't necessarily lead to universal oblivion. But maybe the claustrophobic *slowness* that Stanley Williamson's account evokes in the doomed take-off of the Manchester United Elizabethan is what is most secretly frightening. Flight is the most purely *lively* phenomenon: when gravity pulls a plane back into the ground it is *like* dying: like the life going out of a larger, living body, to leave a heavy, lifeless corpse.

There was no fear of flying, of course, when flying was only done by aviators. Nowadays, the cheapness and convenience – and safety – of modern air travel has made fliers of us all, though none of us knows the first thing about flying. Nor do we want to: we want to arrive, not travel, and break open our duty-frees. The sound barrier, says Chuck Yeager, 'was not in the sky, but in our knowledge and experience ...' These days the speed of modern airliners is not much less, and therefore so great that as well as jet-lag we suffer, like V. S. Naipaul's narrator in *A Bend in the River* arriving mentally as well as temporally almost before he has left, the severest culture shock. Enfranchised by the democracy of cheap passenger air travel, what we have chosen to become experts on is not flying but, banally, the subculture of its institutions. Just as the pub bore has his opinion on the merits of every airline's check-in procedure, so many self-consciously modern novels have taken an interest in airports and departure lounges. Somehow, though, you feel that the only reason Malcolm Bradbury and David Lodge can have chosen to try and deconstruct airports and stewardess argot as fascinating semiology is because these are in every other respect entirely devoid of interest. 'Airport novel' is a modern literary-critical term connoting a blandly undemanding narrative that need not engage the brain. But the experience of flying has certainly been turned on its head: where once it was inescapably solitary, now it is inescapably, suffocatingly social. Even stowing your tray table, as Nicholson Baker discovers, is to punch someone in the back.

As a result, when aviation is written about nowadays, it is mostly with the emphasis on its civic role. 'Barring mechanical failures, turbulent weather and terrorist acts,' declares one of the characters in Don DeLillo's novel *White Noise*, 'an aircraft travelling at the speed of sound may be the last refuge of gracious living and civilized manners known to man.' When the architect Sir Norman Foster was commissioned to make a television programme about his favourite building, he chose the Boeing 747: the jumbo jet. To describe a plane as a building, whatever the lesson of its classically clean lines for future architects, is to recognize, tacitly, just how much of our lives all of us spend actually inhabiting one. And while the B-52 and the Stuka have been demonized in our century, aeroplanes have far more often been hymned as aesthetic paragons and civilizing influences. Our only supersonic airliner, former pilot Brian Calvert reminds us, we always refer to with friendly confidentiality by her name: not *the* Concorde, or *a* Concorde, and never, though there is more than one, Concordes. Just: Concorde. When we see a Battle of Britain Spitfire above us at one of today's air displays, we see more than the pert outlines of those tapered wings and hear more than the liquid clatter of the Merlin engine. We apprehend a profoundly British myth of safety: in 1940, when Nazism menaced our security as never before or since, *aeroplanes saved us*. Roy Jacobsen is not a poet, published or unpublished, but when he became the only British individual to purchase an airworthy specimen of the RAF's amazing delta-wing former nuclear bomber, the Vulcan, its charismatically agile flight inspired him to salute, memorably, 'a giant manta ray wallowing around the sky'. Even the Rolling Stones' Keith Richards was once quoted grumbling about the number of 'Brabazon bands' he'd had the misfortune to listen to. When you know that the Bristol Brabazon was a British bid for the post-war transatlantic airliner market, of all-wooden construction and irredeemably underpowered, whose toiling roar only underlined the labour of hauling itself up off the runway, you see that the leathery rock star has actually been moved to a complex and esoteric poetic metaphor. No one, yet, has written even adequately, let alone transcendently, about an eighth wonder of the world like the Avro Vulcan, and in finding the right words, so far the amateurs are still coming up with the best lines.

But if there is one task for the late-twentieth-century writer, one subject to address and deficit to redress, before the aeroplane's century runs out, it is properly to articulate a special kind of lost grace and civility of the air. J. L. Carr, Ken Follett and Alan Sillitoe have all written novels about flying boats; one of Biggles' finest exploits was to shoot the high falls in one. Howard Hughes's Spruce Goose remains the biggest and most pharaonic aircraft ever built. Nowadays our planes take off from tarmac runways – which is why the whole idea of taking to the air from the buoyant sea has such an extra levity about it, and confers a kind of softness and protectiveness on all the craft that managed to slip from one element into the other. But there is just a page and a half, in Alexander Frater's travel book, about the most poetic flying boat of all, the Short Empire boat, that plied Imperial Airways' legendary route down through Africa along the course of the Nile, each craft personally named after empyrean goddesses like Ceres and Cassiopaeia. Here is half the world comprehended; a beguiling myth of beneficent empire; a true voyage for all those seafaring enthusiasts – but a vessel that dances the skies as well. And there is not one Empire boat preserved for posterity, so it will have to be words now. Let fly many more.

GRAHAM COSTER
London, 1997

H. G. Wells

Mr Butteridge's First Flight

It is curious how the final boom of flying began. It was like the coming of a breeze on a quiet day; nothing started it, it came. People began to talk of flying with an air of never having for one moment dropped the subject. Pictures of flying and flying machines returned to the newspapers; articles and allusions increased and multiplied in the serious magazines. People asked in monorail trains, 'When are we going to fly?' A new crop of inventors sprang up in a night or so like fungi. The Aero Club announced the project of a great Flying Exhibition in a large area of ground that the removal of slums in Whitechapel had rendered available.

The advancing wave soon produced a sympathetic ripple in the Bun Hill establishment. Grubb routed out his flying machine model again, tried it in the yard behind the shop, got a kind of flight out of it, and broke seventeen panes of glass and nine flower pots in the greenhouse that occupied the next yard but one.

And then, springing from nowhere, sustained one knew not how, came a persistent, disturbing rumour that the problem had been solved, that the secret was known. Bert met it one early-closing afternoon as he refreshed himself in an inn near Nutfield, whither his motor-bicycle had brought him. There smoked and meditated a person in khaki, an engineer, who presently took an interest in Bert's machine. It was a sturdy piece of apparatus, and it had acquired a kind of documentary value in these quick-changing times; it was now nearly eight years old. Its points discussed, the soldier broke into a new topic with, 'My next's going to be an aeroplane, so far as I can see. I've had enough of roads and ways.'

'They *tork*,' said Bert.

'They talk – and they do,' said the soldier. 'The thing's coming.'

'It keeps *on* coming,' said Bert; 'I shall believe when I see it.'

'That won't be long,' said the soldier.

The conversation seemed degenerating into an amiable wrangle of contradiction.

'I tell you they *are* flying,' the soldier insisted. 'I see it myself.'

'We've all seen it,' said Bert.

'I don't mean flap up and smash up; I mean real, safe, steady, controlled flying, against the wind, good and right.'

'You ain't seen that!'

'I *'ave*! Aldershot. They try to keep it a secret. They got it right enough. You bet – our War Office isn't going to be caught napping this time.'

Bert's incredulity was shaken. He asked questions, and the soldier expanded.

'I tell you they got nearly a square mile fenced in – a sort of valley. Fences of barbed wire ten feet high, and inside that they do things. Chaps about the camp – now and then we get a peep. It isn't only us neither. There's the Japanese; you bet they got it too – and the Germans! And I never knowed anything of this sort yet that the Frencheys didn't get ahead with – after their manner! They started ironclads, they started submarines, they started navigables, and you bet they won't be far be'ind at this.'

The soldier stood with his legs very wide apart, and filled his pipe thoughtfully. Bert sat on the low wall against which his motor-bicycle was leaning.

'Funny thing fighting'll be,' he said.

'Flying's going to break out,' said the soldier. 'When it *does* come, when the curtain does go up, I tell you you'll find every one on the stage – busy ... Such fighting, too! ... I suppose you don't read the papers about this sort of thing?'

'I read 'em a bit,' said Bert.

'Well, have you noticed what one might call the remarkable case of the disappearing inventor – the inventor who turns up in a blaze of publicity, fires off a few successful experiments, and vanishes?'

'Can't say I 'ave,' said Bert.

'Well, I 'ave, anyhow. You get anybody come along who does

anything striking in this line, and, you bet, he vanishes. Just goes off quietly out of sight. After a bit, you don't hear anything more of 'em at all. See? They disappear. Gone – no address. First – oh! it's an old story now – there was those Wright Brothers out in America. They glided – they glided miles and miles. Finally they glided off stage. Why, it must be nineteen hundred and four, or five, *they* vanished! Then there was those people in Ireland – no, I forget their names. Everybody said they could fly. *They* went. They ain't dead that I've heard tell; but you can't say they're alive. Not a feather of 'em can you see. Then that chap who flew round Paris and upset in the Seine. De Booley, was it? I forget. That was a grand fly, in spite of the accident; but where's he got to? The accident didn't hurt him. Eh? *'E's* gone to cover.'

The soldier prepared to light his pipe.

'Looks like a secret society got hold of them,' said Bert.

'Secret society! *Naw!*'

The soldier lit his match, and drew. 'Secret society,' he repeated in response to these words, with his pipe between his teeth and the match flaring. 'War Departments; that's more like it.' He threw his match aside, and walked to his machine. 'I tell you, sir,' he said, 'there isn't a big Power in Europe, *or* Asia, *or* America, *or* Africa, that hasn't got at least one or two flying machines hidden up its sleeve at the present time. Not one. Real, workable flying machines. And the spying! The spying and manoeuvring to find out what the others have got. I tell you, sir, a foreigner, or, for the matter of that, an unaccredited native, can't get within four miles of Lydd nowadays – not to mention our little circus at Aldershot, and the experimental camp in Galway. No!'

'Well,' said Bert, 'I'd like to see one of them, anyhow. Jest to help believing. I'll believe when I see, that I'll promise you.'

'You'll see 'em fast enough,' said the soldier, and led his machine out into the road.

He left Bert on his wall, grave and pensive, with his cap on the back of his head, and a cigarette smouldering in the corner of his mouth.

'If what he says is true,' said Bert, 'me and Grubb, we been wasting our blessed old time. Besides incurring expense with thet green'ouse.'

*

It was while this mysterious talk with the soldier still stirred in Bert Smallways' imagination that the most astounding incident in the whole of that dramatic chapter of human history, the coming of flying, occurred. People talked glibly enough of epoch-making events; this *was* an epoch-making event. It was the unanticipated and entirely successful flight of Mr Alfred Butteridge from the Crystal Palace to Glasgow and back in a small businesslike-looking machine heavier than air – an entirely manageable and controllable machine that could fly as well as a pigeon.

It wasn't, one felt, a fresh step forward in the matter so much as a giant stride, a leap. Mr Butteridge remained in the air altogether for about nine hours, and during that time he flew with the ease and assurance of a bird. His machine was, however, neither bird-like nor butterfly-like, nor had it the wide lateral expansion of the ordinary aeroplane. The effect upon the observer was rather something in the nature of a bee or wasp. Parts of the apparatus were spinning very rapidly, and gave one a hazy effect of transparent wings; but parts, including two peculiarly curved 'wing-cases' – if one may borrow a figure from the flying beetles – remained expanded stiffly. In the middle was a long, rounded body like the body of a moth, and on this Mr Butteridge could be seen sitting astride, much as a man bestrides a horse. The wasp-like resemblance was increased by the fact that the apparatus flew with a deep, booming hum, exactly the sound made by a wasp at a window pane.

Mr Butteridge took the world by surprise. He was one of those gentlemen from nowhere Fate still succeeds in producing for the stimulation of mankind. He came, it was variously said, from Australia and America and the South of France. He was also described quite incorrectly as the son of a man who had amassed a comfortable fortune in the manufacture of gold nibs and the Butteridge fountain pens. But this was an entirely different strain of

Butteridges. For some years, in spite of a loud voice, a large presence, an aggressive swagger, and an implacable manner, he had been an undistinguished member of most of the existing aeronautical associations. Then one day he wrote to all the London papers to announce that he had made arrangements for an ascent from the Crystal Palace of a machine that would demonstrate satisfactorily that the outstanding difficulties in the way of flying were finally solved. Few of the papers printed his letter, still fewer were the people who believed in his claim. No one was excited even when a fracas on the steps of a leading hotel in Piccadilly, in which he tried to horsewhip a prominent German musician upon some personal account, delayed his promised ascent. The quarrel was inadequately reported, and his name spelt variously Betteridge and Betridge. Until his flight, indeed, he did not and could not contrive to exist in the public mind. There were scarcely thirty people on the look-out for him, in spite of all his clamour, when about six o'clock one summer morning the doors of the big shed in which he had been putting together his apparatus opened – it was near the big model of a megatherium in the Crystal Palace grounds – and his giant insect came droning out into a negligent and incredulous world.

But before he had made his second circuit of the Crystal Palace towers, Fame was lifting her trumpet, she drew a deep breath as the startled tramps who sleep on the seats of Trafalgar Square were roused by his buzz and awoke to discover him circling the Nelson column, and by the time he had got to Birmingham, which place he crossed about half-past ten, her deafening blast was echoing throughout the country. The despaired-of thing was done. A man was flying securely and well.

Scotland was agape for his coming. Glasgow he reached by one o'clock, and it is related that scarcely a shipyard or factory in that busy hive of industry resumed work before half-past two. The public mind was just sufficiently educated in the impossibility of flying to appreciate Mr Butteridge at his proper value. He circled the University buildings, and dropped to within shouting distance of the crowds in West End Park and on the slope of Gilmorehill. The thing flew quite steadily at a pace of about three miles an hour, in a wide circle, making a deep hum that would have drowned his full, rich voice completely had he not provided himself with a megaphone. He avoided churches, buildings, and monorail cables with consummate ease as he conversed.

'Me name's Butteridge,' he shouted; 'B-U-T-T-E-R-I-D-G-E. Got it? Me mother was Scotch.'

And having assured himself that he had been understood, he rose amidst cheers and shouting and patriotic cries, and then flew up very swiftly and easily into the south-eastern sky, rising and falling with long, easy undulations in an extraordinarily wasp-like manner.

His return to London – he visited and hovered over Manchester and Liverpool and Oxford on his way, and spelt his name out to each place – was an occasion of unparalleled excitement. Everyone was staring heavenward. More people were run over in the streets upon that one day than in the previous three months, and a County Council steamboat, the *Isaac Walton*, collided with a pier of Westminster Bridge, and narrowly escaped disaster by running ashore – it was low water – on the mud on the south side. He returned to the Crystal Palace grounds, that classic starting-point of aeronautical adventure, about sunset, re-entered his shed without disaster and had the doors locked immediately upon the photographers and journalists who had been waiting his return.

'Look here, you chaps,' he said, as his assistant did so, 'I'm tired to death, and saddle-sore. I can't give you a word of talk. I'm too – done— My name's Butteridge. B-U-T-T-E-R-I-D-G-E. Get that right. I'm an imperial Englishman. I'll talk to you all tomorrow.'

Foggy snapshots still survive to record that incident. His assistant struggles in a sea of aggressive young men carrying notebooks or upholding cameras and wearing bowler hats and enterprising ties. He himself towers up in the doorway, a big figure with a mouth – an eloquent cavity beneath a vast black moustache – distorted by his shout to those relentless agents of publicity. He towers there, the most famous man in the country. Almost symbolically he holds and gesticulates with a megaphone in his left hand.

Graham Wallace

Alcock and Brown over the Atlantic

3 a.m. Alock and Brown had been airborne for close on eleven hours and all was well. Ireland was barely 600 miles ahead of them, they had plenty of petrol in reserve, thanks to Alcock's careful handling of the Rolls-Royce engines, and they were flying steadily eastwards at a good average speed of 105 knots. The sun would soon be rising in front of them, the monotony and fatigue of the night would soon be past.

Brown to Alcock: 'Immediately you see sun rising point machine straight for it and we'll get its compass bearing.'

3.10 a.m. The darkness of the night slowly merged into the first pearly lustre of dawn. Alcock and Brown could begin to distinguish the shapes of the clouds that hemmed them in. The moon vanished behind the clouds, great drops of rain spattered on the windscreen and drummed on the fabric of the wings and fuselage, driven inside the cockpit by the wind.

The *Vimy* was dodging in and out of the clouds when quite suddenly, as they emerged into a space of clear air, Alcock and Brown saw a great towering mass of cumulonimbus straight ahead, blocking their path like some vast range of black mountains.

There was no time to alter course, the *Vimy* flew straight into the centre of this storm. A sudden turbulence gripped the machine and tossed it around like a falling leaf in an autumnal gale. All around them swirled thick vapour, hiding the wing-tips and, at times, the front of the fuselage. The wings quivered and vibrated, the rigging wires humming in loud sympathy. The dreadful sudden-ness of the storm caused Alcock and Brown to lose all sense of direction and balance. The rain turned to hail which drove into their faces with cruel violence. The *Vimy* was completely out of control, plunging like a crazy horse, and throwing the two men around in the cockpit with only their safety-belts to hold them in place. Alcock fought to regain control and keep the machine on the level, but with no horizon to see and his senses knocked out of balance by the violence of the *Vimy*'s plunge, it was impossible. Their instruments became useless, the bubble of the artificial horizon had long since vanished and there was only the pressure of their seats against their backs to show that they were not hanging upside-down in space. The lightning flashed round the *Vimy*, tracing the shape of the machine in lines of fire, and the hail continued to beat unmercifully into the cockpit.

At this point disaster nearly overtook them and finished off their venture. The storm was at its height when the air speed indicator jammed, showing a reading of 90 knots. Alcock wrestled with the joystick, trying to force the nose of the *Vimy* up, but they were moving too slowly for this to be effective. For one sickening moment the *Vimy* hung motionless in the air, then she stalled, tilting over and dropping in a steep spiral dive down towards the Atlantic. Neither man could see anything through the swirling mass of cloud that had swallowed them up, and the lightning so dazzled their eyes that they could not read their instruments, not that they were of any help. Alcock struggled to centralize joystick and rudder, but he had lost all judgement of balance. The engines roared and vibrated at full revolutions as the *Vimy* gained momentum in the dive and the wind shrieked through the rigging wires. It seemed as if nothing could save them now. The pressure against their backs increased as the *Vimy* tipped forwards, falling almost vertically.

4,000 … 3,000 … 2,000 feet … the *Vimy* was still plunging downwards, completely out of control with both engines roaring and wings threatening to pull away from the fuselage. It was then that Alcock showed what a supremely good pilot he was under these conditions. All his experience of flying through the storms over the Turkish mountains on his nightly bombing raids lay in the touch of his hands and feet on the controls of the *Vimy*. He managed to regain control over the engines and throttle them right back, but he still could not check the headlong plunge of the *Vimy* towards the Atlantic.

1,000 ... 500 ... 250 ... 100 feet. The needle of the altimeter was almost resting on the zero mark when they left the storm as quickly as they had entered it. The *Vimy* fell out of the cloud only 60 feet above the ocean. But to the startled eyes of Alcock and Brown the ocean was not in its customary situation below them, it was standing up sideways, almost vertically to them. Alcock looked up at the waves that seemed to be above him, and at the horizon, and instantaneously regained his sense of balance. Instinctively he centralized the joystick and rudder. The *Vimy* responded at once. Alcock opened the throttles wide, the Rolls-Royce engines roared out and they regained flying speed, skimming the crests of the waves, at times so close that the spray of the white horses beat on the underside of the wings. The danger was past.

Both men were too dazed by their experience to think or act consciously. After a few minutes, Brown regained his composure and looked at the compass. He took another close look and saw that, instead of pointing east, the lubber's line was pointing due west. They were heading back to Newfoundland! He nudged Alcock and pointed to the compass. Alcock looked and burst into a roar of laughter, then he swung the *Vimy* round in a wide turn and back on course for Ireland.

The routine of flight was re-established ... engine inspection ... temperature and pressure readings ... petrol to be pumped ... they were still climbing, passing through one cloud layer after another when, once again, they headed into a storm.

Heavy rain started falling, turning to hail, cutting their faces and rebounding like shot from the wings. After a few minutes' flying time, snow started to fall heavily. The wind drove the snow inside the cockpit and caked over their goggles with a white screen. The wing surfaces and struts became sheathed in ice and 'Lucky Jim' was turned into a shapeless mass of white behind Alcock's head.

Alcock needed all his strength to move the flying controls, heavy with snow, but he continued to climb, hoping to fly out of and over the storm and, perhaps, to catch a glimpse of the sun. The two engines were labouring, feeling the altitude and the deadweight of the ice that encased the *Vimy*. The cold became intense, forcing both men to huddle down behind the windscreen for protection, but the storm continued without let-up.

Altitude . . . 8,800 feet. From his shelter behind the windscreen Brown screwed his head round to look at the engines. It was difficult to see at all clearly through the driving snow and hail but it looked to him as if the fuel intake gauges on the side of the engine nacelles were completely iced over and the air intakes on the engines were becoming blocked with snow. Already the two engines were beating more irregularly, starved of air by the altitude and snow. Reluctantly Brown straightened up in his seat and looked again, taking off his goggles for a better view. He saw that if he did not act quickly, they would be in serious trouble. They would be forced down through lack of power and, by being unable to see the gauges, would fail to regulate the flow of petrol into the engines and so foul up the carburettors. He quickly made up his mind. Alcock could not release the flying controls for an instant, so there was no alternative but for him to leave the cockpit and try to clear both gauges and air intakes. This was the only logical course of action, the fact that they were in a blinding snowstorm over the Atlantic made no difference. If they were to survive he must go out on to those wings.

Brown, the cripple, released his safety-belt and pulled off his mittens to leave his hands free for work. As he stood up in the cockpit and started climbing back on to the fuselage, Alcock looked round and realized what he was trying to do. He tried to pull him back, but Brown savagely pushed him away, and scrambled up on to the centre section of the fuselage, then he lowered himself, inch by inch, onto the wing, gripping the wooden strut that braced the port engine. The snow sheathed his body in a shroud of ice as he clung grimly on to the strut and fumbled in his pockets for a jack-knife. He had to cling on with all his strength, the wind tore at his face and hands, forcing him backwards, his feet were slipping on the icy surface of the wing.

Painfully, with short blows of his knife, he chipped the ice off the gauges. The exertion made him pant and gasp for air, his heart pounded with the altitude and the great gulps of icy air that he breathed in burnt his throat and lungs with cold. Once the gauges were clear he reached up to clear the air intakes. The propeller was only a few inches away from his body and the slipstream became an added force trying to loosen his grip on the *Vimy*. The exhaust was roaring in his face, but somehow Brown managed to clear the air intakes of the port engine to be rewarded by the noise of all twelve cylinders beating regularly.

Meanwhile Alcock had to use all his skill as a pilot to keep the *Vimy* in level flight. One false move, one slight tilt to port or starboard, and Brown would be sent hurtling down to the Atlantic 9,000 feet below. Brown clung gasping to a strut on the port wing, trying to summon up enough strength to tackle the starboard engine. He had to fight every inch of the way, when seconds seemed like minutes and minutes stretched out to hours as he gripped the struts and bracing wires with fingers numb and weak with cold. He had to force his body against the might of the wind, always keeping his weight off his crippled leg. He clung to the starboard engine, almost defeated, with the flaming exhaust only inches over his head. With his last reserve of strength he cleared the air intakes and worked his way back into the cockpit, exhausted but triumphant.

The ordeal of Brown was not finished. The storm continued to rage without a break. Five times more he had to fight his way along the wings.

V. M. Yeates

Rumpties

The Corps School was a restful place, undisturbed by hurly-burlies and war, except for noises incidental to courses in bombing. And the staff mess was the most peaceful spot in the happy valley.

Being introduced into this mess was, to one used to the RFC atmosphere, something like finding oneself in the holy calm of a Pall Mall club miraculously endowed with faint but persistent Moral Purpose, after a New Year hullaballoo in a Regent Street bar. Conversation was leisurely, prolonged, and decorous, and alcohol was used only in such small quantities as stimulated the larynx to this sort of talk. No one swore or discussed women. The profound purity of the mature English gentleman away from his womenfolk reigned.

They were pleased to have a flying man to talk to, being all quite ignorant of flying and having the impression that there was something specially daring and heroic about it.

The usual questions were asked: why had he taken it up? what did he feel like the first time he went up? had he ever looped the loop? had he shot down any Huns? did he know McCudden or Micky Mannock or the Mad Major?

Tom told them the first time he went up was in a Rumpty, that was to say, a Maurice Farman Shorthorn, a queer sort of bus like an assemblage of birdcages. You climbed with great difficulty through a network of wires into the nacelle, and sat perked up there, adorned with a crash helmet, very much exposed to the wondering gaze of men. There did not seem to be any *a priori* reason why this structure should leave the ground, but after dashing across the aerodrome at forty miles an hour for some time the thing did imperceptibly and gradually climb into the air. It was very like a ride on top of an omnibus. A Rumpty was no aeroplane for stunting. The flight was a quiet trip up to three hundred feet and down again. A few daring spirits who had tried stunting were dead. The CO of that squadron, a pompous and bossy penguin, Major Beak, maintained that Rumpties were good buses when you knew how to fly them. He had been on active service on them, in Mesopotamia, where he had contended valiantly with the heat bumps engendered by the fierce sun until the heat made him so bad tempered that he was invalided home to get rid of him. On the home front he was sufficiently senior to be able to avoid flying, and work off his bad temper on junior people who did fly. According to him Rumpties were fine, and it was only damned junior stupidity that jeered at them. They had to be used, for hundreds of them existed, a big order having been placed; and as they were of no use for any practical purpose, the only thing to do with them was to use them for training. The trainees would have to unlearn later all that they learnt then, but young pilots must begin at the beginning, and a Rumpty certainly was only just beginning to be an aeroplane. Flying with their antiquated controls was a mixture of playing a harmonium, working the village pump, and sculling a boat.

However, Tom became habituated to staggering through the atmosphere in these soaring cats'-cradles, and in the fullness of time he took one up by himself, and stayed up for an hour and a half, reaching in this time the eagle-baffling height of three thousand feet, whence he gazed down on the still sleeping western suburbs of London and felt himself to be a pilot. This flight was so successful that after breakfast he was sent up again in another machine.

By this time a fairly strong breeze was blowing from the south-west, and there was a ceiling of cloud at about seven hundred feet; not the weather in which a novice in a Rumpty was likely to enjoy himself. He flew round and round the aerodrome at five hundred feet, being bumped about irksomely by the choppy air. It was a great change from the still clear atmosphere of dawn ... but an hour passed, and he might soon land. Then the engine spluttered and stopped. Tom knew one thing, that he must not stall, and immediately put the nose down into gliding position to maintain speed. The engine did not pick up. This was a forced landing, and by the time he realized the alarming truth he did not seem to have enough height to glide on to the aerodrome so as to land into the wind. There was a field in front that he must make for. The engine gave a splutter but subsided again. The field was rushing up at him. He was going down much too steeply. He was almost in the field. He was doing seventy; he would never get in. Trees were in front. The engine spluttered again. He had left the throttle open. He looked down and pulled it off, and then there was a shock and he was out of the aeroplane, lying on the ground a dozen yards from the remains of it. He had been thrown on his head, but the crash helmet had saved him. He must have flown into the ground; he didn't really know exactly what had happened; he found himself on the ground and the Rumpty smashed. He might have been unconscious for a little while. The nacelle was upside down on the ground with a pile of wreckage on it. He had been strapped in, but the safety belt had given; otherwise his neck must have been broken. But what a mess the old Rumpty was! One more write-off. It was an achievement to smash up a Rumpty like that and not be hurt. He shook himself. Yes, he was quite uninjured; one shoe was missing, and the ankle felt a little bit wrenched. He walked over to the wreck and found his shoe wedged upside down under the nacelle with the toe projecting. He pulled at it, but it was fixed firmly. He got both hands to it and tugged and wriggled it, and suddenly it came away and he rolled over on his back.

Someone flew overhead as he was putting on his shoe, leaning over to look at him. He walked round the wreck, his own wreck. It was a good one. He ought to be dead. Was he, by the way? He couldn't see his dead body about, but it might be under the nacelle. The motor ambulance came jolting over the field towards him, and it was a relief when the orderly spoke to him, and he knew he was not a spirit. The matter ended with a fortnight's sick leave and a few words with Major Beak about his incompetence.

Cecil Lewis

Air Observer at Amiens

I walked down to the Mess and was greeted by the OC.

'Hullo, you're down at last. Orders are just through that we're to send you to No. 9 Squadron – 2Cs.'

'But ... I was to be a Morane pilot ...'

'Well, if you ask me, you're well out of that. They're too damn dangerous. Nos. 1 and 3 have killed a hell of a lot of pilots lately.'

'When am I to go?'

'Right away. They want you urgently. I think you'll find there's a train for Amiens tonight. Better slip along and see the Adjutant. Get your batman to pack your kit.'

A squadron at last! But 2Cs ... That meant artillery observation, dawdling up and down the lines while Archie* took pot-shots at you; that meant photography; that meant beastly long reconnaissances, with Fokkers buzzing about on your tail. The obscure future date on which I should at last go into action had always been remote in my mind, imperfectly realized, even, I suspect, deliberately shut out. Now, suddenly, with a brief order, it had become startlingly clear and close at hand. For months after, with a few brief moments of respite, I was to live hypnotized not so much by the dread of death – for death, like the sun, is a thing you cannot look at steadily for long – as by the menace of the unforeseen. Friends, Mess companions, would go out on patrol and never come back. Archie, hostile aircraft, and machine-gun fire from the ground all took their toll. As the months went by it seemed only a matter of time until your turn came. You sat down to dinner faced by the empty chairs of men you had laughed and joked with at lunch. They were gone. The next day new men would laugh and joke from

* (the common slang for an anti-aircraft battery)

those chairs. Some might be lucky and stick it for a bit, some chairs would be empty again very soon. And so it would go on. And always, miraculously, you were still there. Until tomorrow ... In such an atmosphere you grew fatalistic, and as time went by and left you unscathed, like a batsman who has played himself in, you began to take liberties with the bowling. You took unnecessary risks, you volunteered for dangerous jobs, you provoked enemy aircraft to attack you. You were invulnerable: nothing could touch you. Then, when one of the old hands, as seemingly invulnerable as yourself, went West, you suddenly got cold feet. It wasn't possible to be sure – even of yourself. At this stage it required most courage to go on – a sort of plodding fatalism, a determination, a cold-blooded effort of will. And always alone! No friends right and left, no crowd morale. The lot of the P.B.I.* was hopeless enough; but each in his extremity had at least someone at hand, someone to cheer and to succour.

Besides, we were always at the mercy of the fragility of the machine and the unreliability of the engine. One chance bullet from the ground might cut a thin wire, put the machine out of control, and send us, perfectly whole, plunging to a crash we were powerless to prevent. So, in the later stages, we had to win victories over ourselves long before we won any over the enemy, for it was not impossible to turn back, to tell a lie – not always easy to verify – of faulty engine, bad visibility, jammed guns, and so stave off the inevitable for one day more. We came in for some admiration at that time, just because we were pilots, just because we flew. But flying is pleasurable enough, in short doses, and was even in those days reasonably safe. Truthfully, there was little admirable in that. But to fly on a straight line, taking photos of the enemy trenches, an easy Archie target, within range of the ground machine-guns, bumped by the eddies of passing shells and pestered by enemy scouts, that required nerve. And it would have to be done twice a day, day after day, until you were hit or went home. Small wonder if, under this strain, pilots lived a wild life and wined and

* (P.B.I.: poor bloody infantry)

womanized to excess. Stanhope in *Journey's End* summarizes it perfectly: 'To forget, you bloody little fool, to forget. Do you think there's no limit to what a man can bear?'

The squadron tender met me at Amiens. The driver loaded up my kit. We picked up three other pilots in the Square. They had dined well, and came bundling into the tender with much laughter and began singing songs at the top of their voices. As the tender bumped and slithered over the *pavé* they began to sober up a bit, found out who I was, and looked me over like a new boy at school, answering all my questions about work, machines, casualties, with airy unconcern. It was only later I found out that when you went on a 'blind' to Amiens, talk about the job was taboo. You had come in specifically to forget it. Arrived in the tumbledown village (smell of mud and manure), they took me over to the Mess to report to the OC, who gave me a drink while I told him all about the Fokker, the details of which had not yet reached the squadron. The news was good, and as one of their pilots had been shot down by a Fokker two days previously they were glad of it, and we had another round of drinks. Then I was given a billet at a farm along the muddy street: a musty-smelling room with the windows hermetically sealed and dry rot in the big feather bedstead. I lay for a little before sleeping, wondering about it all. It seemed curious that my training should land me in a stuffy little room in some obscure village in France, and that from here my personal war should begin.

*

Next morning I was allotted a machine and given my orders. I was to put in time – the old story. My Flight-Commander was scandalized at my lack of experience. Twenty hours, the total my logbook showed, was no good to him. I was to take my machine and fly it all day. I was to get the lie of the land, go up with a map and locate all the landmarks, so that I could find my way back from the lines in any weather, like a homing pigeon. I was particularly to familiarize myself with the advance landing ground, so that I could get down safely if the engine should be hit or I should be wounded on patrol. And so on.

So I set off. I browsed round the countryside, visited the FE squadron I had come out with, had my first look at the lines. The next day I went over them at 10,000, and on my way back got completely lost. French maps were different from the English ones I was used to. They were nothing like so accurate, and the nomenclature put me off. Still, how I could have missed Amiens with its great cathedral when I was within twenty miles of it at 10,000 feet I don't know. But I did; and at last resorted to the amateur's refuge – to come down and ask where I was.

So my training went on. Practice at formation flying, locating gun emplacements in a given map square coordinate, practice at reconnaissance formation, at lamp signalling, at forced landings and later, several trips with gunnery officers who came down from their batteries and were taken up to see their targets from the air.

*

After ten hours of this came my first real job – to photograph the enemy second-line trenches. The lines, from the air, had none of the significance they had from the ground, mainly because all contours were nonexistent. The local undulations, valleys, ravines, ditches, hillsides, which gave advantage to one side or the other, were flattened out. All you saw was two more or less parallel sets of trenches, clearer in some places than in others according to the colour of the earth thrown up in making them. These faced each other across the barren strip of no man's land, and behind them started a complicated network of communication trenches, second-line trenches, more communication trenches and then the third-line trenches. The network was more complex at the important positions along the line; but everywhere it was irregular, following the lie of the ground, opening up to a wide mesh at one place, closing up, compact and formidable, at another. As positions were consolidated more trenches were dug, and later, when I came to know my own section of the line as well as the palm of my hand, I could tell at a glance what fresh digging had been done since my last patrol.

The surveying of the German line was difficult from the ground. You couldn't very well walk about with a theodolite and a chain in full view of the enemy, so the making of maps was largely a matter of aerial photography. In the spring of 1916, with the big offensive on the Somme preparing, the accuracy of these maps was of the greatest importance. So our job that day was to go over the front line at 7,500 feet and fly all along the enemy second-line trenches from Montauban, round the Fricourt salient, and up to Boisselle, photographing as we went.

If there was ever an aeroplane unsuited for active service, it was the BE 2C. The pilot sat slightly aft of the main planes and had a fair view above and below, except where the lower main plane obscured the ground forward; but the observer, who sat in front of him, could see practically nothing, for he was wedged under the small centre section, with a plane above, another below and bracing wires all round. He carried a gun for defence purposes; but he could not fire it forward, because of the propeller. Backwards, the centre-section struts, wires and the tailplane cramped his style. In all modern machines the positions are reversed; the pilot sits in front, leaving the observer a good field of fire aft and using his own guns, which can be fired through the propeller, forward. But in 1916 the synchronized gear enabling a machine-gun to be fired through the whirling propeller and still miss the blades had not been perfected.

The observer could not operate the camera from his seat because of the plane directly below him, so it was clamped on outside the fuselage, beside the pilot; a big, square, shiny mahogany box with a handle on top to change the plates (yes, plates!). To make an exposure you pulled a ring on the end of a cord. To sight it, you leaned over the side and looked through a ball and cross-wire finder. The pilot, then, had to fly the machine with his left hand, get over the spot on the ground he wanted to photograph – not so easy as you might think – put his arm out into the 70 m.p.h. wind, and push the camera handle back and forward to change the plates, pulling the string between each operation. Photography in 1916 was somewhat amateurish.

So I set out on that sunny afternoon, with a sergeant gunner in the front seat, and climbed up towards the lines. As I approached them, I made out the place where we were to start on the ground, comparing it with the map. Two miles the other side of the front line didn't look far on paper; but it seemed a devil of a way when you had to fly vertically over the spot. The sergeant knelt on his seat, placed a drum on the Lewis gun and faced round over the tail, keeping a wary eye open for Fokkers. But the sky was deserted, the line quiet. Jerry was having a day off. I turned the machine round to start on my steady course above the trenches, when two little puffs of grey smoke appeared 100 feet below us, on the left. The sergeant pointed and smiled: 'Archie!' Then three others appeared closer, at our own height. It was funny the way the balls of smoke appeared magically in the empty air, and were followed a moment later by a little flat report. If they didn't range us any better than that they were not very formidable, I thought, and began to operate the camera handle.

There are times in life when the faculties seem to be keyed up to superhuman tension. You are not necessarily doing anything; but you are in a state of awareness, of tremendous alertness, ready to act instantaneously should the need arise. Outwardly, that day, I was calm, busy keeping the trenches in the camera sight, manipulating the handle, pulling the string; but inside my heart was pounding and my nerves straining, waiting for something, I did not know what, to happen. It was my first job. I was under fire for the first time. Would Archie get the range? Would the dreaded Fokker appear? Would the engine give out? It was the fear of the unforeseen, the inescapable, the imminent hand of death which might, from moment to moment, be ruthlessly laid upon me. I realized, not then, but later, why pilots cracked up, why they lost their nerve and had to go home. Nobody could stand the strain indefinitely, ultimately it reduced you to a dithering state, near to imbecility. For always you had to fight it down, you had to go out and do the job, you could never admit it, never say frankly: 'I am afraid. I can't face it any more.' For cowardice, because, I suppose, it is the most common human emotion, is the most despised. And you did gain victories over yourself. You won and won and won again, and always there was another to be won on the morrow. They sent you home to rest, and you put it in the background of your mind; but it was not like a bodily fatigue from which you could completely recover, it was a sort of damage to the essential tissue of your being. You might have a greater will-power, greater stamina to fight down your failing; but a thorough-bred that has been lashed will rear at the sight of the whip, and never, once you had been through it, could you be quite the same again.

I went on pulling the string and changing the plates when, out of the corner of my eye, I saw something black ahead of the machine. I looked up quickly: there was nothing there. I blinked. Surely, if my eyes were worth anything, there had been something ... Yes! There it was again! This time I focused. It was a howitzer shell, one of our own shells, slowing up as it reached the top of its trajectory, turning slowly over and over, like an ambling porpoise, and then plunging down to burst. Guns fire shells in a flat trajectory; howitzers fling them high, like a lobbed tennis ball. It follows that, if you happen to be at the right height, you catch the shell just as it hovers at its peak point. If you are quick-sighted you can then follow its course down to the ground. I watched the thing fasci-nated. Damn it, they weren't missing the machine by much, I thought; but I was left little time to consider it, for suddenly there was a sharp tearing sound like a close crack of thunder, and the machine was flung upwards by the force of the explosion of an Archie burst right underneath us. A split second later, and it would have been a direct hit. A long tear appeared in the fabric of the plane where a piece of shrapnel had gone through. There was a momentary smell of acrid smoke. 'Ess! Ess!' shouted the sergeant. 'They've ranged us!' I flung the machine over and flew west, then turned again, and again, and again ... The Archie bursts were distant now. We had thrown them off.

'How many more?' shouted the sergeant, with a jerk of his head to the camera box.

'Two.'

Flying on a steady course is the surest way to get caught by Archie, and we had been, right enough. If we were quick we might snatch the other two photos and get away before he ranged us again. I turned back over the spot, pulled the string and flew on to make the last exposure, when the sergeant suddenly stiffened in his seat, cocked his gun, and pointed: 'Fokker!'

I turned in my seat and saw the thin line of the monoplane coming down on our tail. He had seen the Archie bursts, no doubt, had a look round to see if we were escorted, and, finding it all clear, was coming down for a sitter.

I got the last photo as he opened fire. The distant chatter of his gun was hardly audible above the engine roar. It didn't seem to be directed at us. He was, I know now, an inexperienced pilot, he should have held his fire. We replied with a chatter that deafened me, the muzzle of the Lewis gun right above my head. The Fokker hesitated, pulled over for a moment, and then turned at us again. The sergeant pulled his trigger. Nothing happened. 'Jammed! Jammed!' he shouted. He pulled frantically at the gun, while the stuttering Fokker came up. I put the old 2C right over to turn under him. As I did so, there was a sharp crack, and the little windscreen a foot in front of my face showed a hole with a spider's web in the glass round it.

It was Triplex: no splinters; but another foot behind would have put that bullet through my head – which was not Triplex. A narrow shave. Instinctively I stood the machine on its head and dived for home. At that moment, as if to cap it all, the engine set up a fearful racket. The whole machine felt as if it would fall to pieces.

'Switch off! Switch off!' yelled the sergeant. 'The engine's hit.'

I obeyed, still diving, turning sharply as I did so to offer a more difficult target to the Fokker. But, luckily for us, he decided not to pursue. In those days the Huns did not adventure much beyond their own side of the lines, and now we were back over ours.

We saw him zoom away again. He had us at his mercy, had he known. There was a moment of wonderful relief. We laughed. It had all happened in much less time than it takes to tell, and we were still alive, safe!

'Make for the advance landing ground,' shouted the sergeant. He was furious with the gun jamming, jumpy at our narrow shave and, anyway, didn't relish his job with inexperienced pilots like me, just out from home.

I spotted the advance landing ground – thank Heaven I had been down on it previously – and circled to make my landing. It would have been a fine thing, I thought, if that had happened a few miles further over and I had been forced down in Hunland on my first patrol. I skimmed over the telegraph poles, got down without mishap and jumped out to examine the machine.

The sergeant was apostrophizing the gun: 'These bloody double drums!' he said. 'Always jamming! He had us sitting, God dammit!'

I pulled over the prop. There was a hollow rattle from the inside. Something serious, a big end gone, or a smashed connecting rod, probably. Anyway, they would have to send out another engine . . . But we were down! Here was the ground under my feet; the sky above, serene, impersonal; the machine solid beneath my touch, swaying slightly in the wind. All that remained to bear witness of our escape was the rattle of the engine, the tear in the plane, the smashed windscreen and the tiny perforations of the bullet holes in the body, two down behind my seat, more in the tail. The sergeant came up.

'Are you all right, sir?'

'Fine! And you?'

'Quite, thank you, sir. I thought he'd got us with that second burst. Always turn, sir, as soon as a machine attacks. It can't get its sights on you so easy. And it has to allow for the traverse . . . If you'll phone the squadron, sir, and order out a tender and a repair squad, I'll dismount the camera and get a guard put over the machine. You got all the photos, didn't you, sir?'

'Yes. Twenty-two in all.'

'The Corps will be pleased. They wanted them badly.'

Well, we'd got away with it! We'd done the job! If you'd heard me phoning the squadron ten minutes later, you might have imagined from my casual manner I'd been through that sort of thing every day for a month.

W. B. Yeats

'An Irish Airman Foresees His Death'

I know that I shall meet my fate
Somewhere among the clouds above;
Those that I fight I do not hate,
Those that I guard I do not love;
My country is Kiltartan Cross,
My countrymen Kiltartan's poor,
No likely end could bring them loss
Or leave them happier than before.
Nor law, nor duty bade me fight,
Nor public men, nor cheering crowds,
A lonely impulse of delight
Drove to this tumult in the clouds;
I balanced all, brought all to mind,
The years to come seemed waste of breath,
A waste of breath the years behind
In balance with this life, this death.

A. Harry Griffin

Happy Landing on Helvellyn

20 December 1986

Sixty years ago, at about 1 p.m. on 22 December 1926, an aeroplane landed on the summit of Helvellyn (3,116 feet) and, half an hour later, took off again. It was the first and only time a plane has landed on a British mountain summit – they don't make planes like that nowadays – and on Monday, at precisely one o'clock, a simple ceremony on the summit will mark the occasion with the 'unveiling' of a new memorial.

The old stone tablet about forty yards south of the summit shelter and often hidden by rocks, credited Bert Hinkler, the record-breaking airman who was later killed when he flew into a mountain-side, with the feat, and the monument, with its lettering gradually eroded by the weather, was generally known as the Hinkler Memorial. But in fact the pilot was John F. Leeming, a northern pioneer of flying who also wrote books on gardening and bees; Hinkler was his passenger.

The new memorial credits Leeming and Hinkler, in that order, with the feat. A Keswick stonemason, John Gaskell, carved the tablet and, on one of the few relatively fine days in late November, placed it on the exact site of the landing – thirty yards or so from the steep drop down crags and screes to Red Tarn. The 1926 madcap adventure took place on a cold, windy day with snow on the fells. It was a publicity stunt on behalf of civil aviation, then in its infancy.

The chosen plane was an Avro Gosport two seater fitted with an experimental 100 h.p. engine. Unfortunately, it had no certificate of airworthiness, so a special permit had to be issued – 'valid only for the purpose of a flight from Woodford Aerodrome to the summit of Helvellyn and a return flight to the said aerodrome'. Before the flight Leeming, no mountaineer, climbed the icy mountain on foot to examine the summit area, making rather heavy weather of it, and wrote later that if any credit was due to him, it was for that ascent on foot 'and not for the flying part of the affair'. It was arranged that some rocks should be rolled away from an area just south of the summit and, meanwhile, Leeming, joined by his friend Bert Hinkler, practised landings, trying to touch down as near as possible to the newspaper pegged down on Woodford aerodrome.

The first attempt took place on 15 December, with Leeming flying alone and Hinkler, in a second plane, flying a photographer – Doughty of the *Manchester Guardian* – whose job was to take pictures of the landing or, if anything happened to the first machine, of the crash. On this occasion they ran into bad weather, with thick cloud, and buffeting winds.

Six days later, with rather better weather reports, they tried again, but this time Hinkler's machine failed to start and eventually it was decided – greatly to the disappointment of the redoubtable Doughty – that Hinkler should travel as passenger in Leeming's plane. The *Manchester Guardian* scoop was not to be. Again they had to turn back, within a mile of the mountain, because of gale-force winds, and made a forced landing in a field three miles from Lancaster, where they left the plane tied down by a hedge and trudged into town for the night. At the hotel they discovered, with their wallets left behind, they had precisely six shillings and a penny between them, but the proprietor of a Lancaster garage eventually came to their rescue, paying their hotel bill and servicing their plane.

The next day, with the engine spluttering, they had to come down in a field at Calgarth near Windermere – the children at the hospital nearby thought Leeming, suddenly dropping out of the sky, was Father Christmas – but, finally, after a bumpy flight, with a storm approaching, they reached Helvellyn and Leeming gently put the plane down on the summit itself, and not on the slightly lower area that had been cleared of stones. Later he estimated that his landing speed, due to the strong wind, was little more than 15 m.p.h. but, even so, the landing must have been a considerable shock to the solitary walker who happened to be standing by the summit cairn, a few feet away.

As the startled spectator helped them pile stones under the wheels to stop the plane from running backwards, they discovered that here was a witness of undoubted integrity: the professor of Greek at Birmingham University, Professor E. R. Dodds, who, knowing nothing of the proposed flight, had just happened to climb the mountain for some pre-Christmas exercise.

Leeming only had thirty yards, slightly uphill, in which to get the machine airborne again – over the precipitous drop above Red Tarn. They said goodbye to the professor, adjusted belts and goggles, Leeming pressed the throttle wide open, and they moved forward slowly, then more quickly, towards the edge. 'Five yards from the drop,' Leeming wrote later, 'the wheels were still on the ground and just for an instant the nose seemed to drop as we shot away into space. The next moment we were away, flying, dropping down to gain speed.'

Captain W. E. Johns

Biggles Shoots the Falls

The rays of the rising sun were tingeing the treetops with gold and orange as the amphibian, with her engine purring like a well-oiled sewing machine, swung round in a circle to face the stream in readiness for a take-off.

'It's about time we went,' muttered Biggles to Dickpa, who sat beside him in order to act as guide, and nodded towards a distant bend in the river, around which a launch came into view, two feathers of spray flying back from her bows betraying the urgency of her mission, which was made still more apparent by a group of uniformed men crowding near the bows. 'Well, boys, it's too bad, but you're just too late,' he murmured with mock sympathy as he opened the throttle.

The purr of the engine rose to a deep, vibrating roar that sent a cloud of macaws wheeling and screeching into the air from the trees on the bank. The *Condor* moved forward with swiftly increasing speed, and, after a quick glance at the instrument board to make sure the engine was giving her full revolutions, the pilot drew the joystick back towards his safety belt. The amphibian left the water like a gull and rose gracefully into the air.

Slowly the tropic sun swung upwards into a sky no longer turquoise, but hard steely blue. Its rays struck full upon the polished hull of the amphibian and flashed from time to time in glittering points of light on the goggles of the pilot as he moved his head to scan the savage panorama below. Manaos, shining whitely, soon lay far astern.

For two hours they cruised steadily westwards, following the winding river that wound like a silver snake to the far horizon. From time to time they passed over places where the river assumed a milky whiteness, and Biggles hardly needed Dickpa to tell him that such stretches indicated foaming rapids where the water hurled itself over boulders as it dropped swiftly to the lower level. Occasionally the river disappeared under filmy clouds of spray where it dropped over gigantic falls into boiling whirlpools below. On each side lay the vast, untrodden, primaeval forest, dark and forbidding, hiding the earth under an unpenetrable canopy of mystery. Biggles, as he watched it, could not help reflecting on the strange fascination that urged men like Dickpa to leave home, comfort and security to face its hidden terrors.

He was aroused from his reverie by a light touch on the arm, and turned sharply, to find Dickpa pointing at something ahead upon which he had riveted his gaze. Following the outstretched finger, he saw a wide tributary branching away to the south, and with a sharp inclination of his thumb Dickpa indicated that he was to follow it.

In spite of his habitual coolness, Biggles felt a thrill of excitement run through him. Before them, not far away, lay something which a thousand men had sought in vain, and presently, all being well, it would be his good fortune to see it. Treasure! The very word, charged with the romance of ages, was sufficient to bring a sparkle to the eyes.

Obediently he swung round in a gentle bank to follow the new river. For another half-hour he flew on, once exchanging a grim smile with Dickpa as they passed a foaming cascade. The forest on each side began to give way slowly to more open country, and presently they could see vast stretches of rolling prairie spreading into the far distance.

Biggles suddenly caught his breath as the note of the engine changed. It was slight, so slight that only a pilot or an engineer would have noticed it; he did not move a muscle, but listened intently to the almost imperceptible hesitation in the regular rhythm. Then, without further warning, the engine cut out dead. Before the whirling propeller had run to a standstill Biggles had pushed his joystick forward and was going down in a long, gentle glide towards the river, eyes searching swiftly for the best landing place.

After the first start of surprise when the engine had so unexpectedly stopped, Dickpa remained perfectly still, watching the pilot
for any signal he might make. Once, as Biggles glanced in his
direction, his lips formed the word 'parachute', but the pilot shook
his head severely. The details of the river grew clearer. A long,
straight reach lay before them, and Biggles, losing height steadily,
headed the amphibian towards it.

With his lips set in a straight line, he glued his eyes on the water
for signs of rocks or other obstructions which might rip the bottom
out of the delicate hull, but he relaxed with relief when he saw all
was clear.

Swish ... swish ... swish ... sang the keel, as it kissed the placid
water, and a moment later it had settled down as it ran to a stop in
the middle of the stream.

'Confound it!' snapped Biggles irritably, his voice sounding
strangely unnatural in the silence.

'What is it, do you think – anything serious?' asked Dickpa
anxiously.

'No, I shouldn't think so,' replied Biggles.

'Sounded like magneto to me, sir, the way she cut out so sudden
like,' observed Smyth, climbing into the cockpit and then out onto
the hull behind the engine. 'I shall have to wait a minute or two to
let her cool down before I can do anything,' he added.

'Well, there doesn't appear to be any particular hurry,' said
Biggles. 'We were lucky she cut out where she did and not
somewhere over the forest or one of those places where the river
wound about so much. Have a look at her, Smyth, and tell me if
you want any help.'

For a quarter of an hour or twenty minutes Smyth laboured at
the engine, the others watching him with interest. 'It's the mag, as I
thought,' remarked the mechanic; 'brush has gone. I've a spare,
inside.'

In a few minutes the faulty part was replaced and the cause of
the breakdown remedied. As Smyth reached for the magneto cover,
and a spanner to bolt it on, Biggles turned away casually to return
to his cockpit, but the next moment a shrill cry of alarm broke

from his lips as he pointed to the bank, past which they were floating with ever-increasing speed.

'We've drifted to the head of some rapids,' said Dickpa crisply. 'Get the engine started; we've no time to lose.'

An eddy caught the nose of the *Condor* and spun the machine round on its own length. They swung dizzily round a bend, and as the new vista came into view a cry of horror broke from Algy, and he pointed, white-faced. High in the air, not a quarter of a mile away, hung a great white cloud. A low rumble, like the roll of distant thunder rapidly approaching, reached the ears of the listeners.

'The falls!' cried Biggles. 'The falls! Get that mag jacket on, Smyth, for heaven's sake; if it isn't on in two minutes we're lost.'

The current had now seized the machine in its relentless grip and was whirling it along at terrific speed; from time to time an eddy would swing it round dizzily, a manoeuvre the pilot had no means of checking.

'Look out!' Algy, taking his life in his hands, reached far over the side and fended the *Condor* away from a jagged point of rock that thrust a black, toothlike spur above the surface. By his presence of mind the danger was averted almost before it had arisen, but little flecks of foam marked the positions of more ahead. Straight across their path lay a long, black boulder, a miniature island around which the water seethed and raged in white, lashed fury.

'If we hit that, we're sunk,' snapped Biggles. 'How long will you be, Smyth?'

'One minute, sir.'

'That's thirty seconds too long,' replied Biggles, and the truth of his words was only too apparent to the others, for the *Condor* was literally racing towards the rock as if determined to destroy herself. A bare hundred yards beyond it the river ended abruptly where it plunged out of sight into the mighty, seething cauldron below. The rock seemed to literally leap towards them.

'Steady, Algy! Leave me if I don't make the bank,' barked Biggles, and before the others could realize his intention, he had seized a mooring rope and taken a flying leap onto the rock. He landed on his feet and flung his weight against the nose of the machine. Waterborne, it swung away swiftly. The tail whipped round, the elevators literally grazing the rock, and the next instant it was clear. Biggles took a lightning turn of the rope round a jutting piece of rock and flung himself backward to take the strain.

The rope jerked taut with a twang like a great banjo string, and the *Condor*, nose towards the rock, remained motionless, two curling feathers of spray leaping up from her bow as it cut the raging torrent. Algy, in the cockpit, was winding the self-starter furiously, and looked up as the engine came to life. He opened the throttle, and the machine began to surge slowly towards the rock. For a minute Biggles watched it uncomprehendingly. The rope was slack and the engine was roaring on full throttle, yet the *Condor* was making little or no headway. It seemed absurd, but as the truth became obvious his heart grew cold with horror. Slowly the full significance of what was happening dawned upon him. He realized that against the rapids it was an utter impossibility for the machine to make sufficient headway to get enough flying speed to lift it. They were in the middle of the stream, and to attempt to reach either bank would mean they would inevitably go sideways over the falls before they could reach it. Only one path remained – downstream – and that way lay the falls. For a moment or two Biggles did not even consider it, but then, as he saw it was the only way they *could* go unless they intended to remain for ever as they were, he began to weigh up the chances.

There was no wind. The current was running at perhaps 30 or 40 m.p.h., and that would consequently be the *Condor*'s speed the instant she was released. Another 20 or 30 m.p.h. on top of that and they would be travelling at nearly 70 m.p.h., which was ample for a take-off. The only doubt in his mind was whether or not she would 'unstick'. He knew, of course, that nearly all marine aircraft were slow to leave the water unless they got a 'kick' from a wave or the assistance of broken water. That was a risk he would have to take, he decided.

The *Condor*, still under full throttle, had nearly nosed up to the rock now, and Biggles saw that Algy was shouting. He could not hear what he said for the noise of the engine and the rushing water, but he could guess by his actions what he was trying to convey. Algy was trying to tell him that the machine could not get sufficient flying speed to rise against such a current. 'I know that,' thought Biggles grimly as he examined the course he would have to take as he went downstream. There were several rocks projecting above the water, but fortunately none in a direct line between him and the falls.

The *Condor* was just holding its own against the current, travelling so slowly that it would require far more petrol than they had on board for it to ever get above the rapids. Biggles made up his mind suddenly, and sprang like a cat for the nose of the machine. He jerked down into his seat while Algy stared at him with ashen face. Biggles motioned him into his seat, reached over and cut the rope and then kicked the rudder hard over. The *Condor* bucked like a wild horse as the stream caught her, and the next instant they were tearing through a sea of spray towards apparent destruction.

Eighty yards – seventy – sixty – Biggles bit his lip. Would she never lift? The combined noise of the engine and the falls was devastating, yet the pilot did not swerve an inch. Thirty yards from the bank he glanced at his air speed indicator, and then jerked the stick back into his stomach. The machine lifted, hung for a moment as if undecided as to whether to go on or fall back on the water again, then picked up and plunged into the opaque cloud of spray.

The pilot's heart missed a beat as they rocked and dropped like a stone in the terrific 'bump', or down current, caused by the cold, moisture-soaked atmosphere. The engine spluttered, missed fire, picked up again, missed and Biggles thought the end had come. He knew only too well the cause of the trouble: the spray was pouring into the air intake and choking his engine.*

The *Condor* burst out into the sunshine on the other side of the

* When Biggles was telling me about this particular incident I reminded him that Sir Alan Cobham had a similar narrow escape from the same cause whilst flying over the Victoria Falls on one of his African flights of survey.

cloud, the engine picked up with a shrill crescendo bellow and the machine soared upward like a bird. Out of the corner of his eye Biggles caught a glimpse of the rock-torn maelstrom below, and leaned back limply in his cockpit. He caught Algy's eye and shook his head weakly, as if the matter was beyond words. Algy gave him a sickly grin and disappeared into the cabin, to allow Dickpa to resume his seat in the cockpit in order to point out the way.

Dickpa leaned towards him. 'I thought you said this was the safest form of transport in the world!' he bellowed* sarcastically.

'Quite right,' yelled Biggles. 'Where would you have been in a canoe?'

---

* Normal speech would be impossible with an open cockpit due to the noise of the engine and the rush of air.

Beryl Markham

West With the Night

You can live a lifetime and, at the end of it, know more about other people than you know about yourself. You learn to watch other people, but you never watch yourself because you strive against loneliness. If you read a book, or shuffle a deck of cards or care for a dog, you are avoiding yourself. The abhorrence of loneliness is as natural as wanting to live at all. If it were otherwise, men would never have bothered to make an alphabet, nor to have fashioned words out of what were only animal sounds, nor to have crossed continents – each man to see what the other looked like.

Being alone in an aeroplane for even so short a time as a night and a day, irrevocably alone, with nothing to observe but your instruments and your own hands in semi-darkness, nothing to contemplate but the size of your small courage, nothing to wonder about but the beliefs, the faces and the hopes rooted in your mind – such an experience can be as startling as the first awareness of a stranger walking by your side at night. You are the stranger.

It is dark already and I am over the south of Ireland. There are the lights of Cork and the lights are wet; they are drenched in Irish rain, and I am above them and dry. I am above them and the plane roars in a sobbing world, but it imparts no sadness to me. I feel the security of solitude, the exhilaration of escape. So long as I can see the lights and imagine the people walking under them, I feel selfishly triumphant, as if I have eluded care and left even the small sorrow of rain in other hands.

It is a little over an hour now since I left Abingdon. England, Wales and the Irish Sea are behind me like so much time used up. On a long flight distance and time are the same. But there had been a moment when Time stopped – and Distance too. It was the moment I lifted the blue and silver Gull from the aerodrome, the

moment the photographers aimed their cameras, the moment I felt
the craft refuse its burden and strain towards the earth in sullen
rebellion, only to listen at last to the persuasion of stick and
elevators, the dogmatic argument of blueprints that said she *had* to
fly because the figures proved it.

So she had flown, and once airborne, once she had yielded to
the sophistry of a draughtsman's board, she had said, 'There: I have
lifted the weight. Now, where are we bound?' – and the question
had frightened me.

'We are bound for a place thirty-six hundred miles from here –
two thousand miles of it unbroken ocean. Most of the way it will
be night. We are flying west with the night.'

So there behind me is Cork; and ahead of me is Berehaven
Lighthouse. It is the last light, standing on the last land. I watch it,
counting the frequency of its flashes – so many to the minute. Then
I pass it and fly out to sea.

The fear is gone now – not overcome nor reasoned away. It is
gone because something else has taken its place; the confidence and
the trust, the inherent belief in the security of land underfoot – now
this faith is transferred to my plane, because the land has vanished
and there is no other tangible thing to fix faith upon. Flight is but
momentary escape from the eternal custody of earth.

Rain continues to fall, and outside the cabin it is totally dark. My
altimeter says that the Atlantic is 2,000 feet below me, my Sperry
Artificial Horizon says that I am flying level. I judge my drift at
three degrees more than my weather chart suggests, and fly
accordingly. I am flying blind. A beam to follow would help. So
would a radio – but then, so would clear weather. The voice of the
man at the Air Ministry had not promised storm.

I feel the wind rising and the rain falls hard. The smell of petrol
in the cabin is so strong and the roar of the plane so loud that my
senses are almost deadened. Gradually it becomes unthinkable that
existence was ever otherwise.

At ten o'clock p.m. I am flying along the Great Circle Course for
Harbour Grace, Newfoundland, into a 40-mile headwind at a speed
of 130 m.p.h. Because of the weather, I cannot be sure of how many

more hours I have to fly, but I think it must be between sixteen and eighteen.

At ten thirty I am still flying on the large cabin tank of petrol, hoping to use it up and put an end to the liquid swirl that has rocked the plane since my take-off. The tank has no gauge, but written on its side is the assurance: 'This tank is good for four hours.'

There is nothing ambiguous about such a guarantee. I believe it, but at twenty-five minutes to eleven, my motor coughs and dies, and the Gull is powerless above the sea.

I realize that the heavy drone of the plane has been, until this moment, complete and comforting silence. It is the actual silence following the last splutter of the engine that stuns me. I can't feel any fear; I can't feel anything. I can only observe with a kind of stupid disinterest that my hands are violently active and know that, while they move, I am being hypnotized by the needle of my altimeter.

I suppose that the denial of natural impulse is what is meant by 'keeping calm', but impulse has reason in it. If it is night and you are sitting in an aeroplane with a stalled motor, and there are 2,000 feet between you and the sea, nothing can be more reasonable than the impulse to pull back your stick in the hope of adding to that 2,000, if only by a little. The thought, the knowledge, the law that tells you that your hope lies not in this, but in a contrary act – the act of directing your impotent craft towards the water – seems a terrifying abandonment, not only of reason, but of sanity. Your mind and your heart reject it. It is your hands – your stranger's hands – that follow with unfeeling precision the letter of the law.

I sit there and watch my hands push forward on the stick and feel the Gull respond and begin its dive to the sea. Of course it is a simple thing; surely the cabin tank has run dry too soon. I need only to turn another petcock ...

But it is dark in the cabin. It is easy to see the luminous dial of the altimeter and to note that my height is now 1,100 feet, but it is not easy to see a petcock that is somewhere near the floor of the plane. A hand gropes and reappears with an electric torch, and fingers, moving with agonizing composure, find the petcock and turn it; and I wait.

At 300 feet the motor is still dead, and I am conscious that the needle of my altimeter seems to whirl like the spoke of a spindle winding up the remaining distance between the plane and the water. There is some lightning, but the quick flash only serves to emphasize the darkness. How high can waves reach – twenty feet, perhaps? Thirty?

It is impossible to avoid the thought that this is the end of my flight, but my reactions are not orthodox; the various incidents of my entire life do not run through my mind like a motion-picture film gone mad. I only feel that all this has happened before – and it has. It has all happened a hundred times in my mind, in my sleep, so that now I am not really caught in terror; I recognize a familiar scene, a familiar story with its climax dulled by too much telling.

I do not know how close to the waves I am when the motor explodes to life again. But the sound is almost meaningless. I see my hand easing back on the stick, and I feel the Gull climb up into the storm, and I see the altimeter whirl like a spindle again, paying out the distance between myself and the sea.

The storm is strong. It is comforting. It is like a friend shaking me and saying, 'Wake up! You were only dreaming.'

But soon I am thinking. By simple calculation I find that my motor had been silent for perhaps an instant more than thirty seconds.

I ought to thank God – and I do, though indirectly. I thank Geoffrey De Havilland who designed the indomitable Gipsy, and who, after all, must have been designed by God in the first place.

*

A lighted ship – the daybreak – some steep cliffs standing in the sea. The meaning of these will never change for pilots. If one day an ocean can be flown within an hour, if men can build a plane that so masters time, the sight of land will be no less welcome to the steersman of that fantastic craft. He will have cheated laws that the cunning of science has taught him how to cheat, and he will feel his guilt and be eager for the sanctuary of the soil.

I saw the ship and the daybreak, and then I saw the cliffs of Newfoundland wound in ribbons of fog. I felt the elation I had so long imagined, and I felt the happy guilt of having circumvented the stern authority of the weather and the sea. But mine was a minor triumph; my swift Gull was not so swift as to have escaped unnoticed. The night and the storm had caught her and we had flown blind for nineteen hours.

I was tired now, and cold. Ice began to film the glass of the cabin windows and the fog played a magician's game with the land. But the land was there. I could not see it, but I had seen it. I could not afford to believe that it was any land but the land I wanted. I could not afford to believe that my navigation was at fault, because there was no time for doubt.

South to Cape Race, west to Sydney on Cape Breton Island. With my protractor, my map and my compass, I set my new course, humming the ditty that Tom had taught me: 'Variation West – magnetic best. Variation East – magnetic least.' A silly rhyme, but it served to placate, for the moment, two warring poles – the magnetic and the true. I flew south and found the lighthouse of Cape Race protruding from the fog like a warning finger. I circled twice and went on over the Gulf of St Lawrence.

After a while there would be New Brunswick, and then Maine – and then New York. I could anticipate. I could almost say, 'Well, if you stay awake, you'll find it's only a matter of time now' – but there was no question of staying awake. I was tired and I had not moved an inch since that uncertain moment at Abingdon when the Gull had elected to rise with her load and fly, but I could not have closed my eyes. I could sit there in the cabin, walled in glass and petrol tanks, and be grateful for the sun and the light, and the fact that I could see the water under me. They were almost the last waves I had to pass. Four hundred miles of water, but then the land again – Cape Breton. I would stop at Sydney to refuel and go on. It was easy now. It would be like stopping at Kisumu and going on.

Success breeds confidence. But who has a right to confidence except the gods? I had a following wind, my last tank of petrol was more than three-quarters full and the world was as bright to me as if it were a new world, never touched. If I had been wiser, I might have known that such moments are, like innocence, short-lived. My engine began to shudder before I saw the land. It died, it spluttered, it started again and limped along. It coughed and spat black exhaust towards the sea.

There are words for everything. There was a word for this – airlock, I thought. This had to be an airlock because there was petrol enough. I thought I might clear it by turning on and turning off all the empty tanks, and so I did that. The handles of the petcocks were sharp little pins of metal, and when I had opened and closed them a dozen times, I saw that my hands were bleeding and that the blood was dropping on my maps and on my clothes, but the effort wasn't any good. I coasted along on a sick and halting engine. The oil pressure and the oil temperature gauges were normal, the magnetos working, and yet I lost altitude slowly while the realization of failure seeped into my heart. If I made the land, I should have been the first to fly the North Atlantic from England, but from my point of view, from a pilot's point of view, a forced landing was failure because New York was my goal. If only I could land and then take off, I would make it still . . . if only, if only . . .

The engine cuts again, and then catches, and each time it spurts to life I climb as high as I can get, and then it splutters and stops and I glide once more towards the water, to rise again and descend again, like a hunting sea bird.

I find the land. Visibility is perfect now and I see land forty or fifty miles ahead. If I am on my course, that will be Cape Breton. Minute after minute goes by. The minutes almost materialize; they pass before my eyes like links in a long slow-moving chain, and each time the engine cuts, I see a broken link in the chain and catch my breath until it passes.

The land is under me. I snatch my map and stare at it to confirm my whereabouts. I am, even at my present crippled speed, only twelve minutes from Sydney Airport, where I can land for repairs and then go on.

The engine cuts once more and I begin to glide, but now I am not worried; she will start again, as she has done, and I will gain altitude and fly into Sydney.

But she doesn't start. This time she's dead as death; the Gull settles earthwards and it isn't any earth I know. It is black earth stuck with boulders and I hang above it, on hope and on a motionless propeller. Only I cannot hang above it long. The earth hurries to meet me, I bank, turn, and side-slip to dodge the boulders, my wheels touch, and I feel them submerge. The nose of the plane is engulfed in mud, and I go forward striking my head on the glass of the cabin front, hearing it shatter, feeling blood pour over my face.

I stumble out of the plane and sink to my knees in muck and stand there foolishly staring, not at the lifeless land, but at my watch.

Twenty-one hours and twenty-five minutes.

Atlantic flight. Abingdon, England, to a nameless swamp – nonstop.

Hanna Reitsch

Flying Indoors

Though to fly is one of Humanity's most ancient dreams, it seems extraordinary that the problem of the helicopter had been occupying men's thoughts for centuries before it was finally solved. We can see, for example, from drawings made by Leonardo da Vinci about the year 1500 that he concerned himself not only with the question of flight in general, but also with the problems of vertical ascent, stationary hovering and backward as well as forward movement in the air.

These questions remained in the realm of theory, however, until, in 1937, Professor Focke of Bremen constructed the first helicopter. Using the fuselage of an existing machine, he fitted, instead of the normal wings, two vertically mounted lifting-airscrews, or 'rotors'. These were power-driven and while rotating could be tilted by means of cams, thereby enabling the machine to rise vertically from the ground, remain stationary in midair and fly backwards or forwards.

If one is to appreciate the sensation which this plane caused on its first appearance, it is necessary to remember that to those with experience of flying, an aircraft that could hover in midair without moving seemed a sheer impossibility. How, they asked, could any machine stay up without the 'lift' imparted to it by its movement through the air? To the pilot, surely, sufficient air speed was as essential as life itself, for without it, his aircraft would inevitably stall and crash to the ground?

It is no wonder, then, that Udet, as Head of the Technical Branch of the Ministry of Aviation, was profoundly disturbed and excited by this new development and, indeed, I never remember having seen him so overwrought as he was at this time.

*

I prepared myself for the task of flying the helicopter by making a careful study of the technical material, including the drawings. It soon became clear to me that, both in construction and method of control, the plane was something entirely new and demanded of its pilot the abandonment of all those flying habits which become second nature and the ability to make a completely fresh start.

To reduce the danger to a minimum, the helicopter had been anchored to the ground by a rope, but as it was only a few yards long, the device seemed to me to have the great disadvantage of not allowing the pilot sufficient freedom to get the feel of his plane and explore gradually its characteristics.

When it came to my turn, the helicopter was first disconnected from the rope at my request and then set in the centre of a large white circle described on the ground. There was no covering over the pilot's seat and when I looked out of the open machine, I found that by aligning the tips of the airscrews with the circumference of the circle, I could detect and adjust the smallest backward or forward movement of the plane.

I now opened the throttle slowly to increase the speed of the rotors, being careful, meanwhile, to hold the stick in the normal position. Then I opened up still more, revving the engine in bursts until at last the miracle happened and the helicopter began to rise vertically from the ground, thirty feet, sixty feet, and more, like an express elevator.

Professor Focke and his technicians standing below grew ever smaller as I continued to rise straight up, 150 feet, 250 feet, 300 feet. Then, I began gently to throttle back and the speed of ascent dwindled till I was hovering motionless in midair. This was intoxicating! I thought of the lark, so light and small of wing, hovering over the summer fields. Now Man had wrested from him his lovely secret, how to rise up into the sky and stand there, in the forecourt of the sun, midway between heaven and earth.

*

Meanwhile, some foreign newspapers had sought to discredit the stories about the Focke helicopter and Udet was anxious to find some means of establishing the truth of the claim that Germany was the first country to have found the solution to this centuries-old problem.

An annual springtime event in Berlin was the International Automobile Exhibition, held in the stadium of the Deutschland-halle. Lasting for three weeks, it was attended by a large number of foreign visitors and each evening during its course a variety entertainment was given in the stadium as a special attraction. As part of this programme, Udet now conceived the idea of flying the helicopter inside the Deutschlandhalle, so proving before an inter-national audience that this type of aircraft had, indeed, become a reality.

The first step was to determine whether the proposed flight could be carried out without undue risk and Udet called upon me to make the necessary experiments. If these were successful, the plane was to be flown by myself as a first-night attraction and then, for the remainder of the three weeks, by another pilot.

My co-pilot and I tested together the behaviour of the helicopter inside the Deutschlandhalle and it soon became clear that Udet's plan was quite feasible. At the same time, the methods adopted by my partner and by myself were somewhat different.

To my mind, the effectiveness of the demonstration from the spectators' point of view would depend on whether the plane flew above or below them – and if below, then to many, no doubt, the machine would appear never to have left the ground. I therefore flew as close to the roof as I could.

My partner, on the other hand, thought this was too dangerous and decided on principle not to fly more than a few yards above the ground. My own attitude was as follows: I was absolutely certain of my ability to fly the plane and therefore the only possible source of danger was the helicopter itself. If it was technically unsafe, then the height at which it was flown was immaterial – the risk to thousands of spectators' lives ought not to be taken at all. The technical aspect, however, was not my responsibility, as pilot, but the designer's.

After we had been training on these lines for some days, we were surprised, one Sunday morning, to find the front seats of the stadium filled with Luftwaffe generals. My co-pilot went up first, keeping, as usual, within twenty feet of the ground. But at this height, the air currents set up by the blades of the rotors were reflected off the ground in turbulent eddies, causing the plane to rock in an apparently dangerous manner. This, added to the failure of one of the steel rotor braces on my partner's second flight, caused Göring, rightly or wrongly, to permit the public demonstration of the helicopter to take place only on condition that throughout the three weeks' period I myself flew the plane at every performance.

I must admit that the prospect appalled me. Firstly, I was to become a variety artiste! Every day during February 1938, at every street corner, it seemed, in Berlin, I came upon a vast, garishly coloured poster bearing in giant letters the word: KISUAHELI! – and underneath: 'Deutschlandhalle – Kisuaheli – Through the Tropics at 200 Miles-per-Hour!' Then there was a list of attractions: Dancing Girls, Fakirs, Clowns, Blackamoors, and, 'Last Item – Hanna Reitsch Will Fly the Helicopter'.

When my flying friends heard of this, they were frankly scandalized, while my opponents, I imagined, would give a superior smile, confidently asserting that I would next be heard of in a nightclub cabaret. But it was not for cheap notoriety that I had agreed, with the consent of my parents, to fly the helicopter in this strange setting, but because I realized that the reputation of German technical skill was at stake.

As for the setting, it turned out to be even stranger than I had expected. During rehearsals, the technicians would be perched on their ladders against the helicopter, calculating with their slide rules the correct angle of tilt for the rotors, while all around them in the arena of the Deutschlandhalle a colourful throng of circus folk practised their turns – skinny gymnasts with tennis-ball biceps scaling ropes or twirling on the parallel bars, scantily clad chorus girls, stamping their legs with energetic precision, and a clown, who every now and then would come toddling up, double-somersault and toddle on.

Most intriguing of all were the Negroes – a novelty in Germany before 1945. If they were not watching us at work, they liked to sit round the helicopter reading the newspaper, for most of them had been born in a circus troupe and knew less, even, about the jungle than I!

As the opening night approached, tension steadily mounted and though I tried to remain calm and detached and avoid succumbing to 'footlight-fever', everything seemed to conspire to fray my nerves. There were the posters, for example. Try as I might to get back to my hotel after rehearsals without seeing one, sooner or later, through the window of my car, I would be bound to glimpse that horrid word: KISUAHELI!

Then, there were my friends and fellow airmen, who somehow found their way to me, full of strident and reproachful oratory. There was my brother in the navy, who never ceased to beseech and implore me to withdraw from the show. Finally, a complication was added to the performance itself. At the end, I was told to take leave of the public with a Nazi salute, perfectly timed and perfectly executed. I rehearsed this in front of Udet, comfortably ensconced in an armchair smoking a cigar, and I had plenty of opportunity to realize, before he was finally satisfied, that flying the helicopter in the Deutschlandhalle was not, as I had imagined, the hardest thing in the world.

The first night arrived and I found myself sitting beside Udet in his box in the Deutschlandhalle, watching the first half of the show. Officially, smoking was strictly forbidden, but Udet was nervously lighting one cigarette after another, turning to me between whiles to ask me again and again how I felt. After a while, I could stand it no longer and during the first interval I slipped unnoticed out of the box and watched the performance from another part of the stadium.

At last, at about half-past eleven, the time came for me to get ready.

The theme of the programme was Germany's lost colonies, at that time a much ventilated grievance, and the stadium had been furnished with palm trees, a negro village and other exotic para-phernalia to give the public the illusion of an African landscape.

Into this setting my demonstration with the helicopter had been ingeniously fitted. The plane itself was housed, out of sight, in a native tent. At the end of the Variety Programme proper, there was a complete blackout for a few seconds, then giant searchlights picked out the tent as it slowly opened to reveal the helicopter, which was then pushed into the arena by mechanics in spotless white overalls.

There was an atmosphere of almost solemn tension among the spectators, as if they were expecting some great sensation. The word 'Deutschland' stood, clear and beautiful, on the silver fuselage of the plane and as my eyes read the inscription, my heart lifted in greeting to my country, before I climbed into the cockpit and made ready for my first flight.

Meanwhile, a technical and historical introduction to the helicopter was being given over the loudspeakers. At the end, the public was instructed to hold securely onto hats and other light articles, as a potential source of danger both to the plane and to themselves and as I took off, the effect of thousands of people on the floor and at the sides of the arena, all staring up at me and clutching grimly on to some object or other, was distinctly comic.

But my attention was soon claimed by the engine of the helicopter, which was somehow lacking in power. At first, I could find no explanation and it was only after the phenomenon had repeated itself on the second evening that a possible reason occurred to me – part of the oxygen required by the engine was being used up by the vast audience in the stadium.

Though the technicians at first derided this explanation, it proved to be correct and thereafter, every evening before the flight, I had all entrance doors opened wide to replenish the oxygen in the atmosphere. Only by this means could I ensure the necessary reserve of power to overcome the slight air pockets that were continually present over the arena.

At first, the audience followed the flight intently, but very soon their enthusiasm began to wane until, at the end of the performance, there was only moderate applause.

The good Berliners were disappointed, for, to their mind, I owed

them the sensation that had been promised in the programme –
'Through the Tropics at 200 Miles-per-Hour' – and instead of that,
the plane had risen slowly up, stood still in the air, and, slow as
ever, moved sideways, backwards and forwards, then flopped
leisurely to earth again.

'*Det sollen dreihundert Sachen sin?*' they murmured – 'And they
call that two 'undred what names?'

'Anybody could do *that*! She don' know 'ow to fly wotcha call
fa-arst – why don' she give us some o' the *real* stuff?'

Not only the Berliners were disappointed. Udet had expected
thunderous applause but now was forced to realize that he had
grossly overestimated the capacity of the general public to appreciate a purely technical achievement.

The enthusiasm and interest aroused in the aeronautical and
technical world, on the other hand, were immediate and there both
the difficulties of flying the helicopter indoors and the significance
of this new type of plane were fully appreciated.

G. L. Steer

Guernica

They told us at the General Staff that afternoon of the bombardment of Markina, Bolibar and Arbacegui-Guerricaiz. All the villages
had been smashed up on the way back to Gernika.*

The destruction at Arbacegui barred our way. There were four
dead near the church. Two cottages sprawled in smoking pieces
across the road, and we climbed over them and down the fields to
see the biggest bombholes we had ever seen, warm and stinking of
metal still. They were over twenty feet deep and forty feet wide. They
were mooncraters. We looked in wonder at them. Suddenly on the
hillside behind us the bell of the little church began to tinkle. We saw
the two old priests and a few villagers stumble across debris and torn
green grass into the tower door. Then silence in the village; nothing
to see but the smoking houses and walls smirched grey with fire.

Over the ridge to the north-west, from the direction of Gernika,
came six fighting planes in echelon. They were flying very fast, level
and straight, and their engines made a noise which meant immediate war. In a few seconds they were on the village. They were so
low that one could see with the naked eye the pilots and every
detail of the planes down to the split wheels and characteristic pin-
nose of the German army fighter, Heinkel 51. These were the same
planes that Kienzle and Schulze-Blanck said that they had flown
from Vitoria – six Heinkel 51s in battle formation.

Christopher Corman and I thought that the bombhole was the
best place. We reached the bottom in two jumps. It looked less safe
from down below, for the sides were unusually wide and one could
see too much sky. But it was a hole, and we lay on the shady side
face down in tumbled clay and jagged bomb splinters.

* This is the Basque spelling of 'Guernica'.

There can have been no movement visible in the village, and there was no traffic moving or stationary upon the road, except our car. But they dropped a few light bombs and machine-gunned the place until they must have shot all the dust off the roofs that still stood.

Then they circled and spotted us. For between fifteen and twenty minutes they dived over our hole at full throttle, loosing off their double guns at us from anything down to 200 feet. The only thing was to pretend to be dead already, and sometimes we wondered whether we were. Old Corman was spinning a long story about the ineffectiveness of aerial machine-gunning on entrenched positions, but somehow today he sounded much less impressive, and I asked him to be silent and to wait and see. It struck me, too, as very undignified for an Englishman to eat earth before the German aviation: but I was bothered if I could think of any safe alternative. It was difficult to think at all. As soon as that very material process known as the collection of one's thoughts was nearly complete another bloody little fighter was roaring down at us, and we were spreadeagled and passive again.

Of course, it's all noise. The shooting was wild, and after a quarter of an hour of it we could not find a bullet in the bombhole. And when they had gone we recollected how often the pilots had kept on gunning when the planes were soaring upwards fit to hit the stars. Terror, noise were their weapons, not death.

I had been machine-gunned a few times before and was machine-gunned many times afterwards, but I never figured in so pretty a target. It impressed me. My experience must be much the same as that of any young recruit. Continual strafing from the air does not frighten; it paralyses. We pulled ourselves out of the hole very slowly. We didn't look about us much. We were thinking all the time of the experience which we had suffered, and not a thought did we give to the future or the present. We were raw material for any surprise.

None of the villagers were hurt, but they stayed huddled in the blackness of the church tower, I suppose till nightfall. Their terror was real, not half exorcized like ours. We turned our car in front of the burning barricade. It, too, was untouched. The chauffeur was told to go straight back to Bilbao.

As we made homewards we had to stop twice and wait for enemy aeroplanes to pass. Their type was the light bomber Heinkel 111, and we saw several fly across to our right towards the Gernika inlet. The same alarm chained the peasantry to their holes and hedges; the fields were tragically deserted and bare. As we passed the level crossing we heard bombing to the north, where the inlet settles down into green valley. We saw nothing, for there were hills between. The bombs must have been dropped by the planes which passed us. We had experienced quite enough that day, and we went on without stopping to Bilbao to write our stories.

It was about four thirty by the clock of our car on Monday, April 26th.

*

Monday was the weekly market day of Gernika, when the town existed. At about four thirty the market, in summer, was at its fullest. The civil war had not made a great difference to the Gernika farmers who brought in their animals and produce for sale from the rich valley. Rather there was better business. In Gernika, where the population was usually 7,000, there were now an additional 3,000 refugees and two Basque battalions, who had plenty of pesetas to spend. A few of the factious rich had been jailed or run away, but only a few. Their fine stone houses with the floreate blazons engraved hugely over wide doors were shut: but they never had used the market much, and most of them visited peacetime Gernika little.

Gernika remained a modest Vizcayan country town. The population behaved itself, the priests walked about in the cloth, mass was held in the churches all day and every day. The two Basque Nationalist battalions quartered to the north of the town, where a water-green avenue of plane trees rippled out towards Bermeo, were popular with the people, and in Gernika itself there was the usual post of Basque motorized police. There were no troops retreating through the town. The armies were beyond Markina, miles to the east, and at Oitz, miles to the south. Gernika lay well behind the front, on part of its communications with Bilbao: to destroy it would cut off the retreating armies from the General Staff and their base.

After four there were farm carts coming into Gernika, rolling on solid wooden wheels and drawn by oxen whose heads were shaded under fleeces of sheep. Basque peasants in their long puckered market smocks walked backwards in front of them, mesmerizing the oxen to Gernika with their slim wands, with which they kept touching the horns and yoke gently. They talked to the oxen. Others were driving sheep to market. There was an assembly of animals near the parish church, a stately structure cavernous and dark within, standing upon a flight of thin steps like leaves piled one upon the other.

It is improbable that anyone was thinking about the war, when at four thirty the church bell rang out loud. All over Spain a peal on a single bell is an air raid warning. The population took cover, and the sheep in the square were left to their own devices.

There were numerous air raid shelters in Gernika, constructed after the terrible raid on Durango on March 31st. Any cellar was covered with sandbags, and the entrance protected in the same way: a cardboard at the door painted ornamentally REFUGIO showed where the people had to dive. Though there had been few raid warnings at Gernika since the war began, the whole Basque population by now took their church bells seriously.

In a few minutes a Heinkel 111 came over and dropped six medium bombs, probably fifty-pounders, near the station, with a shower of grenades. A director of the railway company who was in the office rang up Bilbao to inform them that an aeroplane was bombing Gernika.

A few minutes later another Heinkel 111 appeared, to bomb the same area, but nearer the centre. The telephone with Bilbao was now cut. The plane from its slant and speedy sides machine-gunned the town at random, then veered homeward.

The parish priest, Aronategui, left his church with the sacraments, for dying people were reported near the railway station. He went calmly through the deserted streets with the bread. No fires had yet started.

Fifteen minutes passed, and the people were coming out of their shelters. A heavy drumming of engines was heard to the east. It was what we called in lighter moments the *tranvías* – the trams – the Junkers 52s, who were so clumsy that they seemed to clang rather than to fly. These were the heaviest bombers that Germany had sent to Spain.

Over the town, whose streets were once more empty trenches, they dispersed their load a ton at a time. They turned woodenly over Gernika, the bombs fell mechanically in line as they turned. Then came the crack of the explosions; smoke stood up over Gernika like wool on a Negro's head. Everywhere it sprouted, as more heavy bombers came.

Besides many fifty- and hundred-pound bombs, they dropped great torpedoes weighing a thousand. Gernika is a compact little town, and most of these hit buildings, tearing them to pieces vertically from top to bottom and below the bottom. They penetrated refuges. The spirit of the people had been good, but now they panicked.

An escort of Heinkel 51s, the same perhaps that had molested us that afternoon, were waiting for this moment. Till now they had been machine-gunning the roads round Gernika, scattering, killing or wounding sheep and shepherds. As the terrified population streamed out of the town they dived low to drill them with their guns. Women were killed here whose bodies I afterwards saw. It was the same technique as that used at Durango on March 31st, nearly a month back.

The little fighting planes came down in a line, like flashing dancing waves on shingle. They burst in spray on the countryside as they merrily dived. Twenty machine-guns working together in line, and the roar of breakers behind them from ten engines. Always they flew nose towards Gernika. For the pilots it must have been like surfing. The terrified people lay face down in ditches, pressed their backs against tree trunks, coiled themselves in holes, shut their eyes and ran across sweet green open meadow. Many were foolish,

and fled back before the aerial tide into the village. It was then that
the heavy bombing of Gernika began.

It was then that Gernika was smudged out of that rich landscape,
the province of Vizcaya, with a heavy fist.

It was about five fifteen. For two hours and a half flights of
between three and twelve aeroplanes, types Heinkel 111 and Junkers
52, bombed Gernika without mercy and with system. They chose
their sectors in the town in orderly fashion, with the opening points
east of the Casa de Juntas and north of the Arms Factory. Early
bombs fell like a circle of stars round the hospital on the road to
Bermeo: all the windows were blown in by the divine efflatus, the
wounded militiamen were thrown out of their beds, the inner fabric
of the building shook and broke.

On the shattered houses, whose carpets and curtains, splintered
beams and floors and furniture were knocked into angles and ready
for the burning, the planes threw silver flakes. Tubes of two pounds,
long as your forearm, glistening silver from their aluminium and
elektron casing: inside them, as in the beginning of the world in
Prometheus' reed, slept fire. Fire in a silver powder, sixty-five
grammes in weight, ready to slip through six holes at the base of
the glittering tube. So as the houses were broken to pieces over the
people sheathed fire descended from heaven to burn them up.

Every twenty minutes fresh raiders came. And between the
explosions and the spurts of flame as the burning metal seeped into
curtains and beams, doors and carpets, while a grey pall stood over
Gernika supported from below by white pillars where fires were
starting, in the pauses of modern battle the population ran about
the streets to clear away the doors of smothered refuges, to pull
children and other small worthless belongings from houses afire.

There was much groaning in Gernika, much breathless work to
dig out wounded people before the next planes came. Twenty minutes
was the interval between fire, and the priests spoke to the people to
keep them calm. By now something like a spirit of passive resistance
had been built up in them. Gernika's face was turning to ashes,
everybody's face in Gernika was ash-grey, but terror had reached a
condition of submissive stubbornness not seen before in Vizcaya.

In the intervals people moved out of the town, but the fear of the fighting plane and separation from their families persuaded many to remain in Gernika. And then the planes returned with their tinsel tubes to shower over Gernika and another part was destroyed, and more were buried in the *refugios*.

I do not know whether you have ever sat in a railway station having lost one train and waiting for another which will come in two and a half hours' time. A country railway station, where you can buy nothing to read or smoke or eat: and the hours take days to pass if you cannot go to sleep. Now in Gernika it was well-nigh impossible to go to sleep, except in an obligatory sleep which had no morrow in Gernika, or Vizcaya or this world. And since there was nothing to eat or smoke, and fumes prevented one from reading, no other diversion remained but to allow terror to expand those hours past days into months and years. Years half spent in dugouts that might crash at any moment, and half spent in streets of an unrecognizable town looking for people who may now be unrecognizable.

And so you see that to be in Gernika when it was destroyed was, in a limited sense, like waiting for a train in a country station. Time in both cases passed slowly.

Soon there was little of the town to move about in. The Church of San Juan was burning fiercely, with a huge bombhole through its roof and its altar and pulpit rippling fire. Even a few isolated buildings were touched: at the old parish church of Andra Mari, in the corner of the square where the sheep had been gathered, the chapel behind the altar was aflame.

As the people not trapped in the refuges moved northwards before the general fire the planes that raided Gernika came very low. It must have been difficult for them to sight their target in the smoke and grit which rose from the spreading campfire below them. They flew at 600 feet, slowly and steadily shedding their tubes of silver, which settled upon those houses that still stood in pools of intolerable heat; then slipped and dribbled from floor to floor. Gernika was compact as peat to serve as fuel for the German planes. Nobody now bothered to save relatives or possessions: between bombardments they walked out of Gernika in front of the stifling smoke and sat in bewildered hundreds on the roads to Bermeo and Mugika. Mercifully, the fighters had gone. They no longer glanced down to mutilate the population in movement and chase them across the open fields. The people were worn out by noise, heat and terror; they lay about like dirty bundles of washing, mindless, sprawling and immobile. There was nothing to save in Gernika but the few old mattresses and pillows, kitchen tables and chairs which they had dragged out of the fire. By seven thirty that evening fire was eating away the whole of crowded little Gernika but the Casa de Juntas and the houses of the Fascist families. These, being wealthier than the others, lived in stone mansions apart from the rest of the people: their properties did not catch the infection of the running fire, even when under pressure of the wind it stretched its savage arms to stroke them.

At seven forty-five the last plane went away. One could hear now, through ears half-numbed by the engines of the heavy bombers and explosion of the heavy bombs, the nervous crackle of arson all over the town and the totter and trembling collapse of roofs and walls. Gernika was finished, and as night fell and the motorized police stumbled along the road to ring up Bilbao to say that all was over, the total furnace that was Gernika began to play tricks of crimson colour with the night clouds. Very gently and softly they throbbed reflections of her death movement. They lay over her like a crimson-cushioned ceiling, like the hangings of a dying monarch, billowy and rich, stirring to the Gernika light.

Around the corpse of the Basques' oldest village *caseríos* aflame in the hills made candles. The aviation had spent the residue of its fire upon them and had struck many.

Beginning to talk and to try to understand their experience, the Basques asked each other how many planes had attacked their town. Some said eighty, others a hundred, others two hundred, others more. They could not tell: but those who were outside Gernika the whole afternoon say that between fourty and fifty German planes attacked her, including ten fighters. The bombers reappeared again and again with fresh loads.

To the people within Gernika it was not a question of figures, but of inquantitative and immeasurable terror. All they could hear was the drumbeat of the engines and the split of the explosions again and again until they sounded dull enough. They could see no more but the trembling doors of their refuges and their own helpless faces, and sometimes if they were in the streets the points of fire where the silver tubes struck: these fell many at a time, for they were dropped twenty-four together on a single spinning rod. Sometimes, too, before they bolted below they saw through the smoke the stiff, stubborn wings of the planes which molested them and heard the wingless flight of the metal that spurted blindly all over the town, crushing walls and roof tiles and stripping trees of their leaves and branches.

When they crept back to the town between the soft breeze of the flames now blowing on every house they saw what I saw later that night.

*

At Bilbao we sent our day's story off: it dealt with the bombardments all along the communications that day, from Markina to Arbacegui-Guerricaiz. Some time about seven Arbex told me that Gernika was being bombed: he said that they had had news earlier of it, but there were no details. He did not seem to give the bombardment much importance. I did not mention it in my story that night.

We were having dinner at eight thirty in the Torrontegui that evening: quite a number of us. Captain Roberts of the *Seven Seas Spray* and his daughter Fifi, Arbex, Christopher Holme and some other journalists sat down with me in the wide sombre dining room, peopled by the near-ghosts of women and old men of the Right, who talked in a whisper and glided rather than walked. The dinner was going fairly well, when at ten o'clock Antonio Irala rang up.

'Gernika is in flames,' he said.

We got cars, threw our napkins on the floor and drove out into the dark towards Gernika. I recollect the mood in which I went to that fire: the same mood as that with which many people in England heard the news of it. Irala must be exaggerating, I felt. The whole town cannot be burning.

We followed Arbex's car through the countryside along the road which we had followed that morning. Arbex drove like a lunatic, with a cigarette holder sticking out of his open glass. It glowed ahead of us, until we lost it against a brighter sky.

*

Fifteen miles south of Gernika the sky began to impress us. It was not the flat dead sky of night: it seemed to move and carry trembling veins of blood: a bloom of life gave it body, flushed its smooth round skin.

Nearer it became a gorgeous pink. The sort of pink that Parisians have dreamed of for centuries. And it seemed enormously fat: it was beginning to disgust us.

It still had no source. Gernika was hidden behind the hills through which we careered. But we could see now that the fatness was great bellying clouds of smoke and the pinkness the reflection of some great fire upon them. The skies in their vague, all-embracing way were mirroring Gernika, and pulsed more slowly to the destruction that danced a war dance over the home of seven thousand human beings.

Out of the hills we saw Gernika itself. A Meccano framework. At every window piercing eyes of fire: where every roof had stood wild trailing locks of fire. The Meccano framework was trembling, and a wild red disorder was taking the place of its rigid geometry. We drove down the street which led into Gernika from the south carefully, for it was a street no longer. Black or burning beams and tattered telephone wires rolled drunkenly, merrily across it, and the houses on either side streamed fire as vapour rises effortless from Niagara. Four dead sheep lay to our right in a trickle of blood, and as we approached the central place over huge bomb holes and volcanoed fresh earth before the Casa de Juntas, we saw a dazed score of militiamen, Batallón Saseta, standing by the roadside, half waiting for, half incapable of understanding, their orders. The fire of the houses lit up their spent, open faces.

In the plaza, in the dark shadow of the Casa de Juntas which made the only shade in Gernika that night, people sat upon broken chairs, lay on rough tables or mattresses wet with water. Mostly women: some hundreds of them were littered around in the open space, and as we passed they groped about, fiddled with dirty pillows, tried to sleep, tried feebly to talk. We talked to them: they told me all that had happened, this stricken people were my authority for all that I have written. Two priests were with them: Aronategui was not to be found, and they supposed him dead. They conversed in tired gestures and words unnaturally short for Spain, and they made the funny noises of bombers poising, fighters machine-gunning, bombs bursting, houses falling, the tubes of fire spurting and spilling over their town. Such was the weary, sore-eyed testimony of the people of Gernika, and it was only later that people who were never in Gernika thought of other stories to tell.

Some of the witnesses were quite dumb. They were digging them out of ruined houses, families at a time, dead and blue-black with bruising: others were brought in from just outside Gernika with machine-gun bullets in their bodies. One a lovely girl. The militia cried as they laid her out on the ground in the broken hospital: they could give no reason for their tears, they just cried.

A fire brigade with a feeble piddle was playing on the chapel of Andra Mari. I went up into the shades of the Casa de Juntas. The gardens were torn about, windows were broken, but behind the Casa stood the oak of Basque civil liberty. Untouched. The black old trunk, under which when it flowered the Catholic kings promised to respect Basque democracy, stood there in its mummi-fied death, untouched between thick white pillars. The seats engraved with the arms of Vizcaya, tree and lurking wolves, where the Señor of Vizcaya took the oath of suzerainty and respect, untouched. The new-sprung oak from the loins of the older, untouched and green. A few rose petals lay on the stones around, pink confetti blown there in the twilight by the bombardment of Gernika.

In the centre of the town the smaller tongues of fire were tuning into a single roar. The motorized police, with Monzon, Minister of the Interior, stood helpless beyond the plaza, where streets tightened and intertwined to make the heart of our conflagration. We tried to enter, but the streets were a royal carpet of live coals, blocks of wreckage slithered and crashed from the houses, and from their sides that were still erect the polished heat struck at our cheeks and eyes. There were people, they said, to be saved there: there were the frameworks of dozens of cars. But nothing could be done, and we put our hands in our pockets and wondered why on earth the world was so mad and warfare become so easy.

We talked with the people round the great furnace for two hours. I smoked a number of cigarettes to settle my mood, drove back to Bilbao, and slept on my story.

Government lorries and ox carts carried away the refugees. Our headlights illumined the slack shoulders and loose blankets of hundreds who walked slowly towards Bilbao and Munguia.

Between cigarettes I played with three silver tubes picked up that evening in Gernika. The argent thermite distilled itself slowly from their bases; they came from the German RhS factory in 1936, said their stamp. And over the legend stood a symbol in miniature, the Imperial eagle with scarecrow wings spread.

Stephen Spender

'The Landscape Near An Aerodrome'

More beautiful and soft than any moth
With burring furred antennae feeling its huge path
Through dusk, the air liner with shut-off engines
Glides over suburbs and the sleeves set trailing tall
To point the wind. Gently, broadly, she falls,
Scarcely disturbing charted currents of air.

Lulled by descent, the travellers across sea
And across feminine land indulging its easy limbs
In miles of softness, now let their eyes trained by watching
Penetrate through dusk the outskirts of this town
Here where industry shows a fraying edge.
Here they may see what is being done.

Beyond the winking masthead light
And the landing ground, they observe the outposts
Of work: chimneys like lank black fingers
Or figures frightening and mad: and squat buildings
With their strange air behind trees, like women's faces
Shattered by grief. Here where few houses
Moan with faint light behind their blinds,
They remark the unhomely sense of complaint, like a dog
Shut out, and shivering at the foreign moon.

In the last sweep of love, they pass over fields
Behind the aerodrome, where boys play all day
Hacking dead grass: whose cries, like wild birds,
Settle upon the nearest roofs
But soon are hid under the loud city.

Then, as they land, they hear the tolling bell
Reaching across the landscape of hysteria,
To where louder than all those batteries
And charcoaled towers against that dying sky,
Religion stands, the church blocking the sun.

Antoine de St-Exupéry

The Elements

When Joseph Conrad described a typhoon he said very little about towering waves, or darkness or the whistling of the wind in the shrouds. He knew better. Instead, he took his reader down into the hold of the vessel, packed with emigrant coolies, where the rolling and the pitching of the ship had ripped up and scattered their bags and bundles, burst open their boxes and flung their humble belongings into a crazy heap. Family treasures painfully collected in a lifetime of poverty, pitiful mementoes so alike that nobody but their owners could have told them apart, had lost their identity and lapsed into chaos, into anonymity, into an amorphous magma. It was this human drama that Conrad described when he painted a typhoon.

Every airline pilot has flown through tornadoes, has returned out of them to the fold – to the little restaurant in Toulouse where we sat in peace under the watchful eye of the waitress – and there, recognizing his powerlessness to convey what he has been through, has given up the idea of describing hell. His descriptions, his gestures, his big words would have made the rest of us smile as if we were listening to a little boy bragging. And necessarily so. The cyclone of which I am about to speak was, physically, much the most brutal and overwhelming experience I ever underwent; and yet beyond a certain point I do not know how to convey its violence except by piling one adjective on another, so that in the end I should convey no impression at all – unless perhaps that of an embarrassing taste for exaggeration.

It took me some time to grasp the fundamental reason for this powerlessness, which is simply that I should be trying to describe a catastrophe that never took place. The reason why writers fail when they attempt to evoke horror is that horror is something invented after the fact, when one is recreating the experience over again in the memory. Horror does not manifest itself in the world of reality. And so, in beginning my story of a revolt of the elements which I myself lived through, I have no feeling that I shall write something which you will find dramatic.

*

I had taken off from the field at Trelew and was flying down to Comodoro-Rivadavia, in the Patagonian Argentine. Here the crust of the earth is as dented as an old boiler. The high-pressure regions over the Pacific send the winds past a gap in the Andes into a corridor fifty miles wide through which they rush to the Atlantic in a strangled and accelerated buffeting that scrapes the surface of everything in their path. The sole vegetation visible in this thread-bare landscape is a series of oil derricks looking like the after-effects of a forest fire. Towering over the round hills on which the winds have left a residue of stony gravel there rises a chain of prow-shaped, saw-toothed, razor-edged mountains stripped by the elements down to the bare rock.

For three months of the year the speed of these winds at ground level is up to 100 m.p.h. We who flew the route knew that once we had crossed the marshes of Trelew and had reached the threshold of the zone they swept we should recognize the winds from afar by a grey-blue tint in the atmosphere at the sight of which we would tighten our belts and shoulderstraps in preparation for what was coming. From then on we had an hour of stiff fighting and of stumbling again and again into invisible ditches of air. This was manual labour, and our muscles felt it pretty much as if we had been carrying a longshoreman's load. But it lasted only an hour. Our machines stood up under it. We had no fear of wings suddenly dropping off. Visibility was generally good, and not a problem. This section of the line was a stint, yes; it was certainly not a drama.

But on this particular day I did not like the colour of the sky.

*

The sky was blue. Pure blue. Too blue. A hard blue sky that shone over the scraped and barren world while the fleshless vertebrae of the mountain chain flashed in the sunlight. Not a cloud. The blue sky glittered like a new-honed knife. I felt in advance the vague distaste that accompanies the prospect of physical exertion. The purity of the sky upset me. Give me a good black storm in which the enemy is plainly visible. I can measure its extent and prepare myself for its attack. I can get my hands on my adversary. But when you are flying very high in clear weather the shock of a blue storm is as disturbing as if something collapsed that had been holding up your ship in the air. It is the only time when a pilot feels that there is a gulf beneath his ship.

Another thing bothered me. I could see on a level with the mountain peaks not a haze, not a mist, not a sandy fog, but a sort of ash-coloured streamer in the sky. I did not like the look of that scarf of filings scraped off the surface of the earth and borne out to sea by the wind. I tightened my leather harness as far as it would go and I steered the ship with one hand while with the other I hung on to one of the struts that ran alongside my seat. I was still flying in remarkably calm air.

Very soon came a slight tremor. As every pilot knows, there are secret little quiverings that foretell your real storm. No rolling, no pitching. No swing to speak of. The flight continues horizontal and rectilinear. But you have felt a warning drum on the wings of your plane, little intermittent rappings scarcely audible and infinitely brief, little cracklings from time to time as if there were traces of gunpowder in the air.

And then everything round me blew up.

Concerning the next couple of minutes I have nothing to say. All that I can find in my memory are a few rudimentary notions, fragments of thoughts, direct observations. I cannot compose them into a dramatic recital because there was no drama. The best I can do is to line them up in a kind of chronological order.

In the first place, I was standing still. Having veered right in order to correct a sudden drift, I saw the landscape freeze abruptly

where it was and remain jiggling on the same spot. I was making
no headway. My wings had ceased to nibble into the outline of the
earth. I could see the earth buckle, pivot – but it stayed put. The
plane was skidding as if on a toothless cogwheel.

Meanwhile I had the absurd feeling that I had exposed myself
completely to the enemy. All those peaks, those crests, those teeth
that were cutting into the wind and unleashing its gusts in my
direction, seemed to me so many guns pointed straight at my
defenceless person. I was slow to think, but the thought did come
to me that I ought to give up altitude and make for one of the
neighbouring valleys where I might take shelter against a mountain-
side. As a matter of fact, whether I liked it or not I was being
helplessly sucked down towards the earth.

Trapped this way in the first breaking waves of a cyclone about
which I learned, twenty minutes later, that at sea level it was
blowing at the fantastic rate of 150 m.p.h., I certainly had no
impression of tragedy. Now, as I write, if I shut my eyes, if I forget
the plane and the flight and try to express the plain truth about
what was happening to me, I find that I felt weighed down, I felt
like a porter carrying a slippery load, grabbing one object in a jerky
movement that sent another slithering down, so that, overcome by
exasperation, the porter is tempted to let the whole load drop.
There is a kind of law of the shortest distance to the image, a
psychological law by which the event to which one is subjected is
visualized in a symbol that represents its swiftest summing up: I was
a man who, carrying a pile of plates, had slipped on a waxed floor
and let his scaffolding of porcelain crash.

*

I found myself imprisoned in a valley. My discomfort was not less,
it was greater. I grant you that backwash has never killed anybody,
that the expression 'flattened out on the ground by backwash'
belongs to journalism and not to the language of flyers. How could
air possibly pierce the ground? But here I was in a valley at the
wheel of a ship that was three-quarters out of my control. Ahead of
me a rocky prow swung to left and right, rose suddenly high in the

air for a second like a wave over my head and then plunged down below my horizon.

Horizon? There was no longer a horizon. I was in the wings of a theatre cluttered up with bits of scenery. Vertical, oblique, horizontal, all of plane geometry was awhirl. A hundred transversal valleys were muddled in a jumble of perspectives. Whenever I seemed about to take my bearings a new eruption would swing me round in a circle or send me tumbling wing over wing and I would have to try all over again to get clear of all this rubbish. Two ideas came into my mind. One was a discovery: for the first time I understood the cause of certain accidents in the mountains when no fog was present to explain them. For a single second, in a waltzing landscape like this, the flyer had been unable to distinguish between vertical mountainsides and horizontal planes. The other idea was a fixation: the sea is flat; I shall not hook anything out at sea.

I banked – or should I use that word to indicate a vague and stubborn jockeying through the east–west valleys? Still nothing pathetic to report. I was wrestling with disorder, was wearing myself out in a battle with disorder, struggling to keep in the air a gigantic house of cards that kept collapsing despite all I could do. Scarcely the faintest twinge of fear went through me when one of the walls of my prison rose suddenly like a tidal wave over my head. My heart hardly skipped a beat when I was tripped up by one of the whirling eddies of air that the sharp ridge darted into my ship. If I felt anything unmistakably in the haze of confused feelings and notions that came over me each time one of these powder magazines blew up, it was a feeling of respect. I respected that sharp-toothed ridge. I respected that peak. I respected that dome. I respected that transversal valley opening out into my valley and about to toss me God knew how violently as soon as its torrent of wind flowed into the one on which I was being borne along.

What I was struggling against, I discovered, was not the wind but the ridge itself, the crest, the rocky peak. Despite my distance from it, it was the wall of rock I was fighting with. By some trick of invisible prolongation, by the play of a secret set of muscles, this was what was pummelling me. It was against this that I was butting

my head. Before me on the right I recognized the peak of
Salamanca, a perfect cone which, I knew, dominated the sea. It
cheered me to think I was about to escape out to sea. But first I
should have to wrestle with the wind off that peak, try to avoid its
down-crushing blow. The peak of Salamanca was a giant. I was
filled with respect for the peak of Salamanca.

There had been granted me one second of respite. Two seconds.
Something was collecting itself into a knot, coiling itself up, growing
taut. I sat amazed. I opened astonished eyes. My whole plane
seemed to be shivering, spreading outward, swelling up. Horizontal
and stationary it was, yet lifted before I knew it 1,500 feet straight
into the air in a kind of apotheosis. I who for forty minutes had not
been able to climb higher than 200 feet off the ground was suddenly
able to look down on the enemy. The plane quivered as if in boiling
water. I could see the wide waters of the ocean. The valley opened
out into this ocean, this salvation. – And at that very moment,
without any warning whatever, half a mile from Salamanca, I was
suddenly struck straight in the midriff by the gale off that peak and
sent hurtling out to sea.

*

There I was, throttle wide open, facing the coast. At right angles to
the coast and facing it. A lot had happened in a single minute. In
the first place, I had not flown out to sea. I had been spat out to sea
by a monstrous cough, vomited out of my valley as from the mouth
of a howitzer. When, what seemed to me instantly, I banked in
order to put myself where I wanted to be in respect of the coastline,
I saw that the coastline was a mere blur, a characterless strip of
blue; and I was five miles out to sea. The mountain range stood up
like a crenellated fortress against the pure sky while the cyclone
crushed me down to the surface of the waters. How hard that wind
was blowing I found out as soon as I tried to climb, as soon as I
became conscious of my disastrous mistake: throttle wide open,
engines running at maximum, which was 150 m.p.h., my plane
hanging sixty feet over, the water, I was unable to budge. When a
wind like this one attacks a tropical forest it swirls through the

branches like a flame, twists them into corkscrews and uproots giant trees as if they were radishes. Here, bounding off the mountain range, it was levelling out the sea.

Hanging on with all the power in my engines, face to the coast, face to that wind where each gap in the teeth of the range sent forth a stream of air like a long reptile, I felt as if I were clinging to the tip of a monstrous whip that was cracking over the sea.

In this latitude the South American continent is narrow and the Andes are not far from the Atlantic. I was struggling not merely against the crushing winds that blew off the east-coast range, but more likely also against a whole sky blown down upon me off the peaks of the Andean chain. For the first time in four years of airline flying I began to worry about the strength of my wings. Also, I was fearful of bumping the sea – not because of the down-currents which, at sea level, would necessarily provide me with a horizontal air mattress, but because of the helplessly acrobatic positions in which this wind was buffeting me. Each time that I was tossed I became afraid that I might be unable to straighten out. Besides, there was a chance that I should find myself out of fuel and simply drown. I kept expecting the petrol plungers to stop priming, and indeed the plane was so violently shaken up that in the half-filled tanks as well as in the feed pipes the petrol was having trouble coming through and the engines, instead of their steady roar, were giving forth a sort of dot-and-dash series of uncertain explosions.

I hung on, meanwhile, to the controls of my heavy transport plane, my attention monopolized by the physical struggle and my mind occupied by the very simplest thoughts. I was feeling practically nothing as I stared down at the imprint made by the wind on the sea. I saw a series of great white puddles, each perhaps 800 yards in extent. They were running towards me at a speed of 150 m.p.h. where the down-surging wind-spouts broke against the surface of the sea in a succession of horizontal explosions. The sea was white and it was green – white with the whiteness of crushed sugar and green in puddles the colour of emeralds. In this tumult one wave was indistinguishable from another. Torrents of air were pouring down upon the sea. The winds were sweeping past in giant gusts as when, before the autumn harvests, they blow a great flowing change of colour over a wheatfield. Now and again the water went incongruously transparent between the white pools, and I could see a green and black sea bottom. And then the great glass of the sea would be shattered anew into a thousand glittering fragments.

It seemed hopeless. In twenty minutes of struggle I had not moved forward a hundred yards. What was more, with flying as hard as it was out here five miles from the coast, I wondered how I could possibly buck the winds along the shore, assuming I was able to fight my way in. I was a perfect target for the enemy there on shore. Fear, however, was out of the question. I was incapable of thinking. I was emptied of everything except the vision of a very simple act. I must straighten out. Straighten out. Straighten out.

*

There were moments of respite, nevertheless. I dare say those moments themselves were equal to the worst storms I had hitherto met, but by comparison with the cyclone they were moments of relaxation. The urgency of fighting off the wind was not quite so great. And I could tell when these intervals were coming. It was not I who moved towards those zones of relative calm, those almost green oases clearly painted on the sea, but they that flowed towards me. I could read clearly in the waters the advertisement of a habitable province. And with each interval of repose the power to feel and to think was restored to me. Then, in those moments, I began to feel I was doomed. Then was the time that little by little I began to tremble for myself. So much so that each time I saw the unfurling of a new wave of the white offensive I was seized by a brief spasm of panic which lasted until the exact instant when, on the edge of that bubbling cauldron, I bumped into the invisible wall of wind. That restored me to numbness again.

*

Up! I wanted to be higher up. The next time I saw one of those green zones of calm it seemed to me deeper than before and I began to be hopeful of getting out. If I could climb high enough, I thought, I would find other currents in which I could make some headway. I took advantage of the truce to essay a swift climb. It was hard. The enemy had not weakened. 300 feet. 600 feet. If I could get up to 3,000 feet I was safe, I said to myself. But there on the horizon I saw again that white pack unleashed in my direction. I gave it up. I did not want them at my throat again; I did not want to be caught off balance. Too late, though. The first blow sent me rolling over and over and the sky became a slippery dome on which I could not find a footing.

*

One has a pair of hands and they obey. How are one's orders transmitted to one's hands?

I had made a discovery which horrified me: my hands were numb. My hands were dead. They sent me no message. Probably they had been numb a long time and I had not noticed it. The pity was that I had noticed it, had raised the question. That was serious.

Lashed by the wind, the wings of the plane had been dragging and jerking at the cables by which they were controlled from the stick, and the stick in my hands had not ceased jerking a single second. I had been gripping the stick with all my might for forty minutes, fearful lest the strain snap the cables. So desperate had been my grip that now I could not feel my hands.

What a discovery! My hands were not my own. I looked at them and decided to lift a finger: it obeyed me. I looked away and issued the same order: now I could not feel whether the finger had obeyed or not. No message had reached me. I thought: 'Suppose my hands were to open: how would I know it?' I swung my head round and looked again: my hands were still locked round the wheel. Nevertheless, I was afraid. How can a man tell the difference between the sight of a hand opening and the decision to open that hand, when there is no longer an exchange of sensations between the hand and the brain? How can one tell the difference between an image and an act of the will? Better stop thinking of the picture of open hands. Hands live a life of their own. Better not offer them this monstrous temptation. And I began to chant a silly litany which went on uninterruptedly until this flight was over. A single thought. A single image. A single phrase tirelessly chanted over and over again: 'I shut my hands. I shut my hands. I shut my hands.' All of me was condensed into that phrase and for me the white sea, the whirling eddies, the saw-toothed range ceased to exist. There was only; 'I shut my hands.' There was no danger, no cyclone, no land unattained. Somewhere there was a pair of rubber hands which, once they let go the wheel, could not possibly come alive in time to recover from the tumbling drop into the sea.

I had no thoughts. I had no feelings, except the feeling of being emptied out. My strength was draining out of me and so was my impulse to go on fighting. The engines continued their dot-and-dash explosions, their little crashing noises that were like the intermittent cracklings of a splitting canvas. Whenever they were silent longer than a second I felt as if a heart had stopped beating. There! that's the end. No, they've started up again.

The thermometer on the wing, I happened to see, stood at twenty below zero, but I was bathed in sweat from head to foot. My face was running with perspiration. What a dance! Later I was to discover that my storage batteries had been jerked out of their steel flanges and hurtled up through the roof of the plane. I did not know then, either, that the strips on my wings had come unglued and that certain of my steel cables had been filed down to the last thread. And I continued to feel strength and will oozing out of me. Any minute now I should be overcome by the indifference born of utter weariness and by the mortal yearning to take my rest.

What can I say about this? Nothing. My shoulders ached. Very painfully. As if I had been carrying too many sacks too heavy for me. I leaned forward. Through a green transparency I saw sea bottom so close that I could make out all the details. Then the wind's hand brushed the picture away.

In an hour and twenty minutes I had succeeded in climbing to 900 feet. A little to the south – that is, on my left – I could see a long trail on the surface of the sea, a sort of blue stream. I decided to let myself drift as far down as that stream. Here where I was, facing west, I was as good as motionless, unable either to advance or retreat. If I could reach that blue pathway, which must be lying in the shelter of something not the cyclone, I might be able to move in slowly to the coast. So I let myself drift to the left. I had the feeling, meanwhile, that the wind's violence had perhaps slackened.

It took me an hour to cover the five miles to the shore. There in the shelter of a long cliff I was able to finish my journey south. Thereafter I succeeded in keeping enough altitude to fly inland to the field that was my destination. I was able to stay up at 900 feet. It was very stormy, but nothing like the cyclone I had come out of. That was over.

On the ground I saw a platoon of soldiers. They had been sent down to watch for me. I landed nearby and we were a whole hour getting the plane into the hangar. I climbed out of the cockpit and walked off. There was nothing to say, I was very sleepy. I kept moving my fingers, but they stayed numb. I could not collect my thoughts enough to decide whether or not I had been afraid. Had I been afraid? I couldn't say. I had witnessed a strange sight. What strange sight? I couldn't say. The sky was blue and the sea was white. I felt I ought to tell someone about it, since I was back from so far away! But I had no grip on what I had been through. 'Imagine a white sea ... very white ... whiter still.' You cannot convey things to people by piling up adjectives, by stammering.

You cannot convey anything because there is nothing to convey. My shoulders were aching. My insides felt as if they had been crushed in by a terrific weight. You cannot make drama out of that, or out of the cone-shaped peak of Salamanca. That peak was charged like a powder magazine; but if I said so people would laugh. I would myself. I respected the peak of Salamanca. That is my story. And it is not a story.

There is nothing dramatic in the world, nothing pathetic, except in human relations. The day after I landed I might get emotional, might dress up my adventure by imagining that I who was alive and walking on earth was living through the hell of a cyclone. But that would be cheating, for the man who fought tooth and nail against that cyclone had nothing in common with the fortunate man alive the next day. He was far too busy.

I came away with very little booty indeed, with no more than this meagre discovery, this contribution: how can one tell an act of the will from a simple image when there is no transmission of sensation?

I could perhaps succeed in upsetting you if I told you some story of a child unjustly punished. As it is, I have involved you in a cyclone, probably without upsetting you in the least. This is no novel experience for any of us. Every week men sit comfortably at the cinema and look on the bombardment of some Shanghai or other, some Guernica, and marvel without a trace of horror at the long fringes of ash and soot that twist their slow way into the sky from those man-made volcanoes. Yet we all know that together with the grain in the granaries, with the heritage of generations of men, with the treasures of families, it is the burning flesh of children and their elders that, dissipated in smoke, is slowly fertilizing those black cumuli.

The physical drama itself cannot touch us until someone points out its spiritual sense.

Richard Hillary

Of Crashes

Of crashes. It was after an armament lecture in one of the huts when we heard, very high, the thin wailing scream of a plane coming down fast. The corporal sat down and rolled himself a cigarette. He took out the paper and made of it a neat trough with his forefinger, opened the tin of tobacco and sprinkled a little on to the paper, ran his tongue along the paper edge and then rolled it. As he put it in his mouth we heard the crash, maybe a mile away. The corporal lit a match and spoke: 'I remember the last time we had one of those. I was on the salvage party. It wasn't a pretty sight.'

We learned later that the man had been on a war-load height test and had presumably fainted. They did not find much of him, but we filled up the coffin with sand and gave him a grand funeral.

John Gillespie Magee

'High Flight'

Oh! I have slipped the surly bonds of earth
    And danced the skies on laughter-silvered wings;
Sunward I've climbed, and joined the tumbling mirth
    Of sun-split clouds – and done a hundred things
You have not dreamed of – wheeled and soared and swung
    Hung in the sunlit silence. Hov'ring there
I've chased the shouting wind along, and flung
    My eager craft through footless halls of air.

Up, up the long, delirious, burning blue
    I've topped the windswept heights with easy grace
Where never lark, nor even eagle flew –
    And while with silent, lifting mind I've trod
The high, untrespassed sanctity of space,
    Put out my hand and touched the face of God.

Paul Nash

The Personality of Planes

I first became interested in the war pictorially when I realized the machines were the real protagonists. Although vast human forces were involved – even at the beginning, their operations were directed mechanically, and they themselves assumed increasingly a mechanical appearance. Pictorially, they seemed to me unimportant compared with the personality of the machines they employed as weapons, for so powerful were these agents of war that, once set in motion, they very soon dominated the immense stage, even though this was divided into three distinct elements, the earth, the water and the air. Everywhere one looked, alarming and beautiful monsters appeared, the tank, the aeroplane, the submarine, the torpedo and the mine, all had individual beauty in terms of colour, form and line, but beyond, or was it *behind*, that actual appearance, these things possessed each a personality, difficult to define and yet undeniable. It was not wholly a matter of mechanistic character. There seemed to be involved some *other* animation – 'a life of their own' is the nearest plain expression I can think of – which often gave them the suggestion of human or animal features.

Of all the many machine personages I quickly found the kind which most strongly appealed to me. For me the aeroplanes seemed paramount. But the discovery did not come quite spontaneously. For the first three months of the war I was unable to paint, being otherwise engaged and otherwise interested. But with the termination of my work and the forming of Sir Kenneth Clark's Advisory Committee for appointing war artists, an opportunity occurred which seemed almost miraculously providential. I was offered the post of official war artist to the Air Ministry. Further, it was understood that my work would be expected to give an imaginative interpretation of the subject. Other artists working upon equal terms would attend to the factual and documentary records. Thus it was I became suddenly intimately interested in a study of aerial creatures.

It was some weeks before my appointment became, as it were, absolute. During my enforced delay I lost no time in making myself acquainted with the character of aeroplanes, of whose construction I then knew nothing whatever. By nature I am unable to appreciate even simple mechanical contrivances. Until I was able to study machines at close range, photographs and pictures were my only guide. But for this I had a mine of inexhaustible yield and infinite variety – the Photograph Division at the Ministry of Information. To become familiar and friendly with these aerial creatures I made a large array of their images in my room, changing the prints from time to time and gaining gradually, I thought, through their constant presence, a sense of their essential nature and behaviour. I did not trouble to learn their names, and to follow their actual anatomy was often beyond me. But all the time I could see the fighter tearing across the spaces of the sky and the bomber ploughing through the clouds, or the mighty Sunderland, most animal of all planes, charging along the coast with its great snout thrust out, defiant and terrible. I was always glad that that one was on our side. But I do not see how so noble a beast could belong to any but Albion.

At last my appointment was confirmed, my permits and passes issued.

My method was to decide upon the aspects of the plane I wished to record and take photographs at once. I would then make a free, rough drawing in line, generally upon a dark paper which would 'take' both a hard wax chalk and water colour in thin washes.

By these means, and a certain amount of reading in such papers as *Flight* and the *Aeroplane*, I began to know something of the character of planes and decided to begin a series of studies, to be called *Aerial Creatures*, with the heavy and medium bombers. The first species on the list happened to be the Vickers Wellington. The Wellington has become almost boringly popular. It gets all the searchlight as it were. I can understand this to a certain extent.

The Wellington is very human in one way. It is jolly, it is on the plump side, I see that now. But when I first tried to stare a Wellington out of countenance, I was shaken. This baleful creature filled me with awe. Its chief characteristic is a look of purpose, of unswerving concentration upon its goal. Its big mammalian head and straight pointed wings, its proud fin and strong level flight, like that of an avenging angel, all make up a personality of great strength, a formidable machine, heroic and justly popular. On the other hand, if we seek an animal equivalent for the Wellington, it resembles the whale so nearly that there seems no reason why it should not start spouting in the sky at any moment. To watch the dark silhouette of a Wellington riding the evening clouds is to see almost the exact image of the great killer whale hunting in unknown seas.

Even so the Wellington is *not* a whale. It is a Wellington, and for two pins it can look like some other creature. I must insist here that these 'resemblances' should not be regarded literally; they are indications merely of that other life which, to the imaginative sense, modern aeroplanes seem to possess.

While I was making my studies of the Wellingtons, I was often aware of a strange silhouette in the distance, of a body, elongated and rigid, proceeding at a slow pace and at what at first appeared to be a rather precarious angle; the nose depressed, the queer, wide tail up-tilted. When the phenomenon came my way and the air began to pulsate with its heavy engines, I saw it was a plane of curious distinction; in form very long, very narrow, with a wide wingspan and well-balanced tail features. Looking up, as it passed in the sunlight, I saw two flashes come from its bow. Once from the crown of its spine then again, when the beam of light was thrown back from a front of glass at a lower level, right forward – what seemed to me the true helm. Obviously quite another beast from the Wellington whale . . .

I recognized this interesting creature as a Whitley, the next in order, as it turned out, of my series of bombers.

By the time I came to make studies of the Whitley, my technique had developed. I now pursued my quarry in a staff car accompanied by an officer or NCO, whenever this was possible. This method not only saved time and eliminated space but supplied the very necessary element of education I still needed for intelligent interpretation of mechanical facts into pictorial equivalents.

A Whitley, as Blake said of a tear, is an intellectual thing, and as obscurely so, perhaps. Planes have their permanent moods, some active, others passive. Pride, in the proper sense, ferocity and cunning, dignified range or a quiet, ominous detachment, cerebral and deadly. Such, in part, is the Whitley's psyche. Yet, with all this, it is a queer birdlike creature, reminding me of a dove! Look at its head and lovely birdlike wings. As it sails through the low clouds at sunset, it might be the dove returning to the Ark on Mount Ararat. But it is more than this. If it is a dove, it is a dove of death. It is known as the Flying Coffin for more than obvious reasons. Look again, as she lifts into the sky, how menacing is that dark profile! I never see a Whitley low overhead without a thought of how the Boches must cower and scurry at the approach of that baleful shade.

Unfortunately the space of this essay does not allow an adequate review of this subject, and a consideration of the new types of machines must be postponed for another occasion. Here there is room left, however, to examine two more well-known species – the Blenheim and the Hampdens.

The two varieties of the first, the short-nosed and the long-nosed Blenheims, are equally first-rate operational aircraft, I should imagine. From the moment I encountered them they impressed me as being reliable characters. They seemed friendly, trustworthy and entirely efficient. They had the air of creatures of good stock, their proportions were fine, their poise and balance sure and satisfying. In comparison with Wellingtons and Whitleys they are of smaller scale, but they look very sturdy and resilient. As to animal equivalents, the short-nose Blenheim is, naturally, enigmatical. You might say it has *no* face – which is true, in a sense, and also terrifying – but I would prefer to say it wears a mask, or that behind a mask it is *growing* a face which, when at last it appears, may eclipse that of all others for its dire beauty.

The long-nosed Blenheim, however, has, literally, no end of a face. Of all planes it possesses most facial features. For instance, it shows clearly a mouth, two wide nostrils, a beaked nose and at least one glaring eyeball. When I began to draw this machine, from which the pilot had just descended, it occurred to me to find out how long he was staying. Only a few minutes it appeared. I abandoned drawing and used up a spool on my camera; taking the plane at various angles and distances. Back in the car I had time to make two rapid studies and note down the colours. The pilot returned and, as he had his foot on the ladder, I asked if he had ever noticed what sort of animal his aeroplane resembled. He said no, that was a new one on him. 'Well, it's like a shark,' I said. 'Good God!' he cried, 'so it is,' and took one leap into the cockpit as if he expected it would bite him. As a matter of fact, this shark-face is rather a superficial resemblance. It depends greatly upon the livid colour of the underparts and the fishlike eyeball. As the Blenheim swung round and, taxiing past, mounted into the sky, I drew a few frenzied lines to fix that flying image from which later was evolved the watercolour called *Appearance of Long-nosed Blenheim*. By this, partly, it may be judged.

At the last, there comes among my aerial creatures, perhaps the strangest of them all. The lineaments of its design are not very prepossessing. It lacks the symmetry of some planes I have described; it is rather clumsy. And, in Heaven's name, what does it look like? No fish, not a bird, not quite a reptile, not wholly an insect. Yet all these negatives suggest a positive. We can only find the equivalent of the Hampden bomber in the mists of prehistory. It is plainly some sort of pterodactyl. It has something of the reptile and yet – apart from being a plane – it is a creature of the skies. I love it because it is a devil. It sets out across the darkling fields soaring into the dusk with its great satanic nose snuffing the upper air. Presently the moon rises, and there goes the flying lizard, gliding across the cloud edge, its pale eyes flickering in the lunar ray. Flying against Germany.

Paul Richey

The Battle of France

I could not sleep that night, which was unusual for me. The others were restless too, tossing about, muttering, perhaps dreaming of the morning's job. We were all so completely exhausted that we couldn't relax. Eventually I sank into dream land – or nightmare-land, as it was nowadays.

We were up again at 2 a.m., staggering about groping for our tunics in the dark. Our bodies must be crawling by now, I thought, for we hadn't taken off more than our sweaty tunics for ten days, and we'd slept in all sorts of unlikely places. We piled silently into the transport and drove off to the airfield. We knew it was cold because it always was, but we couldn't feel it; only that trembling in the stomach that made one weak and slightly nauseated.

On the airfield we lay round the base of a haystack to wait for dawn and the order to take off. We waited, but no order came. It was one of the loveliest dawns I have ever seen; I lay still in the hay and watched it. By the time the sun appeared on the horizon the order to take off still hadn't come. We grew restless and fidgeted uneasily. Waiting was bad for us: it strung us up. We weren't used to being given orders to brood on all night, and then hour by hour next day; we were trained to carry out an order on the spot and in double-quick time.

Exasperated, I jumped up and wandered over to my Hurricane. The Bull's parachute was in it, as he wasn't going on this trip, and we were short of packed parachutes for obvious reasons. Thank God we had a splendid parachute-packer – a little Irishman. It had been the peacetime custom to tip our packer ten shillings in the unusual event of making a jump. Now we tipped him a hundred francs a time, so he was waxing rich. I spent an hour pottering about my Hurricane, checking this and that and altering the parachute harness to fit as tightly as possible. I'd learnt the lesson of having a loose harness on my first jump, when I got such a wrench in the groin I thought I'd been shot there.

I went unwillingly back to the hay, longing for some sort of diversion. I tried to sleep, but couldn't, and kept frizzling over the forthcoming trip. I had never felt like this before and I didn't like it. I thought I was losing my nerve and that my morale was low. From previous experience I thought some food might help. I tried to sleep again; no good. I lectured myself severely and called myself a yellow dog. In reply I confessed that I was afraid. I told myself that fear was inadmissible. I answered that it was there regardless. 'All right,' I said to myself, 'get it under control!' I knew all this backwards, but it was therapeutic to go over it again.

I fell to contemplating the quality of courage as it applied to us. I was often afraid before a job, and though none of us admitted it, I knew we all felt the same. Once in the cockpit, though, strapping in, switching on petrol, checking oxygen, starting the engine and checking instruments, the fear turned to the tension of excitement, which was subjugated in its turn by the concentration needed to take off and join up in the air. From then on there was no time to think of anything but finding the enemy, searching every cubic inch of air, and seeing him before he saw me. When I did see him, all the tension and concentration in my body focused in a wild leap of my heart, a flicking-over in the pit of my stomach. It always made me swallow hard a couple of times. After that it was a simple matter: sights switched on, range and wingspan indicators checked, gun button on 'fire', a quick look at the engine instruments and altimeter, an adjustment on the propeller control.

Of course we normally flew with most of these things ready, and sometimes there was no time for fiddling about, but usually we had a few seconds while manoeuvring for position. Then into action, body taut against the straps, teeth clenched, thumb on the gun-button, narrowed eyes intent on getting that black-crossed Hun in the sights and holding him there. I felt my pounding heart turn to a block of ice. Not in fear. My brain became coldly clear, and in an instant I was transformed into a cool, calculating killer. You'd think an aerial combat was a hot-blooded, thrilling affair. It isn't. I've never felt a fighter in a fight – except perhaps in the moment of victory, when I experienced a savage, primitive exaltation. It's not very edifying ...

Thank heaven breakfast arrived: bread, bully beef and hot tea. We didn't touch the beef, but drank that tea in a trice, then lay back on the hay refreshed. And yet I could see the boys were still jumpy. It was absurd, but I solemnly cursed the unfortunate staff officer who had given us our orders, apparently quite unnecessarily, the previous night. For the next two hours I was continually troubled by something proclaiming itself as a premonition. I moped about kicking things and throwing stones aimlessly, much to Killy's annoyance. 'For Christ's sake, Paul, keep still, will you!' he shouted.

At last, at ten o'clock, after a wait of seven and a half hours, the order to take off came through. We doubled across to our machines. It was the first time I'd seen Johnny looking so taut, or any of the boys for that matter. I threw my tin hat and respirator on the ground beside my Hurricane and climbed in. In a few minutes we were off and formed up. This was the first time we had operated as a complete squadron, and I couldn't help wondering whether our present orders had anything to do with my suggestions to Bill Williams a few days earlier. Anyway, we would be able to assess the moral effect of numbers on our own side for once.

As we climbed up through four-tenths of cumulus cloud at 12,000 feet I saw five unescorted Heinkels, in close formation, crossing above and ahead of us from right to left, and called Johnny up to tell him. It broke our hearts to have to leave them alone, but we had to and that was that. Shortly afterwards Hilly, who was Arse-end Charlie with Soper, shouted: 'Look out! They're behind us! Behind us!' We turned individually in a circle, then Hilly called: 'All serene – they're going away.' We closed up again and resumed our climb.

We reached the patrol line at 20,000 feet and spent our time there getting a little extra height. Now and then we caught sight of formations in the distance, but saw none near us. Under the scattered clouds below there was a slight haze, and we couldn't see our bombers at all.

When our allotted time was up Johnny turned us for home, and we started diving gently but quite fast. At 16,000 feet we suddenly spotted a formation of twenty-five Blenheims below us, going the same way. They were just under the cloudbase at 12,000 feet, and we cheered at the sight. Someone called up, 'Good show! There they go!' Yes, it *was* a good show: it was nice to see some British bombers for a change. They looked strong, deadly and brave in their fine compact formation. We came down behind them in a series of S-turns in close formation, smiling to ourselves. We intended to escort them back to base, or, at any rate, as far as we could.

As we came down closer and examined them in detail as they slid along steadily, in and out of the small clouds, we began to think there was something fishy about those Blenheims. Suddenly Johnny ordered: 'Echelon starboard – Echelon starboard – Go! They're bloody Heinkels!'

We could now see the black crosses on their gunmetal-grey wings. I was No. 3 in 'A' Flight, i.e. on Johnny's left, and I slid underneath him to come up on Hilly's right in echelon starboard. This was the first formation attack we'd had a chance of making, and the first unescorted bombers we'd come across. Twenty-five Heinkels versus a squadron of Hurricanes! Nice work! Now perhaps we'd be able to dish out a decent dose of their own medicine to the bombers.

We went in astern of them in good formation, Johnny taking the left-hand aircraft of the enemy formation, Hilly the second, and myself the third, leaving Yellow Section of 'A' Flight to come up on our right. We'd practised this attack dozens of times in peacetime, and it almost seemed like practice now, except that the Hun rear-gunners were shooting. The Huns had closed up into subformations of threes in Vic, some having a fourth 'in the box' (i.e. below and behind the leader of three). The subformations were stepped down and spread out from the leading formation, which consisted of one

Vic of three, and each subformation appeared to be covering another one with its fire. Their formation was most impressive.

As we went in, steadily closing the range and holding our fire, the smoke of the Huns' tracer bullets snaked through the air towards us. Remorselessly closing in, I was tempted almost to pity the German bombers – but clearly they weren't feeling sorry for us, for the fire got hotter. I was coming up behind the left-hand aircraft of a subformation of four Heinkels when I noticed with considerable uneasiness that I seemed to be the focal point of a lot of tracer-lines. At that point I showed poor discipline, but good sense, by swerving slightly to a position astern of the right-hand aircraft of the subformation. Just then Soper called out: 'Look out behind! Behind you!' and before we had even fired a shot we broke up, thinking fighters were attacking us from the rear. (It was ascertained afterwards that a Hurricane got in Soper's sights as he was about to fire, and I think it must have been me, but shouting over the R/T was damned stupid, and surprising in a pilot of Soper's experience.)

That wrecked our chance for a formation attack, and the fight recommenced on a basis of individual attacks. This was all the more unfortunate because the German formation were using 'fire control' (a 'fire controller' in one aircraft, usually the leader's, directs all the rear-gunners to fire at one particular enemy aircraft, so that they can concentrate as a group on one). Obviously the most effective counter to fire control was a simultaneous attack by as many fighters as possible, and this was best achieved in some sort of formation.

I had pulled away above, to the right of the Heinkels, to get out of their effective range. As I decided which one to go for, I saw several drop out of formation with Hurricanes firing astern of them, two with their engines smoking and a third with its wheels down. I dived left and turned right again to come up astern of a Hun who had dropped back in the middle of the formation. I was closing and just about to open fire when I heard Hilly shout: 'Behind you! Behind you! Watch out, for Christ's sake!' I pulled up to the right and saw another Hurricane pulling away violently to the left. Then I saw what Hilly had been shouting about – and I was glad he had!

A damaged Heinkel had dropped astern but had somehow managed to pull himself together again. He had been belting along flat out behind me; he would probably have got me but for Hilly's warning. I heard Hilly say, 'The bastard!' and saw his Hurricane attack the Heinkel, which I think went down. I thought the Hun had put up rather a good show and was sorry in a way to see him go, but thanks, Hilly!

I tried again. I went in astern of the extreme right-hand Heinkel of a rear subformation of three, fired several bursts and was closing fast when I got in the Heinkel's slipstream and my sights came off. I was nearly on top of him, and judging by the way he suddenly lost speed I must have damaged his engines. I pulled out quickly to the left and turned in on him again, steeply banked to the right, to fire a good deflection burst into his front cockpit. I pulled away to his right, banked smartly left and saw him do a sort of cartwheel, quarter-rolling to the right and dropping his nose simultaneously to the vertical. He went straight into a vertical spiral, and though I saw no smoke or flames, I think he'd had it – heavy bombers don't do that for fun. Probably the pilot was dead or wounded; anyway he was out of the formation.

I now took a quick look round and saw only one Hurricane still with us. I'd been rather long-winded and presumed most of 'A' Flight had run out of ammunition and gone home. I still had plenty left, and went in astern of a lagging Heinkel on the left of the formation. Just as I was closing, a dense clump of flak exploded in the rear of the formation, extending all around me. I glanced left and saw the other Hurricane similarly surrounded with bursts but pressing straight on. A shell burst just beneath me and I heard a muffled bang as an assortment of bits came up through my port wing. The aircraft jerked from the shock, but I wasn't going to lose that seductively lagging Heinkel, and kept on after him. He was flat out to catch up, and had nearly made it, when I had him in range and opened fire.

Between bursts I noticed I was drawing a hell of a lot of crossfire from the formation. I heard several pops and saw more holes appear in both my wings. I was astonished to hear a loud bang as a cannon shell opened a decent-sized hole in my port wing. Tough, these boys! But I was surprised how calm I felt, and how coolly I was thinking. I remember making a mental note of that rear cannon, and thinking that these Heinkels must be Mark Vs. Suddenly smoke belched from both my Heinkel's engines, his wheels dropped and he went down in a shallow right-hand diving turn. I let him go and pulled up left.

I still had about a hundred rounds to each gun left, I judged, and I was excited to see a Heinkel swerve and break formation as a clump of flak burst in his subformation. He dropped back below the formation, but immediately regained control and opened up to full throttle to catch up. But he'd lost a couple of hundred yards, and naturally I pounced, going in astern and opening fire almost straight away. I noted another subformation of three, with one in the box, ahead and above right, throwing everything they had at me.

I concentrated on my Heinkel. I had him beautifully steady in the sights and poured short savage bursts into him as I closed. I was wondering why he showed no sign of being hit, because I knew I was hitting him. He had nearly caught his formation up when grey smoke streamed from both his engines, then from his wing-roots and fuselage, and in a second he was completely enveloped. I felt that savage thrill again and said: 'And that for luck, you sod!' as I fired a final burst into the burning mass. It was only half a burst, because I ran out of ammunition with a hiss of compressed air. As I broke lazily away to the left, feeling pretty pleased with myself, I glanced at the still-firing subformation and mentally put two fingers up in derision. It was then I learnt a lesson I should have known and will never forget.

Just as I rolled – too slowly – over to the left to dive away, I saw a sudden flash of tracer very close, and in the same second heard several pops, then a deafening 'Bang!' in my right ear. (I think it came from the boys above right, but it's just possible that the rear-gunner of the blazing Heinkel was still firing, and if so I raise my hat yet again!) In that instant I knew they'd hit my aeroplane. A shower of blood spurted down my right side. My Hurricane was diving almost vertically, and I was surprised to see my right arm, drenched in blood, raised up in front of me against the hood. There was no feeling in it – the hand was hooked like a dead bird's claw. All this happened in a flash; but so quickly does the mind work that in the same moment I guessed at and assessed the damage and decided how to act. That 'Bang!' still echoed in my right ear, and I said aloud, 'Cannon shell in right shoulder – arm may be almost severed – write that off – pull out of dive with left hand, and if necessary bale out, pulling ripcord with left hand.'

But to my horror I found my left arm wouldn't move either! It hung limp and straight down my side. I looked up to find the aircraft plunging earthwards out of control; it was repeatedly diving, gaining speed, flattening out, losing speed and diving again. I had the extraordinary sensation of my head being isolated from the rest of my body inside the cockpit. I was perfectly conscious and could hear the hiss of the airflow rise and fall over the cockpit roof. I looked at my inert body and tried with all my strength to move my arms. My right hand, or claw, was within four inches of the hood handle, but strain as I might I couldn't get it any nearer. The ground was coming up; I could hear myself grunting and straining to move. Then suddenly I heard myself scream. Muffled but clearly audible, I heard myself mutter it, then say it, then shout it: 'God! God! I'm going to be killed! God!'

I stopped shouting abruptly and looked into the bottom of the cockpit, thinking, 'I won't feel it!' I looked up again and saw the ground rushing up now – and suddenly my left arm moved. So obsessed had I become with the idea of escape that my hand flew to the hood handle to pull it back. It was jammed! I heaved frantically with the manic strength of desperation, but it didn't budge an inch. I looked again into the cockpit, frightened of fire. Then my right hand suddenly flopped on to the stick, pulled it back, and out of that hellish dive I came. None too soon either, though not desperately low – at about 2,000 feet, to be exact.

I chattered away to myself: 'My God! That's the narrowest squeak *I* ever want! Now get down smartly – you may be on fire – and your engine's stopped.' I glanced over the instruments and noticed the air speed indicator wasn't registering at all – a bullet or shell must have got the pitot head or some part of the air speed indicator system. I had lots of holes in my wings, and a bullet hole in the windscreen to the right of the bulletproof section. I wondered where the bullet had gone . . .

I was beginning to feel severe pain in the right side of my neck and face, and thought a cannon shell had struck the side of the cockpit and blown a chunk out of me. I still couldn't get the hood open. I circled as I glided down, picked a field near a village so that I could get help quickly, pumped my flaps down and went in to land with my wheels up. As I held off over a harrowed field I braced myself with my left hand against the sight bar. We touched, bounced and bucketed across the field, grinding along in a cloud of dust. Blood splashed over the dashboard and windscreen. Then, just as I thought we were going over, the tail came down with a thump and we came to rest.

I whipped the pin out of my Sutton harness, unclipped my parachute and tried to open the hood. It was still stuck firm, so I jammed both feet against the instrument panel and tugged. No: it wouldn't move. My neck and shoulder throbbed and I was feeling weak, so I rested a moment. From the bottom of the cockpit little wisps of smoke or dust – I wasn't sure which – were rising. I seized the hood handles once more, heaving and straining with all my remaining strength, but the thing held stubbornly firm and I had to rest again. This was bloody! It looked as though I had escaped a comparatively pleasant death by diving into the ground only to be burnt alive. I wondered if the first lick of flame would give me the strength to bust out of this damned cockpit, or, if not, whether death would come quickly in the heat and smoke. Once again I redoubled my efforts: no good. The emergency panel would not come out with the hood closed, but I bashed out the small break-out panel in the left side of the hood with my fist and put my arm through it, for no reason other than to have access to the outside world.

Why the hell didn't those bloody Frenchmen get a move on? I could hear something dripping and smelt petrol. This galvanized me into one final effort – and suddenly, with a jerk, the hood came half-open. I hauled myself out on to the starboard wing and ran away from the aeroplane, expecting an explosion. Panting and exhausted, I stumbled towards a wooded stream. Then I stopped and looked back. No sign of smoke or fire. I went slowly back. I noticed odd things, such as the quiet and the heat, very clearly; others, such as the holes in my aircraft, not at all. Presumably a bullet had damaged the hood runners, but I forgot to look. I stood on the wing and leaned into the cockpit, switching off the reflector sight, turning off the petrol and main engine switches, putting the gun button to 'Safe', and taking out my maps, all in a methodical and automatic way. I walked round to the other side, carrying my helmet and maps. I was getting a good deal of pain now and was staggering. I kicked in the panel where the first-aid kit was kept to get at the morphia; but it was a new aeroplane from England and they hadn't bothered to put in the first-aid kit. I swore graphically, then told myself not to be a bloody sissy, that I only had a minor flesh wound in the neck anyway.

All the same, it hurt. I had no idea at the time, but I had been shot in the neck by an armour-piercing bullet. It nicked the angle of my jaw in entering, exposed the carotid artery and lodged against the front of the spine at the base of the neck. The shock to the spine had caused temporary paralysis. A little more pressure, and the paralysis would have been permanent – that is, until I hit the ground. A fraction of a millimetre to one side and I would have bled to death from a severed carotid within minutes. A little less height and I would have dived in. A fire, or an uncontrollable aircraft, and I couldn't have baled out. A little more or a little less of this or that – but what the hell? I was lucky.

Elizabeth Bowen

Love in the Blitz

They had met one another, at first not very often, throughout that heady autumn of the first London air raids. Never had any season been more felt; one bought the poetic sense of it with the sense of death. Out of mists of morning charred by the smoke from ruins each day rose to a height of unmisty glitter; between the last of sunset and first note of the siren the darkening glassy tenseness of evening was drawn fine. From the moment of waking you tasted the sweet autumn not less because of an acridity on the tongue and nostrils; and as the singed dust settled and smoke diluted you felt more and more called upon to observe the daytime as a pure and curious holiday from fear. All through London, the ropings-off of dangerous tracts of street made islands of exalted if stricken silence, and people crowded against the ropes to admire the sunny emptiness on the other side. The diversion of traffic out of blocked main thoroughfares into byways, the unstopping phantasmagoric streaming of lorries, buses, vans, drays, taxis past modest windows and quiet doorways set up an overpowering sense of London's organic power – somewhere here was a source from which heavy motion boiled, surged and, not to be dammed up, forced for itself new channels.

The very soil of the city at this time seemed to generate more strength: in parks the outsize dahlias, velvet and wine, and the trees on which each vein in each yellow leaf stretched out perfect against the sun blazoned out the idea of the finest hour. Parks suddenly closed because of time bombs – drifts of leaves in the empty deckchairs, birds afloat on the dazzlingly silent lakes – presented, between the railings which still girt them, mirages of response. All this was beheld each morning more lightheadedly: sleeplessness disembodied the lookers-on.

In reality there were no holidays; few were free however light-headedly to wander. The night behind and the night to come met across every noon in an arch of strain. To work or think was to ache. In offices, factories, ministries, shops, kitchens the hot yellow sands of each afternoon ran out slowly; fatigue was the one reality. You dared not envisage sleep. Apathetic, the injured and dying in the hospitals watched light change on walls which might fall tonight. Those rendered homeless sat where they had been sent; or, worse, with the obstinacy of animals retraced their steps to look for what was no longer there. Most of all the dead, from mortuaries, from under cataracts of rubble, made their anonymous presence – not as today's dead but as yesterday's living – felt through London. Uncounted, they continued to move in shoals through the city day, pervading everything to be seen or heard or felt with their torn-off senses, drawing on this tomorrow they had expected – for death cannot be so sudden as all that. Absent from the routine which had been life, they stamped upon that routine their absence – not knowing who the dead were you could not know which might be the staircase somebody for the first time was not mounting this morning, or at which street corner the news-vendor missed a face or which trains and buses in the home-going rush were this evening lighter by at least one passenger.

These unknown dead reproached those left living not by their own death, which might any night be shared, but by their unknownness, which could not be mended now. Who had the right to mourn them, not having cared that they had lived? So, among the crowds still eating, drinking, working, travelling, halting, there began to be an instinctive movement to break down indifference while there was still time. The wall between the living and the living became less solid as the wall between the living and the dead thinned. In that September transparency people became transparent, only to be located by the just darker flicker of their hearts. Strangers saying, 'Good night, good luck,' to each other at street corners, as the sky first blanched then faded with evening, each hoped not to die that night, still more not to die unknown.

That autumn of 1940 was to appear, by two autumns later,

apocryphal, more far away than peace. No planetary round was to bring again that particular conjunction of life and death; that particular psychic London was to be gone for ever; more bombs would fall, but not on the same city. War moved from the horizon to the map.

*

For Stella, her early knowing of Robert was associated with the icelike tinkle of broken glass being swept up among the crisping leaves, and with the charred freshness of every morning. She could recapture that 1940 autumn only in sensations; thoughts, if there had been any, could not be found again.

More loss had not seemed possible after that fall of France. On through the rest of that summer in which she had not rallied from that psychological blow, and forward into this autumn of the attack on London, she had been the onlooker with nothing more to lose – out of feeling as one can be out of breath. She had had the sensation of being on furlough from her own life. Throughout these September raids she had been awed, exhilarated, cast at the very most into a sort of abstract of compassion – only what had been very small indeed, a torn scrap of finery, for instance, could draw tears. To be at work built her up, and when not at work she was being gay in company whose mood was at the pitch of her own – society became lovable; it had the temperament of the stayers-on in London. The existence, surrounded by one another, of these people she nightly saw was fluid, easy, holding inside itself a sort of ideality of pleasure. These were campers in rooms of draughty dismantled houses or corners of fled-from flats – it could be established, roughly, that the wicked had stayed and the good had gone. This was the new society of one kind of wealth, resilience, living how it liked – people whom the climate of danger suited, who began, even, all to look a little alike, as they might in the sun, snows and altitude of the same sports station, or browning along the same beach in the south of France. The very temper of pleasures lay in their chanciness, in the canvaslike impermanence of their settings, in their being off-time – to and fro between bars and grills, clubs and each other's places moved the little shoal through the noisy nights. Faces came and went. There was a diffused gallantry in the atmosphere, an unmarriedness: it came to be rumoured about the country, among the self-banished, the uneasy, the put-upon and the safe, that everybody in London was in love – which was true, if not in the sense the country meant. There was plenty of everything in London – attention, drink, time, taxis, most of all space.

Into that intimate and loose little society of the garrison Stella and Robert both gravitated, and having done so could hardly fail to meet. They for the first time found themselves face to face in a bar or club – afterwards they could never remember which. Both were in their element, to which to have met instantaneously added more. It was a characteristic of that life in the moment and for the moment's sake that one knew people well without knowing much about them: vacuum as to future was offset by vacuum as to past; life stories were shed as so much superfluous weight – this for different reasons suited both her and him. (Information, that he had before the war lived, worked abroad, in a branch of his father's or a friend of his father's business accumulated gradually, later on.) At the first glance they saw in each other's faces a flash of promise, a background of mystery. While his eyes, in which mirror-refracted lighting intensified a curious blue, followed the one white lock slowly back from her forehead, she found herself not so much beginning to study as in the middle of studying this person – communicative, excitable – from whom she only turned away to wave goodbye to the friend who had brought her across the room.

That gesture of goodbye, so perfunctory, was a finalness not to appear till later. It comprehended the room and everybody, everything in it which had up to now counted as her life: it was an unconscious announcement of the departure she was about to take – a first and last wave, across widening water, from a liner. Remembered, her fleeting sketch of a gesture came to look prophetic; for ever she was to see, photographed as though it had been someone else's, her hand up. The bracelet slipping down and sleeve falling back, against a dissolving background of lights and faces, were vestiges, and the last, of her solidity. She returned to Robert –

both having caught a breath, they fixed their eyes expectantly on each other's lips. Both waited, both spoke at once, unheard.

Overhead, an enemy plane had been dragging, drumming slowly round in the pool of night, drawing up bursts of gunfire – nosing, pausing, turning, fascinated by the point for its intent. The barrage banged, coughed, retched; in here the lights in the mirrors rocked. Now down a shaft of anticipating silence the bomb swung whistling. With the shock of detonation, still to be heard, four walls of in here yawped in then bellied out; bottles danced on glass; a distortion ran through the view. The detonation dulled off into the cataracting roar of a split building: direct hit, somewhere else.

It was the demolition of an entire moment: he and she stood at attention till the glissade stopped. What they *had* both been saying, or been on the point of saying, neither of them ever now were to know. Most first words have the nature of being trifling; theirs from having been lost began to have the significance of a lost clue. What they next said, what they said instead, they forgot: there are questions which if not asked at the start are not asked later; so those they never did ask. The top had been knocked off their first meeting – perhaps later they exonerated themselves a little because of that. Nothing but the rising exhilaration of kindred spirits was, after all, to immortalize for them those first hours: and even forward into the time when meetings came to count for too much to be any more left to chance, they were still liking each other for their alikeness' sake. Into their attraction to one another entered their joy *in* attraction, in everything that was flattering and uncertain. There existed between them the complicity of brother and sister twins, counterpart flowerings of a temperament identical at least with regard to love. That unprecedented autumn, in which in everything round them feeling stood at full tide, made the movement of their own hearts imperceptible: in their first weeks of knowing each other they did not know how much might be the time, how much themselves. The extraordinary battle in the sky transfixed them; they might have stayed for ever on the eve of being in love.

Don Charlwood

Lancaster Navigator

In the morning the first of them circled Elsham. We watched them sweep down to our runway, clean-lined and ladylike, a contrast with the more robust, masculine lines of the Halifaxes. We saw them coming like relief coming to a hard-pressed army; they were unconquerable; the days of heavy losses were over. Soon there was a Lancaster at each dispersal point and no sign of the Halifaxes. Perhaps they were not sufficiently superior to Halifaxes to warrant our enthusiasm, but we would have been cheered by any change that held hope of lower losses.

One day, soon after the changeover, I sat in a swivel chair before the large, green navigator's table of B Beer waiting to set out on an eight-hour cross-country flight, the last exercise of our conversion. It was midafternoon, clear over Lincolnshire, but banked with cloud along the northern horizon. The fields and villages shrank below as we climbed to 6,000 feet. We crossed the coast at Whitby and turned nor'-nor'-west for Kinnairds Head. Within half an hour we were over cloud, white and unbroken for as far north as we could see. The fields and hedges had gone and gone too were the coast and the crawling steamers; we were England's no longer, but flew alone with the sun in an empty sky.

All the way to Kinnairds Head I worked steadily at the chart, checking first on Gee, that mysterious radar aid then coming into general use, and then by radio bearings on northern stations. Once, for no more than a minute, I joined Geoff and Doug in the glass-enclosed cockpit. Cloud still lay below us, a deep-piled carpet beneath the dome of the sky. West beyond the Scottish lowlands the sun was blazing its last, flushing the whole remote world. The crew was watching intently, staring northward.

I worked inside for twenty minutes more, then returned to the cockpit. Outside the scene had changed. The sun had gone, leaving the floor below us grey and very lonely. The sky above was empty of clouds and as yet of stars. Geoff peered more intently ahead, his eyes puckered. At his right knee the face of the compass glowed green, the needle oscillating on 338°, the course I had given him. As I stood there the darkness thickened and the stars appeared, cold droplets of light in an empty world. The full realization settled on me that these other men were trusting me to guide them through this inhospitable sky, and that such would be my task until our operational life was over.

Our first operation from the squadron passed uneventfully. Somehow we reached Frankfurt and somehow we returned. Over the target one sentence from the Master Bomber reached us in a precise but troubled voice. 'You are bombing away to hell south—' Then the voice – and perhaps the speaker – was swallowed up in the onslaught.

On the long return journey bursts of horizontal tracer from nearby air-to-air battles frequently split the night, ending sometimes in midair explosions. But our own journey was uneventful, so uneventful that I was concerned that the crew might imagine ops navigation to be little different from the cross-country exercises to which we were so accustomed.

On our return, Lincolnshire lay beneath fog. We were diverted soon after dawn to Middleton-St-George, in County Durham, the home aerodrome of a Canadian bomber squadron. There we remained for two more days, grounded by fog. Although we borrowed collars and ties from the Canadians and spent those two days in the pubs and cinemas of Middlesbrough, the realization was with me constantly that my ops navigation was haphazard and dangerous. It was obvious that to have any chance of surviving a tour we could not afford to meander across Europe with little real idea of our whereabouts.

On our return we were briefed for Mannheim. Again we meandered across Europe, found our target and bombed. But on the return journey the blow I had anticipated fell.

About an hour out from the target, an astro fix showed us forty miles south of track. On training flights my star shots had brought good results, but I regarded this fix with extreme doubt. Astro on operations was a different proposition. With surprise attacks by fighters always a probability, none of us regarded straight and level flight with much enthusiasm, with the result I tended to work hurriedly and less accurately. To alter course on this one check appeared to be inviting trouble. To get another fix was soon complicated by the development of high cloud. Our Gee and our radio were both out of order, and, in any event, we were beyond the range of British transmitters. I continued with dead reckoning for almost two hours. For all that time a strong wind blew us further and further south of track. Supposedly at Caen, we turned for Dungeness, and supposedly at Dungeness, we turned for Elsham. We must in fact have been in the northern reaches of the Bay of Biscay. Below us there was still a layer of cloud; above, windblown cirrus.

I was waiting to hear Ted's reassuring announcement, 'I can see a beacon through a break in the cloud – probably somewhere on the south coast,' when there was a cry from the rear turret, 'Flak dead astern!'

I jumped to my feet. We should by this time have crossed the English coast.

'Flak coming straight up!'

We swung off course.

'Navigator, where the hell are we? When we get out of this muck, what about a bit of astro?'

I shuffled to the astrodome, panting as though deprived of air. The dome was almost over the W. Op.'s head, being shielded from his light by a black curtain. The curtain was closely drawn, as beneath the light Max was trying to find the fault in his set.

'I need a star shot,' I said.

'How the hell am I going to work in the dark?'

'We must have a check.'

'Well, do you want this set fixed, or don't you?'

'Give me two minutes.'

Growling something, he switched off the light. I pulled back the curtain and raised my head into the glass bubble.

Sometimes those moments return to me. With sudden clarity I see Max Burcher trying to repair his set and feel the sextant again cold in my hands, and hear the voices of Geoff and Doug discussing our fuel. With that, the emotions of that night come flooding back: I am to blame for our predicament; I am flinging away the lives of a crew.

'Hello, Darkie; hello, Darkie; hello, Darkie! This is Hazel B Beer calling; Hazel B Beer. Are you receiving me? Are you receiving me? Are you receiving me? Over to you, over!'

Geoff's distress call was familiar from our training. I strained my ears, but there was no suggestion of a reply.

Max touched my leg. 'Haven't you finished yet?'

'One more shot.'

I looked outside again. There was now no light of any kind. Dimly I could see the airscrews thrusting us further into the unknown. The thought struck me that we could be heading north between England and the Continent with land falling away on either side. This sudden suspicion brought a moment of paralysis. I stood for perhaps ten seconds staring at the now unclouded array of stars, doing nothing. Geoff was finishing his call for the second time.

'Are you receiving me? Are you receiving me? Over to you, over!'

There was still no reply. The men were silent. I realized then that my chief fear of ops had been this fear, the fear of wasting the lives of other men. I cast about urgently for Spica to complete my fix. Again Geoff was calling. I listened closely but heard nothing. Then 'Shag', who was isolated from the engine noise, suddenly called us.

'There was an answer! Call again!'

The call was repeated. This time we heard a voice, but what it said we were unable to tell. Again 'Shag' had heard more clearly.

'It's in English, but I can't get it!'

Geoff called again. Clearly from below came the voice of a girl.

'Hello; Hazel B Beer! Hello; Hazel B Beer! This is Thorney Island replying; Thorney Island replying.'

Ahead through breaking cloud we saw the searchlights of Portsmouth. Somehow we reached Waddington, our six hours' petrol stretched to seven hours forty-five minutes.

*

Twice we were briefed for Wilhelmshaven and twice the operation was cancelled. Though news of the previous briefings had probably reached Germany, we were briefed again for the same target on the third successive night.

But again the operation was cancelled.

Next day we were briefed for Wilhelmshaven for the fourth time. This time we got off.

'Where are we, navigator?'

'Over midway across the North Sea – 7° East. ETA Point X now 2205.'

'Thanks.'

To reach Point X on ETA, that is my sole ambition. Beyond Point X my mind does not reach. That is the turning point for our final run to the target. I remember a night over southern Germany when the Pathfinders were to lay yellow flares at just such a point as tonight's Point X. They were to lay them at 0130. At 0122 Geoff asked, 'When are those flares to go down?'

'0130,' I said.

'You're sure of that?'

'Yes,' I said.

'It's bloody quiet round here.'

Doug added, 'I haven't seen another kite for an hour.'

The rest of the crew were accusingly silent. Until then I had worked confidently; now I began to have doubts. 'Any hope of a pinpoint, Ted?'

'No,' he replied, 'we're still over that sheet of cloud.'

Silence again. I worked back over my chart; recomputed winds; replotted fixes.

'Navigator, I make it 0127 and there's not a sign of those bloody flares. No other kites about either,' added Doug again.

A hand seized my throat. I muttered something about making another check, but I felt as if the aircraft were a runaway horse and I had lost both reins and stirrups.

'Still cloud below.'

It was now 0129. We must be miles out. We could be over the Mediterranean. I picked up my computer and gazed at it for several seconds. A shout startled me, 'There go the flares!'

Then Geoff's voice alone, 'Dead ahead, navigator. Nice work!'

'You bastards,' I said.

That was a long time ago. Tonight the Gee is working beyond its usual range and navigation is simple.

'What's that noise?'

'Ice breaking off the props.' It crashes along the fuselage.

B is climbing sluggishly, sheathed in ice. The crashing comes again, hollow-sounding on our shell.

'If there are any Stirlings on tonight they'll end up in the drink – they'll never top this stuff.'

'I believe the cloud is thinner above us.'

'Yes, that could be moonlight.'

'Where are we, navigator?'

'Five minutes from Point X. We're a couple of minutes early.'

'Thanks.'

'That *is* moonlight, Skipper. We'll be clear in another minute.'

'Good!'

We emerge from cloud into the amphitheatre of the sky. The moon rides above a white floor, paling the stars. Ahead the cloud is breaking.

'Navigator, I'll get rid of that two minutes with an orbit. It's clear enough to do it.'

'OK.'

I feel B turning to port. She is sluggish still in her cocoon of ice. The moonlight glitters on her wings.

'Fighter climbin', port quarter up! ME109.'

I stop working and listen. Shag is panting into his microphone as if he had run a long way.

Geoff's voice: 'Jettison cookie!'

'Bomb doors open!'

B leaps upward.

'Fighter comin' in! See 'im, Frank?'

'See 'im, Shag!'

'Prepare to turn port!'

Our nose is down, but the protecting cloud is now far below.

'Turn port, go!'

The air speed indicator begins turning clockwise, 200, 250, 300; but even without the 4,000-pound bomb, B is sluggish. Over the intercom comes the deathly chatter of our guns.

'Just missed us!'

''E's breakin' off, Frank!'

''E's comin' in again! Keep turnin', Geoff.'

The firing again; a long burst from both turrets.

''E's on fire!'

'Got the bassted!'

The fighter comes within sight of the cockpit. 'Good work! He's dropping into the sea!'

The floor of cloud reflects a sudden glare, then the fighter is swallowed up and the night is as before, clear, moonlit and empty. I find that I have been pressed against the wall behind my chair by our violent turn. The pressure eases; I take deep gulps of oxygen; I pick up my chart from the floor.

'Good show, gunners!'

'That damn fighter was waitin'.'

'Too many Wilhelmshaven briefings.'

Perhaps it is so. Perhaps through the secret channels of the land below us the message has gone, 'Wilhelmshaven tonight, attacking from the north.'

I wonder how many German lives the dead pilot saved. He forced us to drop our main bomb into the sea and now he is beside it.

'It's hardly worth taking these incendiaries alone.'

'Bad luck, Skip. Might's well drop them, though.'

'There goes the flare!'

'Nice work, navigator. We'll keep away from it, eh? Might be fighters round it.'

'The cloud is breaking. I can see the Wilhelmshaven searchlights on the horizon.'

'Thanks, Ted.'

'Enemy coast coming up.'

I turn out my light and stand behind Geoff and Doug. Ahead is a forest of searchlights, moving ceaselessly. To enter it is to walk with death. We do not go to cities, we go always to this forest. It lies at the end of every journey. I feel a little incredulous each time I see it. I cannot believe that any of us will emerge from it alive.

'Course out, navigator?'

Always before we enter the target Geoff sets the next course on his compass, in case in the confusion of the attack a mistake is made. I pass it quickly.

'There goes the Pathfinder marker!'

It falls to the ground and lies there, blood red, marking the place we must bomb. It lies like an exposed heart. The flak has started in its streams of red, yellow and orange.

Beside us a Lancaster is heading into the target, a silhouette against the searchlights and the incendiaries spangling the ground. Her movements appear unhurried and confident, but as I watch, a blue searchlight snaps onto her, fastens on like a dog. The Lancaster swings to starboard, but a dozen other beams spring up and pinion her.

'They're coned!'

'We'll run in while those searchlights are occupied.'

The Lancaster has swung away from us. She is silvered by light and appears like a moth plunging at a candle flame. Shells are climbing unhurriedly into the cone of searchlights and bursting there, orange and black. Seven men are sitting on thousands of pounds of explosive and there is nothing we can do for them.

Perhaps later they will be able to say, 'Over the target we were coned – had a hell of a job to get out of it.' Or perhaps tonight—

'They're hit!'

A flame, a little flame, at the root of their wing. And the shells are climbing still.

'Twelve seconds for a shell to reach 20,000 feet,' I repeat to myself. 'Twelve seconds for a shell to reach 20,000 feet.'

'We'll start our run in, Ted.'

'OK. About starboard onto our heading.'

The little flame is growing.

'He's hit again – near the rear turret,' I say.

'Quiet while Ted runs in.'

'Further right, Geoff.'

Geoff kicks B round.

'Coming along nicely now.'

A parachute opens under the nose of the Lancaster and a man dangles there in the light. I look closely, but no more men appear. The aircraft begins dripping with red fluid, like blood.

'He must be a Pathfinder. His target indicators are running out of him!'

'Shut up!'

'Left, left. Hold it steady now.'

Still no more men appear. The propellers are turning, but the Lancaster could be a ghost ship, her crew dead. But no, she turns a little, first one way and then the other.

'Steady, steady.'

A brilliant flash and she has gone. Now I can see nothing; no fragments; no smoke. The man on the parachute has vanished. Seven men are dead. The searchlights swing away and grope in our direction.

Huskily from the rear turret, 'Searchlight on our tail! Hurry it up, Batten!'

'Left a little. Good! The target is coming down the drift wires nicely.'

'Bloody lot of trouble for a few incendiaries!'

'Shut up!'

'Flak dead below us!'

I hear the *crumpf!* under my feet, then a quick series – *crumpf! crumpf! crumpf!*

'Steady! Steady! Bombs gone!'

I go back to the cabin and write it down, 'Bombs gone'; and in the Remarks column: 'Lancaster at approx 18,000 feet hit by flak, exploded. Appeared to be carrying T/Is. One man got out but disappeared after explosion.'

'Hold it steady for the photo.'

We are over the striking point of our bombs.

'Searchlights again! Blue bassted right in my face!'

An explosion swings the whole fuselage to port. Through our masks we can smell cordite.

'Steady a couple more seconds. Steady! Steady! Steady! OK, Geoff, all yours.'

'Turning out, navigator.'

Below us the city is dying. Its searchlights still seek us and its shells still explode, but its streets and houses and hospitals and factories are an inferno. As we watch it is suddenly no longer night. For an instant day has come with a light day never had. The harbour, the city, the swarms of attacking planes, are printed on our eyes. Then it is dark again.

'Log that explosion, navigator. Must have been a gasworks or a mine dump.'

We are out again, the sea below. I find my mouth is dry and my body suddenly exhausted.

Randall Jarrell

'Eighth Air Force'

If, in an odd angle of the hutment,
A puppy laps the water from a can
Of flowers, and the drunk sergeant shaving
Whistles *O Paradiso!* – shall I say that man
Is not as men have said: a wolf to man?

The other murderers troop in yawning;
Three of them play Pitch, one sleeps, and one
Lies counting missions, lies there sweating
Till even his heart beats: One; One; One.
O murderers! . . . Still, this is how it's done:

This is a war . . . But since these play, before they die,
Like puppies with their puppy; since, a man,
I did as these have done, but did not die –
I will content the people as I can
And give up these to them: Behold the man!

I have suffered, in a dream, because of him,
Many things; for this last saviour, man,
I have lied as I lie now. But what is lying?
Men wash their hands, in blood, as best they can:
I find no fault in this just man.

Randall Jarrell

'A Front'

Fog over the base: the beams ranging
From the five towers pull home from the night
The crews cold in fur, the bombers banging
Like lost trucks down the levels of the ice.
A glow drifts in like mist (how many tons of it?),
Bounces to a roll, turns suddenly to steel
And tyres and turrets, huge in the trembling light.
The next is high, and pulls up with a wail,
Comes round again – no use. And no use for the rest
In drifting circles out along the range;
Holding no longer, changed to a kinder course,
The flights drone southward through the steady rain.
The base is closed . . . But one voice keeps on calling,
The lowering pattern of the engines grows;
The roar gropes downward in its shaky orbit
For the lives the season quenches. Here below
They beg, order, are not heard; and hear the darker
Voice rising: *Can't you hear me? Over. Over—*
All the air quivers, and the east sky glows.

Roald Dahl

The Battle of Athens

My logbook records that from Elevsis aerodrome

> on 17 April I went up three times
> on 18 April I went up twice
> on 19 April I went up three times
> on 20 April I went up four times.

Each one of those sorties meant running across the airfield to wherever the Hurricane was parked (often 200 yards away), strapping in, starting up, taking off, flying to a particular area, engaging the enemy, getting home again, landing, reporting to the Ops Room and then making sure the aircraft was refuelled and rearmed immediately so as to be ready for another take-off.

Twelve separate sorties against the enemy in four days is a fairly hectic pace by any standards, and each one of us knew that every time a sortie was made somebody was probably going to get killed, either the Hun or the man in the Hurricane. I used to figure that the betting on every flight was about even money against my coming back, but in reality it wasn't even money at all. When you are outnumbered by at least ten to one on nearly every occasion, then a bookmaker, had there been one on the aerodrome, would probably have been willing to lay something like five to one against your return on each trip.

Like all the others, I was always sent up alone. I wished I could sometimes have had a friendly wing-tip alongside me, and more importantly, a second pair of eyes to help me watch the sky behind and above. But we didn't have enough aircraft for luxuries of that sort.

Sometimes I was over Piraeus harbour, chasing the Ju88s that were bombing the shipping there. Sometimes I was around the

Lamia area, trying to deter the Luftwaffe from blasting away at our retreating army, although how anyone could think that a single Hurricane was going to make any difference out there was beyond me. Once or twice, I met the bombers over Athens itself, where they usually came along in groups of twelve at a time. On three occasions my Hurricane was badly shot up, but the riggers in 80 Squadron were magicians at patching up holes in the fuselage or mending a broken spar. We were so frantically busy during these four days that individual victories were hardly noticed or counted. And unlike the fighter aircraft back in Britain, we had no camera-guns to tell us whether we had hit anything or not. We seemed to spend our entire time running out to the aircraft, scrambling, dashing off to some place or other, chasing the Hun, pressing the firing-button, landing back at Elevsis and going up again.

My logbook records that on 17 April we lost Flight Sergeant Cottingham and Flight Sergeant Rivelon and both their aircraft.

On 18 April Pilot Officer Oofy Still went out and did not return. I remember Oofy Still as a smiling young man with freckles and red hair.

That left us with twelve Hurricanes and twelve pilots with which to cover the whole of Greece from 19 April onwards.

17, 18 and 19 April seem to be all jumbled up together in my memory, and no single incident has remained vividly with me. But 20 April was quite different. I went up four separate times on 20 April, but it was the first of these sorties that I will never forget. It stands out like a sheet of flame in my memory.

On that day, somebody behind a desk in Athens or Cairo had decided that for once our entire force of Hurricanes, all twelve of us, should go up together. The inhabitants of Athens, so it seemed, were getting jumpy and it was assumed that the sight of us all flying overhead would boost their morale. Had I been an inhabitant of Athens at that time, with a German army of over 100,000 advancing swiftly on the city, not to mention a Luftwaffe of about 1,000 planes all within bombing distance, I would have been pretty jumpy myself, and the sight of twelve lonely Hurricanes flying overhead would have done little to boost my morale.

However, on 20 April, on a golden springtime morning at ten o'clock, all twelve of us took off one after the other and got into a tight formation over Elevsis airfield. Then we headed for Athens, which was no more than four minutes' flying time away.

I had never flown a Hurricane in formation before. Even in training I had only done formation flying once in a little Tiger Moth. It is not a particularly tricky business if you have had plenty of practice, but if you are new to the game and if you are required to fly within a few feet of your neighbour's wing-tip, it is a dicey experience. You keep your position by jiggling the throttle back and forth the whole time and by being extremely delicate on the rudder bar and the stick. It is not so bad when everyone is flying straight and level, but when the entire formation is doing steep turns all the time, it becomes very difficult for a fellow as inexperienced as I was.

Round and round Athens we went, and I was so busy trying to prevent my starboard wing-tip from scraping against the plane next to me that this time I was in no mood to admire the grand view of the Parthenon or any of the other famous relics below me. Our formation was being led by Flight Lieutenant Pat Pattle. Now Pat Pattle was a legend in the RAF. At least he was a legend around Egypt and the Western Desert and in the mountains of Greece. He was far and away the greatest fighter ace the Middle East was ever to see, with an astronomical number of victories to his credit. It was even said that he had shot down more planes than any of the famous and glamorized Battle of Britain aces, and this was probably true. I myself had never spoken to him and I am sure he hadn't the faintest idea who I was. I wasn't anybody. I was just a new face in a squadron whose pilots took very little notice of each other anyway. But I had observed the famous Flight Lieutenant Pattle in the Mess tent several times. He was a very small man and very soft-spoken, and he possessed the deeply wrinkled doleful face of a cat who knew that all nine of its lives had already been used up.

On that morning of 20 April, Flight Lieutenant Pattle, the ace of aces, who was leading our formation of twelve Hurricanes over Athens, was evidently assuming that we could all fly as brilliantly as he could, and he led us one hell of a dance around the skies above the city. We were flying at about 9,000 feet and we were doing our very best to show the people of Athens how powerful and noisy and brave we were, when suddenly the whole sky around us seemed to explode with German fighters. They came down on us from high above, not only 109s but also the twin-engined 110s. Watchers on the ground say that there cannot have been fewer than 200 of them around us that morning. We broke formation and now it was every man for himself. What has become known as the Battle of Athens began.

I find it almost impossible to describe vividly what happened during the next half-hour. I don't think any fighter pilot has ever managed to convey what it is like to be up there in a long-lasting dog fight. You are in a small metal cockpit where just about everything is made of riveted aluminium. There is a plexiglas hood over your head and a sloping bulletproof windscreen in front of you. Your right hand is on the stick and your right thumb is on the brass firing-button on the top loop of the stick. Your left hand is on the throttle and your two feet are on the rudder bar. Your body is attached by shoulder-straps and belt to the parachute you are sitting on, and a second pair of shoulder-straps and a belt are holding you rigidly in the cockpit. You can turn your head and you can move your arms and legs, but the rest of your body is strapped so tightly into the tiny cockpit that you cannot move. Between your face and the windscreen, the round orange-red circle of the reflector sight glows brightly.

Some people do not realize that although a Hurricane had eight guns in its wings, those guns were all immobile. You did not aim the guns, you aimed the plane. The guns themselves were carefully sighted and tested beforehand on the ground so that the bullets from each gun would converge at a point about 150 yards ahead. Thus, using your reflector sight, you aimed the plane at the target and pressed the button. To aim accurately in this way requires skilful flying, especially as you are usually in a steep turn and going very fast when the moment comes.

Over Athens on that morning, I can remember seeing our tight little formation of Hurricanes all peeling away and disappearing among the swarms of enemy aircraft, and from then on, wherever I looked I saw an endless blur of enemy fighters whizzing towards me from every side. They came from above and they came from behind and they made frontal attacks from dead ahead, and I threw my Hurricane around as best I could and whenever a Hun came into my sights, I pressed the button. It was truly the most breathless and in a way the most exhilarating time I have ever had in my life. I caught glimpses of planes with black smoke pouring from their engines. I saw planes with pieces of metal flying off their fuselages. I saw the bright-red flashes coming from the wings of the Messerschmitts as they fired their guns, and once I saw a man whose Hurricane was in flames climb calmly out onto a wing and jump off. I stayed with them until I had no ammunition left in my guns. I had done a lot of shooting, but whether I had shot anyone down or had even hit any of them I could not say. I did not dare to pause for even a fraction of a second to observe results. The sky was so full of aircraft that half my time was spent in actually avoiding collisions. I am quite sure that the German planes must have often got in each other's way because there were so many of them, and that, together with the fact that there were so few of us, probably saved quite a number of our skins.

When I finally had to break away and dive for home, I knew my Hurricane had been hit. The controls were very soggy and there was no response at all to the rudder. But you can turn a plane after a fashion with the ailerons alone, and that is how I managed to steer the plane back. Thank heavens the undercarriage came down when I engaged the lever, and I landed more or less safely at Elevsis. I taxied to a parking place, switched off the engine and slid back the hood. I sat there for at least one minute, taking deep gasping breaths. I was quite literally overwhelmed by the feeling that I had been into the very bowels of the fiery furnace and had managed to claw my way out. All around me now the sun was shining and wild flowers were blossoming in the grass of the airfield, and I thought how fortunate I was to be seeing the good earth again. Two airmen, a fitter and a rigger, came trotting up to my machine. I watched them as they walked slowly all the way round it. Then the rigger, a balding middle-aged man, looked up at me and said, 'Blimey, mate, this kite's got so many 'oles in it, it looks like it's made out of chicken-wire!'

I undid my straps and eased myself upright in the cockpit. 'Do your best with it,' I said. 'I'll be needing it again very soon.'

I remember walking over to the little wooden Operations Room to report my return and as I made my way slowly across the grass of the landing field I suddenly realized that the whole of my body and all my clothes were dripping with sweat. The weather was warm in Greece at that time of year and we wore only khaki shorts and khaki shirt and stockings even when we flew, but now those shorts and shirt and stockings had all changed colour and were quite black with wetness. So was my hair when I removed my helmet. I had never sweated like that before in my life, even after a game of squash or rugger. The water was pouring off me and dripping to the ground. At the door of the Ops Room three or four other pilots were standing around and I noticed that each one of them was as wet as I was. I put a cigarette between my lips and struck a match. Then I found that my hand was shaking so much I couldn't put the flame to the end of the cigarette. The doctor, who was standing nearby, came up and lit it for me. I looked at my hands again. It was ridiculous the way they were shaking. It was embarrassing. I looked at the other pilots. They were all holding cigarettes and their hands were all shaking as much as mine were. But I was feeling pretty good. I had stayed up there for thirty minutes and they hadn't got me.

They got five of our twelve Hurricanes in that battle. One of our pilots baled out and was saved. Four were killed. Among the dead was the great Pat Pattle, all his lucky lives used up at last. And Flight Lieutenant Timber Woods, the second most experienced pilot in the squadron, was also among those killed. Greek observers on the ground as well as our own people on the airstrip saw the five Hurricanes going down in smoke, but they also saw something else. They saw twenty-two Messerchmitts shot down during that battle, although none of us ever knew who got what.

So we now had seven half-serviceable Hurricanes left in Greece, and with these we were expected to give air cover to the entire British Expeditionary Force which was about to be evacuated along the coast. The whole thing was a ridiculous farce.

Guy Gibson

The Möhne Dam

As we passed on into the Ruhr Valley we came to more and more trouble, for now we were in the outer light-flak defences, and these were very active, but by weaving and jinking we were able to escape most of them. Time and again searchlights would pick us up, but we were flying very low and, although it may sound foolish and untrue when I say so, we avoided a great number of them by dodging behind the trees. Once we went over a brand-new aerodrome which was very heavily defended and which had not been marked on our combat charts. Immediately all three of us in front were picked up by the searchlights and held. Suddenly Trevor, in the rear turret, began firing away trying to scare them enough to turn out their lights, then he shouted that they had gone behind some tall trees. At the same time Spam was yelling that he would soon be shaving himself by the tops of some corn in a field. Hutch immediately sent out a flak warning to all the boys behind so that they could avoid this unattractive area. On either side of me, Mickey and Hoppy, who were a little higher, were flying along brightly illuminated; I could see their letters quite clearly, 'T.A.J.' and 'M.A.J.', standing out like Broadway signs. Then a long string of tracer came from Hoppy's rear turret and I lost him in the momentary darkness as the searchlights popped out. One of the pilots, a grand Englishman from Derbyshire, was not so lucky. He was flying well out to the left. He got blinded in the searchlights and, for a second, lost control. His aircraft reared up like a stricken horse, plunged onto the deck and burst into flames; five seconds later his mine blew up with a tremendous explosion. Bill Astell had gone.

The minutes passed slowly as we all sweated on this summer's night, sweated at working the controls and sweated with fear as we flew on. Every railway train, every hamlet and every bridge we passed was a potential danger, for our Lancasters were sitting targets at that height and speed. We fought our way past Dortmund, past Hamm – the well-known Hamm which has been bombed so many times; we could see it quite clearly now, its tall chimneys, factories and balloons capped by its umbrella of flak like a Christmas tree about five miles to our right; then we began turning to the right in between Hamm and the little town of Soest, where I nearly got shot down in 1940. Soest was sleepy now and did not open up, and out of the haze ahead appeared the Ruhr hills.

'We're there,' said Spam.

'Thank God,' said I, feelingly.

As we came over the hill, we saw the Möhne Lake. Then we saw the dam itself. In that light it looked squat and heavy and unconquerable; it looked grey and solid in the moonlight, as though it were part of the countryside itself and just as immovable. A structure like a battleship was showering out flak all along its length, but some came from the powerhouse below it and nearby. There were no searchlights. It was light flak, mostly green, yellow and red, and the colours of the tracer reflected upon the face of the water in the lake. The reflections on the dead calm of the black water made it seem there was twice as much as there really was.

'Did you say these gunners were out of practice?' asked Spam, sarcastically.

'They certainly seem awake now,' said Terry.

They were awake all right. No matter what people say, the Germans certainly have a good warning system. I scowled to myself as I remembered telling the boys an hour or so ago that they would probably only be the German equivalent of the Home Guard and in bed by the time we arrived.

It was hard to say exactly how many guns there were, but tracers seemed to be coming from about five positions, probably making twelve guns in all. It was hard at first to tell the calibre of the shells, but after one of the boys had been hit, we were informed over the RT that they were either 20 mm type or 37 mm, which, as everyone knows, are nasty little things.

We circled around stealthily, picking up the various landmarks upon which we had planned our method of attack, making use of some and avoiding others; every time we came within range of those bloody-minded flak-gunners they let us have it.

'Bit aggressive, aren't they?' said Trevor.

'Too right they are.'

I said to Terry, 'God, this light flak gives me the creeps.'

'Me, too,' someone answered.

For a time there was a general bind on the subject of light flak, and the only man who didn't say anything was Hutch, because he could not see it and because he never said anything about flak, anyway. But this was not the time for talking. I called up each member of our formation and found, to my relief, that they had all arrived, except, of course, Bill Astell. Away to the south, Joe McCarthy had just begun his diversionary attack on the Sorpe. But not all of them had been able to get there; both Byers and Barlow had been shot down by light flak after crossing the coast; these had been replaced by other aircraft of the rear formation. Bad luck, this being shot down after crossing the coast, because it could have happened to anybody; they must have been a mile or so off track and had got the hammer. This is the way things are in flying; you are either lucky or you aren't. We, too, had crossed the coast at the wrong place and had got away with it. We were lucky.

Down below, the Möhne Lake was silent and black and deep, and I spoke to my crew.

'Well, boys, I suppose we had better start the ball rolling.' This with no enthusiasm whatsoever. 'Hello, all Cooler aircraft. I am going to attack. Stand by to come in to attack in your order when I tell you.'

Then to Hoppy: 'Hello, M Mother. Stand by to take over if anything happens.'

Hoppy's clear and casual voice came back. 'OK, Leader. Good luck.'

Then the boys dispersed to the prearranged hiding spots in the hills, so that they should not be seen either from the ground or from the air, and we began to get into position for our approach. We circled wide and came around down moon, over the high hills at the eastern end of the lake. On straightening up we began to dive towards the flat, ominous water two miles away. Over the front turret was the dam silhouetted against the haze of the Ruhr Valley. We could see the towers. We could see the sluices. We could see everything. Spam, the bomb aimer, said, 'Good show. This is wizard.' He had been a bit worried, as all bomb aimers are, in case they cannot see their aiming points, but as we came in over the tall fir trees his voice came up again rather quickly. 'You're going to hit them. You're going to hit those trees.'

'That's all right, Spam. I'm just getting my height.'

To Terry: 'Check height, Terry.'

To Pulford: 'Speed control, flight engineer.'

To Trevor: 'All guns ready, gunners.'

To Spam: 'Coming up, Spam.'

Terry turned on the spotlights and began giving directions – 'Down – down – down. Steady – steady.' We were then exactly at sixty feet.

Pulford began working the speed; first he put on a little flap to slow us down, then he opened the throttles to get the air speed indicator exactly against the red mark. Spam began lining up his sights against the towers. He had turned the fusing switch to the 'On' position. I began flying.

The gunners had seen us coming. They could see us coming with our spotlights on for over two miles away. Now they opened up and their tracers began swirling towards us; some were even bouncing off the smooth surface of the lake. This was a horrible moment: we were being dragged along at four miles a minute, almost against our will, towards the things we were going to destroy. I think at that moment the boys did not want to go. I know I did not want to go. I thought to myself, 'In another minute we shall all be dead – so what?' I thought again, 'This is terrible – this feeling of fear – if it is fear.' By now we were a few hundred yards away, and I said quickly to Pulford, under my breath, 'Better leave the throttles open now and stand by to pull me out of the seat if I get hit.' As I glanced at him I thought he looked a little glum on hearing this.

The Lancaster was really moving and I began looking through the special sight on my windscreen. Spam had his eyes glued to the bombsight in front, his hand on his button; a special mechanism on board had already begun to work so that the mine would drop (we hoped) in the right spot. Terry was still checking the height. Joe and Trev began to raise their guns. The flak could see us quite clearly now. It was not exactly inferno. I have been through far worse flak fire than that; but we were very low. There was something sinister and slightly unnerving about the whole operation. My aircraft was so small and the dam was so large; it was thick and solid, and now it was angry. My aircraft was very small. We skimmed along the surface of the lake, and as we went my gunner was firing into the defences, and the defences were firing back with vigour, their shells whistling past us. For some reason, we were not being hit.

Spam said, 'Left – little more left – steady – steady – steady – coming up.' Of the next few seconds I remember only a series of kaleidoscopic incidents.

The chatter from Joe's front guns pushing out tracers which bounced off the left-hand flak tower.

Pulford crouching beside me.

The smell of burnt cordite.

The cold sweat underneath my oxygen mask.

The tracers flashing past the windows – they all seemed the same colour now – and the inaccuracy of the gun positions near the power station; they were firing in the wrong direction.

The closeness of the dam wall.

Spam's exultant, 'Mine gone.'

Hutch's red Very lights to blind the flak gunners.

The speed of the whole thing.

Someone saying over the RT, 'Good show, leader. Nice work.'

Then it was all over, and at last we were out of range, and there came over us all, I think, an immense feeling of relief and confidence.

Trevor said, 'I will get those bastards,' and he began to spray the dam with bullets until at last he, too, was out of range. As we circled round we could see a great 1,000-foot column of whiteness still hanging in the air where our mine had exploded. We could see with satisfaction that Spam had been good, and it had gone off in the right position. Then, as we came closer, we could see that the explosion of the mine had caused a great disturbance upon the surface of the lake and the water had become broken and furious, as though it were being lashed by a gale. At first we thought that the dam itself had broken, because great sheets of water were slopping over the top of the wall like a gigantic basin. This caused some delay, because our mines could only be dropped in calm water, and we would have to wait until all became still again.

We waited.

We waited about ten minutes, but it seemed hours to us. It must have seemed even longer to Hoppy, who was the next to attack. Meanwhile, all the fighters had now collected over our target. They knew our game by now, but we were flying too low for them; they could not see us and there were no attacks.

At last— 'Hello, M Mother. You may attack now. Good luck.'

'OK. Attacking.'

Hoppy, the Englishman, casual, but very efficient, keen now on only one thing, which was war. He began his attack.

He began going down over the trees where I had come from a few moments before. We could see his spotlights quite clearly, slowly closing together as he ran across the water. We saw him approach. The flak, by now, had got an idea from which direction the attack was coming, and they let him have it. When he was about 100 yards away someone said, hoarsely, over the R/T: 'Hell! He has been hit.'

M Mother was on fire; an unlucky shot had got him in one of the inboard petrol tanks and a long jet of flame was beginning to stream out. I saw him drop his mine, but his bomb aimer must have been wounded, because it fell straight onto the powerhouse on the other side of the dam. But Hoppy staggered on, trying to gain altitude so that his crew could bale out. When he had got up to about 500 feet there was a livid flash in the sky and one wing fell off; his aircraft disintegrated and fell to the ground in cascading, flaming fragments. There it began to burn quite gently and rather sinisterly in a field some three miles beyond the dam.

Someone said, 'Poor old Hoppy!'

Another said, 'We'll get those bastards for this.'

A furious rage surged up inside my own crew, and Trevor said, 'Let's go in and murder those gunners.' As he spoke, Hoppy's mine went up. It went up behind the powerhouse with a tremendous yellow explosion and left in the air a great ball of black smoke; again there was a long wait while we watched for this to clear. There was so little wind that it took a long time.

Many minutes later I told Mickey to attack; he seemed quite confident, and we ran in beside him and a little in front; as we turned, Trevor did his best to get those gunners as he had promised.

Bob Hay, Mickey's bomb aimer, did a good job, and his mine dropped in exactly the right place. There was again a gigantic explosion as the whole surface of the lake shook, then spewed forth its cascade of white water. Mickey was all right; he got through. But he had been hit several times and one wing tank lost all its petrol. I could see the vicious tracer from his rear gunner giving one gun position a hail of bullets as he swept over. Then he called up, 'OK. Attack completed.' It was then that I thought that the dam wall had moved. Of course we could not see anything, but if Jeff's theory had been correct, it should have cracked by now. If only we could go on pushing it by dropping more successful mines, it would surely move back on its axis and collapse.

Once again we watched for the water to calm down. Then in came Melvyn Young in D Dog. I yelled to him, 'Be careful of the flak. It's pretty hot.'

He said, 'OK.'

I yelled again, 'Trevor's going to beat them up on the other side. He'll take most of it off you.'

Melvyn's voice again. 'OK. Thanks.' And so as D Dog ran in we stayed at a fairly safe distance on the other side, firing with all guns at the defences, and the defences, like the stooges they were, firing back at us. We were both out of range of each other, but the ruse seemed to work, and we flicked on our identification lights to let them see us even more clearly. Melvyn's mine went in, again in exactly the right spot, and this time a colossal wall of water swept right over the dam and kept on going. Melvyn said, 'I think I've done it. I've broken it.' But we were in a better position to see than he, and it had not rolled down yet. We were all getting pretty excited by now, and I screamed like a schoolboy over the R/T: 'Wizard show, Melvyn. I think it'll go on the next one.'

Now we had been over the Möhne for quite a long time, and all the while I had been in contact with Scampton Base. We were in close contact with the Air Officer Commanding and the Commander-in-Chief of Bomber Command, and with the scientist, observing his own greatest scientific experiment in Damology. He was sitting in the Operations Room, his head in his hands, listening to the reports as one after another the aircraft attacked. On the other side of the room the Commander-in-Chief paced up and down. In a way their job of waiting was worse than mine. The only difference was that they did not know that the structure was shifting as I knew, even though I could not see anything clearly.

When at last the water had all subsided I called up No. 5 – David Maltby – and told him to attack. He came in fast, and I saw his mine fall within feet of the right spot; once again the flak, the explosion and the wall of water. But this time we were on the wrong side of the wall and could not see what had happened. We watched for about five minutes, and it was rather hard to see anything, for by now the air was full of spray from these explosions, which had settled like mist on our windscreens. Time was getting short, so I called up Dave Shannon and told him to come in.

As he turned I got close to the dam wall and then saw what had happened. It had rolled over, but I could not believe my eyes. I heard someone shout, 'I think she has gone! I think she has gone!' Other voices took up the cry and quickly I said, 'Stand by until I make a recce.' I remembered that Dave was going into attack and told him to turn away and not to approach the target. We had a closer look. Now there was no doubt about it; there was a great breach 100 yards across, and the water, looking like stirred porridge in the moonlight, was gushing out and rolling into the Ruhr Valley towards the industrial centres of Germany's Third Reich.

Nearly all the flak had now stopped, and the other boys came down from the hills to have a closer look to see what had been done. There was no doubt about it at all – the Möhne Dam had been breached and the gunners on top of the dam, except for one man, had all run for their lives towards the safety of solid ground; this remaining gunner was a brave man, but one of the boys quickly extinguished his flak with a burst of well-aimed tracer. Now it was all quiet, except for the roar of the water which steamed and hissed its way from its 150-foot head. Then we began to shout and scream and act like madmen over the R/T, for this was a tremendous sight, a sight which probably no man will ever see again.

Quickly I told Hutch to tap out the message, 'Nigger', to my station, and when this was handed to the Air Officer Commanding there was (I heard afterwards) great excitement in the Operations Room. The scientist jumped up and danced round the room.

Then I looked again at the dam and at the water, while all around me the boys were doing the same. It was the most amazing sight. The whole valley was beginning to fill with fog from the steam of the gushing water, and down in the foggy valley we saw cars speeding along the roads in front of this great wave of water, which was chasing them and going faster than they could ever hope to go. I saw their headlights burning and I saw water overtake them, wave by wave, and then the colour of the headlights underneath the water changing from light blue to green, from green to dark purple, until there was no longer anything except the water bouncing down in great waves. The floods raced on, carrying with them as they went – viaducts, railways, bridges and everything that stood in their path. Three miles beyond the dam the remains of Hoppy's aircraft were still burning gently, a dull red glow on the ground. Hoppy had been avenged.

Then I felt a little remote and unreal sitting up there in the warm cockpit of my Lancaster, watching this mighty power which we had unleashed; then glad, because I knew that this was the heart of Germany, and the heart of her industries, the place which itself had unleashed so much misery upon the whole world.

We knew, as we watched, that this flood water would not win the war; it would not do anything like that, but it was a catastrophe for Germany.

I circled round for about three minutes, then called up all aircraft and told Mickey and David Maltby to go home and the rest to follow me to Eder, where we would try to repeat the performance.

John Pudney

'The Ratio'

They were not speaking of God in the hangar
But of a ratio
Between what they had built and natural forces,
That everlasting cast by man
Between the unknown and known resources.
And they spoke humbly, as Phoenician sailors
Or the shipbuilders of Tyre,
As they talked of stress and the fatigue of metals.
To God they did not aspire.

Yet there was some of the fear of God in every one,
In the echoing hangar or on the airfield where the choir
Of larks lifted as blithely in their sweet element
As dolphins once in the water rolled in fun
For navigators setting sail for an unknown continent
Beyond the sun.

John Pudney

'The Siege of Malta'

Distantly, by navigator's calculation
Pinpointing rock in the waters, the target
Mistily seen through the panels of air's dimension.
A point or so to starboard. That's there all right.
The expected, our landfall, Malta.

Look! Malta spun on the sea, shaping to sight
Fragilely as a promise, framed by metal
And the deft handling of airmanship.
Nudge. Nod. That's there all right. A petal
Yellow, all veined with green in the sea's hard
Flooring of other element, of timeless running.
Malta, upon the blood-invested water, cactus, nettle-
Leafed, old prickle, guard.

Fly in to circuit the runways, scarred
And scored sparsely on land hard won,
Beaten out amid ridges and walls like wrinkles
In ancient faces sweetened by the sun.
From lofts of air, here hover over the stones
Fashioned and catacombed, lidding the eye that twinkles
And watches with Phoenician patience over the years,
Casting a count of nations' dust and bones.
Not much of a size, this rock. Some nine by seventeen.
O witness to the Mediterranean glory, to the tears,
And the learning and the swagger. All watched: all seen.

Now circuit once the sallow veined-with-green
Pale rock, pale builded block, flushed dome and steeple,

The monuments of saints, the dappled lemon groves,
The air-bleached mannerisms of baroque,
And the jet shadows on the roads of people:
By Saint Paul guided, by the stone folds of bastions guarded,
Tillers and toilers, minders of scanty droves,
So little needed new, so much less old discarded,
In poor tilth found, in timeless age provided.
Wheels down. Full flaps: and glide to ground.
Phoenician-eyed, these saw Carthage and Rome,
Greeks, infidels and Normans in their humours:
Nor shall we rouse them when these engines sound
Along the ruthless skyline of an aerodrome.

Death is our mission and, at the long last, home,
Unshadowed by the killing, by the organic wrong,
Unawed by glory or the mice-whispers of fear.
Home we desire, and the most of us young, armed, strong,
With these weapons proving an older integrity,
No bolder for death being near.
Watch the old eyes now, like the clang of the bell
In your sleep or the sirens of an alert
Deep in your body's keep of silence. Watch them well:
These work hard, these peasants, scratching at dirt,
And take little notice of flying. Older, stranger,
One here saw Carthage dying, lying under the plough:
One here saw Tyrian Astoreth, lusting, fall;
One here saw Rome in danger;
One faltered, knelt at the shipwreck of Saint Paul.

Jack Airman, at leisure now, no avenger,
With a whatsyours and the silken popsy reclining
On fancy's cushion, no killing
To ward off happiness, no challenger shining,
The mission is death. Your careful lining
And personal armoury saves you whole
From the too-dear erosion, love or friendship,

From the parting, the too-long-lingering, the confusion
Of grief and loving life. No toll
Ever was taken but here these eyes looked on,
And the waters were troubled with blood and oil.
Death blooms in Mediterranean profusion:
We are old where nothing is new, now, Airman John.

Zeppu leans over against the soil,
Where airscrews', ailerons' pattern throws
Our emblem on the light of evening. Easily
Moves man ploughing, in meagreness, furrows
Watered and terraced by ancient husbandry.
Not all by Saints and Powers, Zeppu knows
– It's wonderful what people will believe –
How night or death assemble in the light,
How bean crops bloom or blemish, how the rose,
Most previous birth-rose in a bowl of water,
Smile or grieve.

Not many of them killed, considering. Just those
By law of average. Zeppu will forget
And Grez, barefooted, carrying her shoes,
Will pray for some till harvest. If we set
A time and limit to our fear. A time to choose,
A limit for the body's luck against the force
Of bombardment by thought and deed and thought;
We might be bold with the old eyes. We might not lose
Our singleness for fear of being caught.

So they trampled the Three Cities about the port,
And Valetta built by gentlemen for gentlemen, and the quays
And the garnished churches, and the alleys of stairs
Where noble quarterings passed which could not be bought,
And rooms where parchments faded with the family trees.
So that the carven limestone of the little houses
Clogs the fair prospects, stumbles on to squares,

Wind in an elegiac chandelier carouses,
A brocaded remnant curdles upon the breeze.
Knights, galley slaves, middlemen, pimps, corsairs
Contributed dust to dust, the yellow volley to heaven,
The must and reek of smoke that pillared and settled
Over the old waters, blood-invested, unawares.

No more the young man's hunger for the marvellous seas
Or the air's stairs and extremes is set and sealed
By sixteen knightly quarterings, tempered and mettled,
We will fly away one day
And get us back to our homes and to the grace
Of tenderness, the sap which moves in the wood,
The balance of the head upon the daffodil,
The truth which was understood
In our indeterminate passion,
In the Saturday street or under the hill.
In our own fashion
We will be at peace and be still.
Jack Airman, if there be destiny for good
Among us, you have the power, the prowess, navigator's skill.
We will fly away one day with no need to kill.

Samuel Hynes

Landscape; Open Cockpit; Solitude

Memories of flying are almost always memories of landscape. It isn't that you think, 'I am flying over this state or that one,' but that you are moving above a landscape pierced by a mountain, or patched with woodlands or edged by the sea. The earth is always there below, apart and beautiful (no land is ugly from the air), revealing its private features in a way that it never does to the traveller on its surface. A pilot can see where a road goes, what is over that hill, the shapes of lakes and towns; and I suppose this knowledge of the earth's face is a part of the feeling of dominion that a pilot feels when his plane reaches a commanding altitude and he looks down on the world that stretches out beneath him.

*

I learned the intense delight of flying an open plane. I'm not sure that I can explain why it is so different from a closed cockpit, but it has to do with the intimate presence of the air itself, the medium you fly in, streaming past and around you. You can thrust your whole arm out into the slipstream and press back against the flow of air; you can lean to the side, and the air will force the tears from your eyes and rush into your lungs. And you can look straight into space, down to the earth and up to the sky, with nothing between you and the whole world. The plane is not a protective shell, as an automobile is, but an extension of your own body, moving as you move; and your head is the brain of the whole stretched and vibrating organism. Flying alone in an open plane is the purest experience of flight possible.

*

Once, flying alone, I wandered above a bank of cloud, and learned how it feels to be separated completely from the earth, how anonymous and signless clouds are and how uncomforting the sun is when it shines down on unbroken, trackless whiteness. This kind of experience, of separation from the comfortable and the familiar, is a part of the price of flying. The pilot has to accept the stretches of loneliness and isolation, when the earth is erased by cloud or darkness, or is facelessly strange or hostile, when his will to fly has thrust him into void space.

I felt this separation most intensely on the navigation flights that were a part of the final training programme. First we flew, in flights of three planes, out over the Gulf on a triangular course that, if we were proper navigators, would return us precisely to the field. Since there were other planes involved, this was not really a separating experience, though it did offer one new kind of feeling that was disquieting – the feeling you get when the last bit of land disappears behind you, of the shapelessness and endlessness of space. Below you is the flat and uninformative sea; all around you the air extends its emptiness. Why go one way rather than another, when it is all the same, and goes on for ever? People have committed suicide by flying straight out to sea, and I can understand that it could have a right feeling, that it would be a gesture that would express the feeling of suicide, as well as a way of dying.

The other navigation flight was flown alone, and overland. This time, too, the pattern was a triangle – inland to one town, across to another, and back. No doubt the solitariness was a part of the flight's strange feeling, but it was more than that. I was flying over the pine woods of Florida and south Alabama, a surface that stretched unbroken to the horizon, as flat and featureless as the sea. The Gulf behind me became what the land had been before, a friendly and familiar landmark. When I lost sight of it I felt as though I had flown out of measurable space into the boredom of infinity.

I could see the shadow of my plane sliding along below me on the tops of the trees, and its insubstantial, steady movement seemed a part of the emptiness. Occasionally a railroad track appeared, making a diagonal mark across the pines; but railroads are as identical as pine trees, and it did nothing to alter my mood. I checked the calculations on my plotting board, and I watched the clock on the instrument panel, and at the predicted time the right town appeared, an island of tin roofs and a water tower floating in the sea of pine trees. But I could feel no necessity in that appearance; it might as well have been some other town, or no town at all. I turned, found the second landmark, and headed south. When I could see the Gulf once more beyond the trees I felt that I was reentering the real, distinguishable world.

Joseph Heller

Milo Minderbinder

Milo Minderbinder's planes flew in from everywhere, the pursuit planes, bombers and cargo ships streaming into Colonel Cathcart's field with pilots at the controls who would do what they were told. The planes were decorated with flamboyant squadron emblems illustrating such laudable ideals as Courage, Might, Justice, Truth, Liberty, Love, Honor and Patriotism that were painted out at once by Milo's mechanics with a double coat of flat white and replaced in garish purple with the stencilled name M & M ENTERPRISES, FINE FRUITS AND PRODUCE. The 'M & M' in 'M & M ENTERPRISES' stood for Milo & Minderbinder, and the & was inserted, Milo revealed candidly, to nullify any impression that the syndicate was a one-man operation. Planes arrived for Milo from airfields in Italy, North Africa and England, and from Air Transport Command stations in Liberia, Ascension Island, Cairo and Karachi. Pursuit planes were traded for additional cargo ships or retained for emergency invoice duty and small-parcel service; trucks and tanks were procured from the ground forces and used for short-distance road hauling. Everybody had a share, and men got fat and moved about tamely with toothpicks in their greasy lips. Milo supervised the whole expanding operation by himself. Deep otter-brown lines of preoccupation etched themselves permanently into his care-worn face and gave him a harried look of sobriety and mistrust. Everybody but Yossarian thought Milo was a jerk, first for volunteering for the job of mess officer and next for taking it so seriously. Yossarian also thought that Milo was a jerk; but he also knew that Milo was a genius.

One day Milo flew away to England to pick up a load of Turkish halva and came flying back from Madagascar leading four German bombers filled with yams, collards, mustard greens and black-eyed

Georgia peas. Milo was dumbfounded when he stepped down to the ground and found a contingent of armed MPs waiting to imprison the German pilots and confiscate their planes. *Confiscate!* The mere word was anathema to him, and he stormed back and forth in excoriating condemnation, shaking a piercing finger of rebuke in the guilt-ridden faces of Colonel Cathcart, Colonel Korn and the poor battle-scarred captain with the sub-machine-gun who commanded the MPs.

'Is this Russia?' Milo assailed them incredulously at the top of his voice. '*Confiscate?*' he shrieked, as though he could not believe his own ears. 'Since when is it the policy of the American government to confiscate the private property of its citizens? Shame on you! Shame on all of you for even thinking such a horrible thought.'

'But, Milo,' Major Danby interrupted timidly, 'we're at war with Germany, and those are German planes.'

'They are no such thing!' Milo retorted furiously. 'Those planes belong to the syndicate, and everybody has a share. *Confiscate?* How can you possibly confiscate your own private property? *Confiscate,* indeed! I've never heard anything so depraved in my whole life.'

And sure enough, Milo was right, for when they looked, his mechanics had painted out the German swastikas on the wings, tails and fuselages with double coats of flat white and stencilled in the words M & M ENTERPRISES, FINE FRUITS AND PRODUCE. Right before their eyes he had transformed his syndicate into an international cartel.

Milo's argosies of plenty now filled the air. Planes poured in from Norway, Denmark, France, Germany, Austria, Italy, Yugoslavia, Romania, Bulgaria, Sweden, Finland, Poland – from everywhere in Europe, in fact, but Russia, with whom Milo refused to do business. When everybody who was going to had signed up with M & M Enterprises, Fine Fruits and Produce, Milo created a wholly owned subsidiary, M & M Fancy Pastry, and obtained more aeroplanes and more money from the Mess funds for scones and crumpets from the British Isles, prune and cheese Danish from Copenhagen, éclairs, cream puffs, Napoleons and *petits fours* from Paris, Reims and Grenoble, *Kugelhopf*, pumpernickel and

Pfefferkuchen from Berlin, *Linzer* and *Dobos Torten* from Vienna, *Strudel* from Hungary and *baklava* from Ankara. Each morning Milo sent planes aloft all over Europe and North Africa hauling long red tow signs advertising the day's specials in large square letters: 'EYE ROUND, 79¢ ... WHITING, 21¢.' He boosted cash income for the syndicate by leasing tow signs to Pet Milk, Graines Dog Food and Noxzema. In a spirit of civic enterprise, he regularly allotted a certain amount of free aerial advertising space to General Peckem for the propagation of such messages in the public interest as NEATNESS COUNTS, HASTE MAKES WASTE and THE FAMILY THAT PRAYS TOGETHER STAYS TOGETHER. Milo purchased spot radio announcements on Axis Sally's and Lord Haw Haw's daily propaganda broadcasts from Berlin to keep things moving. Business boomed on every battlefront.

Milo's planes were a familiar sight. They had freedom of passage everywhere, and one day Milo contracted with the American military authorities to bomb the German-held highway bridge at Orvieto and with the German military authorities to defend the highway bridge at Orvieto with anti-aircraft fire against his own attack. His fee for attacking the bridge for America was the total cost of the operation plus six per cent, and his fee from Germany for defending the bridge was the same cost-plus-six agreement augmented by a merit bonus of $1,000 for every American plane he shot down. The consummation of these deals represented an important victory for private enterprise, he pointed out, since the armies of both countries were socialized institutions. Once the contracts were signed, there seemed to be no point in using the resources of the syndicate to bomb and defend the bridge, inasmuch as both governments had ample men and material right there to do so and were perfectly happy to contribute them, and in the end Milo realized a fantastic profit from both halves of his project for doing nothing more than signing his name twice.

The arrangements were fair to both sides. Since Milo did have freedom of passage everywhere, his planes were able to steal over in a sneak attack without alerting the German anti-aircraft gunners;

and since Milo knew about the attack, he was able to alert the German anti-aircraft gunners in sufficient time for them to begin firing accurately the moment the planes came into range. It was an ideal arrangement for everyone but the dead man in Yossarian's tent, who was killed over the target the day he arrived.

'I didn't kill him!' Milo kept replying passionately to Yossarian's angry protest. 'I wasn't even there that day, I tell you. Do you think I was down there on the ground firing an anti-aircraft gun when the planes came over?'

'But you organized the whole thing, didn't you?' Yossarian shouted back at him in the velvet darkness cloaking the path leading past the still vehicles of the motor pool to the open-air movie theatre.

'And I didn't organize anything,' Milo answered indignantly, drawing great agitated sniffs of air in through his hissing, pale, twitching nose. 'The Germans have the bridge, and we were going to bomb it, whether I stepped into the picture or not. I just saw a wonderful opportunity to make some profit out of the mission, and I took it. What's so terrible about that?'

'What's so terrible about it? Milo, a man in my tent was killed on that mission before he could even unpack his bags.'

'But I didn't kill him.'

'You got a thousand dollars extra for it.'

'But I didn't kill him. I wasn't even there, I tell you. I was in Barcelona buying olive oil and skinless and boneless sardines, and I've got the purchase orders to prove it. And I didn't get the thousand dollars. That thousand dollars went to the syndicate, and everybody got a share, even you.' Milo was appealing to Yossarian from the bottom of his soul. 'Look, I didn't start this war, Yossarian, no matter what that lousy Wintergreen is saying. I'm just trying to put it on a businesslike basis. Is anything wrong with that? You know, a thousand dollars ain't such a bad price for a medium bomber and a crew. If I can persuade the Germans to pay me a thousand dollars for every plane they shoot down, why shouldn't I take it?'

'Because you're dealing with the enemy, that's why. Can't you understand that we're fighting a war? People are dying. Look around you, for Christ's sake!'

Milo shook his head with weary forbearance. 'And the Germans are not our enemies,' he declared. 'Oh, I know what you're going to say. Sure, we're at war with them. But the Germans are also members in good standing of the syndicate, and it's my job to protect their rights as shareholders. Maybe they did start the war, and maybe they are killing millions of people, but they pay their bills a lot more promptly than some allies of ours I could name. Don't you understand that I have to respect the sanctity of my contract with Germany? Can't you see it from my point of view?'

'No,' Yossarian rebuffed him harshly.

Milo was stung and made no effort to disguise his wounded feelings. It was a muggy, moonlit night filled with gnats, moths and mosquitoes. Milo lifted his arm suddenly and pointed towards the open-air theatre, where the milky, dust-filled beam bursting horizontally from the projector slashed a conelike swath in the blackness and draped in a fluorescent membrane of light the audience tilted on the seats there in hypnotic sags, their faces focused upward toward the aluminized movie screen. Milo's eyes were liquid with integrity, and his artless and uncorrupted face was lustrous with a shining mixture of sweat and insect repellent.

'Look at them,' he exclaimed in a voice choked with emotion. 'They're my friends, my countrymen, my comrades in arms. A fellow never had a better bunch of buddies. Do you think I'd do a single thing to harm them if I didn't have to? Haven't I got enough on my mind? Can't you see how upset I am already about all that cotton piling up on those piers in Egypt?' Milo's voice splintered into fragments, and he clutched at Yossarian's shirt front as though drowning. His eyes were throbbing visibly like brown caterpillars. 'Yossarian, what am I going to do with so much cotton? It's all your fault for letting me buy it.'

The cotton was piling up on the piers in Egypt, and nobody wanted any. Milo had never dreamed that the Nile Valley could be so fertile or that there would be no market at all for the crop he had bought. The Mess halls in his syndicate would not help; they rose up in uncompromising rebellion against his proposal to tax them on a per capita basis in order to enable each man to own his own share of the Egyptian cotton crop. Even his reliable friends the Germans failed him in this crisis: they preferred ersatz. Milo's Mess halls would not even help him store the cotton, and his warehousing costs skyrocketed and contributed to the devastating drain upon his cash reserves. The profits from the Orvieto mission were sucked away. He began writing home for the money he had sent back in better days; soon that was almost gone. And new bales of cotton kept arriving on the wharves at Alexandria every day. Each time he succeeded in dumping some on the world market for a loss it was snapped up by canny Egyptian brokers in the Levant, who sold it back to him at the original price, so that he was really worse off than before.

M & M Enterprises verged on collapse. Milo cursed himself hourly for his monumental greed and stupidity in purchasing the entire Egyptian cotton crop, but a contract was a contract and had to be honoured, and one night, after a sumptuous evening meal, all Milo's fighters and bombers took off, joined in formation directly overhead and began dropping bombs on the group. He had landed another contract with the Germans, this time to bomb his own outfit. Milo's planes separated in a well-coordinated attack and bombed the fuel stocks and the ordnance dump, the repair hangars and the B-25 bombers resting on the lollipop-shaped hardstands at the field. His crews spared the landing strip and the Mess halls so that they could land safely when their work was done and enjoy a hot snack before retiring. They bombed with their landing lights on, since no one was shooting back. They bombed all four squadrons, the officers' club and the Group Headquarters building. Men bolted from their tents in sheer terror and did not know in which direction to turn. Wounded soon lay screaming everywhere. A cluster of fragmentation bombs exploded in the yard of the officers' club and punched jagged holes in the side of the wooden building and in the bellies and backs of a row of lieutenants and captains standing at the bar. They doubled over in agony and dropped. The rest of the officers fled toward the two exits in panic and jammed up the doorways like a dense, howling dam of human flesh as they shrank from going farther.

Colonel Cathcart clawed and elbowed his way through the unruly, bewildered mass until he stood outside by himself. He stared up at the sky in stark astonishment and horror. Milo's planes, ballooning serenely in over the blossoming treetops with their bomb-bay doors open and wing-flaps down and with their monstrous, bug-eyed, blinding, fiercely flickering, eerie landing lights on, were the most apocalyptic sight he had ever beheld. Colonel Cathcart let go a stricken gasp of dismay and hurled himself headlong into his Jeep, almost sobbing. He found the gas pedal and the ignition and sped toward the airfield as fast as the rocking car would carry him, his huge flabby hands clenched and bloodless on the wheel or blaring his horn tormentedly. Once he almost killed himself when he swerved with a banshee screech of tyres to avoid ploughing into a bunch of men running crazily toward the hills in their underwear with their stunned faces down and their thin arms pressed high around their temples as puny shields. Yellow, orange and red fires were burning on both sides of the road. Tents and trees were in flames, and Milo's planes kept coming around interminably with their blinking white landing lights on and their bomb-bay doors open. Colonel Cathcart almost turned the Jeep over when he slammed the brakes on at the control tower. He leaped from the car while it was still skidding dangerously and hurtled up the flight of steps inside, where three men were busy at the instruments and the controls. He bowled two of them aside in his lunge for the nickel-plated microphone, his eyes glittering wildly and his beefy face contorted with stress. He squeezed the microphone in a bestial grip and began shouting hysterically at the top of his voice,

'Milo, you son of a bitch! Are you crazy? What the hell are you doing? Come down! Come down!'

'Stop hollering so much, will you?' answered Milo, who was

standing there right beside him in the control tower with a microphone of his own. 'I'm right here.' Milo looked at him with reproof and turned back to his work. 'Very good, men, very good,' he chanted into his microphone. 'But I see one supply shed still standing. That will never do, Purvis – I've spoken to you about that kind of shoddy work before. Now, you go right back there this minute and try it again. And this time come in slowly ... slowly. Haste makes waste, Purvis. Haste makes waste. If I've told you that once, I must have told you that a hundred times. Haste makes waste.'

The loudspeaker overhead began squawking. 'Milo, this is Alvin Brown. I've finished dropping my bombs. What should I do now?'

'Strafe,' said Milo.

'*Strafe?*' Alvin Brown was shocked.

'We have no choice,' Milo informed him resignedly. 'It's in the contract.'

'Oh, OK, then,' Alvin Brown acquiesced. 'In that case I'll strafe.'

This time Milo had gone too far. Bombing his own men and planes was more than even the most phlegmatic observer could stomach, and it looked like the end for him. High-ranking government officials poured in to investigate. Newspapers inveighed against Milo with glaring headlines, and Congressmen denounced the atrocity in stentorian wrath and clamoured for punishment. Mothers with children in the service organized into militant groups and demanded revenge. Not one voice was raised in his defence. Decent people everywhere were affronted, and Milo was all washed up until he opened his books to the public and disclosed the tremendous profit he had made. He could reimburse the government for all the people and property he had destroyed and still have enough money left over to continue buying Egyptian cotton. Everybody, of course, owned a share. And the sweetest part of the whole deal was that there really was no need to reimburse the government at all.

'In a democracy, the government is the people,' Milo explained. 'We're people, aren't we? So we might just as well keep the money and eliminate the middleman. Frankly, I'd like to see the government get out of war altogether and leave the whole field to private industry. If we pay the government everything we owe it, we'll only be encouraging government control and discouraging other individuals from bombing their own men and planes. We'll be taking away their incentive.'

Martha Gellhorn

The Black Widow

In the daytime the Thunderbolts, snarling bulldog planes, roared on and off this field, and the pilots poured into the briefing shack and announced their kills to the interrogating officer, or stood huddled around a big map getting last-minute instructions before the next mission. Across the field, a fleet of C-47s was lined up and ambulances moved slowly and carefully over the deep frozen ruts, and orderlies lifted the blanketed wounded into the planes. When the cargo was completed, tier after tier of pain, the heavy freight planes moved down the runway en route to England. Nothing broke the wind and it swept in waves over the iron mud of the field and swirled the snow in dusty clouds. The field was as ugly as all forward airfields are, with the claptrap buildings of the squadrons and a tent hospital outlining its edges. The air hammered with the noise of planes and everyone looked small, eaten with cold and intently busy.

When darkness came, the field was silent and nothing moved and this place then seemed a wasteland in Siberia, a plateau on the moon, the very end of the world. When darkness came, the Black Widows took over.

Now the major in command of these Black Widow night fighters, a man of twenty-six but with the ageless hard tired look one is used to seeing on the faces of all the young, was making a speech. His squadron headquarters had been pieced together from the wood of a German barracks and it was very cold, with one iron stove to heat the room, and badly lighted by a few unshaded bulbs. 'Everybody shoots at us,' he said. 'Friendly bombers and friendly flak and enemy flak and enemy fighters. Just anybody at all; they all got a right to shoot at us. I wouldn't advise it.'

Last night one of their planes had been shot down, and the

squadron doctor, who drove over to the place where the plane crashed, returned to report that nothing remained of the pilot and radio operator except four feet and two hands. There is never any time for pity or sorrow, at least there is no time to show these feelings; death only seems to make the survivors angrier and more aware of what is after all a constant danger. Death reminds you that it can happen to you too, and everyone fears and resents this reminder.

'Well,' said the Major, 'if you're going, you better come with me. I'm on the first mission.'

We ate supper at five, and it was already night. Americans call any sizeable building a château and they had their mess in a château, which was nothing but a large untidy dark icy house. The pilots and radio operators ate in a big room, wearing their flying clothes, and they passed heavy dishes of lukewarm unpalatable food around the long tables and laughed and shouted to each other, eating in haste. A captain beside me began to list again the horrors of night flying, until the Major said, 'She's coming with us now, so leave her alone. Tell her something good.'

The Captain said at once, 'It will be beautiful anyhow. It's certainly beautiful up there, and it's going to be a fine night.'

I handed a bowl of congealed mashed potatoes to the Major and thought that the myth of the glamorous lives of pilots is the silliest myth of all. Probably we got it from the movies about pilots in the last war, who always seemed to live in authentic châteaux and eat at fine tables loaded with cut glass and china and ornamented with occasional champagne buckets. Pilots, according to myth, return from their hazardous work and have a hot bath and step into perfectly tailored uniforms and while away their spare time in a frolic of stout-hearted laughter and singing. Actually they live like hell at these forward fields. It is only one step better than the foxhole. Mostly they sleep in tents and there is no escaping the cold and there is nothing to do but fly, sleep, eat and wait in black discomfort to fly again. They always speak with pity of the infantry, who have a really 'rugged' life.

After supper, during which everyone except myself ate heartily, we went back to Squadron Headquarters. I was zipped into flying pants, flying boots and a flying jacket, feeling more and more like a breathless package. The Major appeared with an oxygen mask and there was some difficulty in fitting the thing on. 'They didn't make these for ladies,' he said. 'Can you breathe?' Someone was stuffing gloves into my hand, and someone else was attempting to fasten a parachute on me. I found myself choking inside the mask and shook my head and the Major said, 'OK, that'll do.' He put an escape kit in my pocket and led me to the map, which was enormous and incomprehensible, and picked up a piece of string that was attached to the map; where the string was attached was our base. He described a rough semicircle to the east with the string and said, 'We'll be patrolling this area. If anything happens, walk southwest.'

We now piled into a jeep, the Major, the radio operator, the driver and I. It was difficult to hoist one's body around and there was a marked tendency to sit down when one meant to stand up, due to the weight of the parachute. It was so cold that one shrank into one's clothes and felt oneself shrivelling in the wind. Now we could see the sleek sharp outlines of the black plane ahead. It is a beautiful plane, with two upcurling tails and long narrow wings, and it looked in the night like a delicate deadly dragonfly. The name of these P-61s, the Black Widow, seemed all wrong for such beauty of line. No one spoke in the jeep. Then the radio operator said thoughtfully, 'This is the worst part of any mission.' After that we were too busy to think about better or worse.

The Major climbed into the cockpit and began getting the plane ready. The radio operator was delegated to give me the necessary information. This was all so hopelessly mad that it could only be taken as a joke. He said in the dark, 'If anything happens you turn this handle.' What handle? Where? 'That will open the trap. Then turn this other handle on the right – it's wired, but you won't have any trouble. That will drop the ladder out and then all you have to do is fall out backwards. You know where your ripcord is, don't you?'

'Yes,' I said sadly.

'If anything goes wrong with those two, you turn this handle on the cowling and that whole piece of glass will fall out and you can climb out through that. It's a little narrow with all those clothes on, but it will be all right, I guess. Well, that's about all,' said he. 'Have you got a cushion for her?' he asked the crew chief, and from nowhere a flat little sofa cushion appeared and was put on top of the wooden crate which was to be my seat. They had found it impractical to carry a gunner here in the glass bulb between the twin tails and there was no seat or safety belt.

'Oh, and your oxygen mask,' said the radio operator. 'It plugs in here, and this is your earphone plug-in.'

I had given up hope by now; it was all too complicated and I thought gloomily that every one of these damned wires would come undone, I would fall out without meaning to or get hurled off my crate and mashed against the confused steel sides of my little glass cage, and I was already cold and so I decided to try hard to think of something else. Meanwhile a brisk businesslike conversation was going on in the cockpit; voices came through the earphones so deafeningly that I could scarcely distinguish words, but from the tone it sounded as calm and sensible as if you were talking about whether there was enough gas in the car to get to the country club.

We hurtled into the night and soared for the stars. I have never been part of such a take-off; the actual feeling of flying became so intense that one felt free of the plane, and as if one were moving nakedly and with no hindrance through a sky that was bigger than any sky ever seen before. It was beautiful too, with a glowing moon and the stars very close. I knew that the beauty was not going to soothe my spirit or hold my attention. The beauty was a vast emptiness in which we roared alone, and the beauty was a good deal too scary for my taste.

A conversation began on the radio; or rather it had been going on all along, only it seemed clearer now. Somewhere on the distant dark snow-covered earth, men would be sitting in a hidden caravan crouched over instruments of black magic – the radar – and a voice came from wherever they were, speaking a most technical code, and this plane obeyed that voice. At 265 m.p.h. we fled blindly through the night, and our eyes were some place behind us in Luxemburg on the ground. A night fighter pilot is directed by radar to his quarry, which he cannot see, and he must not fire until he has a visual target (that is, until he actually sees and identifies the other plane) and he can be as close as 200 yards from the enemy plane before he is certain of it. Until that time, the Black Widow swerves and swoops, climbs and falls alone like a strange mad bird, obeying the voice of the ground controller.

The conversation between ground and sky was weird beyond believing. Since it was all code, it cannot be repeated; but these odd and mystical sentences filtered through the air in rather loud matter-of-fact voices, and when the ground spoke the plane responded. We were over Germany, and a blacker, less inviting piece of land I never saw. It was covered with snow, there were mountains, there was no light and no sign of human life, but the land itself looked actively hostile. Then the voice from the ground said something; the pilot said, 'Roger,' and the plane vaulted up the sky. This ranked easily as one of the nastiest sensations I have ever felt. We climbed, in a matter of seconds, from 11,000 to 22,000 feet. One's body turned to iron and was crushed down, feeling as if an enormous weight were pressing on something that would not yield. My oxygen mask was too large and had to be held on, and as I held it with my right hand, and held onto some kind of steel shelf with my left hand (so as not to fall backwards off my darling little crate) I thought that (a) my stomach was going to be flattened against my backbone and (b) that I was going to strangle. This loathsome set of feelings went on and meanwhile the radio conversation sharpened and went faster and louder, and I knew, though the words were muddled, that we were being led to our quarry.

I had reached a stage of dull resignation and only prayed that we would stop doing whatever we were doing and do something else. The plane stopped climbing and now it was just hard to breathe. An added charm is that one's nose, a reasonably earthy instrument, flows steadily in this cold and of course is unwipeable; presently, since the temperature inside the plane was thirty below zero, one finds oneself with a small frozen river on one's face. This is

mentioned only in passing, because it is a very minor matter, but
there it is. One is anyhow so cold that one more misery doesn't
count. The plane, driven on by the loud ground voice, was roaring
high and straight through the sky. Then, for no reason I could
discover, we turned over on a wing and dropped sideways a few
miles toward the ground. That too was an undesirable sensation;
one's insides seemed to drain away, leaving one empty and weak
and not at all certain which side was upright. The pilot said
something to me, in a nice cosy voice, but I did not understand. He
repeated it. I gathered that we had just dropped through the sky
that way in order to avoid flak at Cologne. It appeared that we had
been following a friendly plane which must have been a bomber
and was copping the Cologne flak. It seemed restful to be flying
level at 11,000 feet again. The radio voices chatted to each other,
apparently saying what a pity the whole thing had been, and better
luck next time.

Everything was calm now, except for the fact that we were still
over Germany. Then the pilot called to me on the intercom, and,
looking where he told me, I saw the trail of a V-2. It came from
somewhere deeper inside Germany and was at this distance a red
ball of fire, and it rose perpendicularly from the ground and passed
out of sight over the top of the sky in a few seconds. Then there
were gun flashes to the west, where the front seemed to be waking
up. One huge gun opened like a blast furnace, but I could not tell
whether it was theirs or ours. On the ground I saw fixed flares, and
again I did not know what they were; then there would be the
sudden quaking soundless fire of the guns. There was also a
frightening star, which I believed to be following us. I was
considering how to call it to the pilot's attention when finally I
decided it was a star, once and for all, and could be classed as
harmless.

The ground was not saying anything much and the pilot seemed
to have more time, for he started an amiable conversation over the
intercom, practically none of which I understood, but his voice and
manner of speaking filled me with admiration. It was as if he were
making friendly talk with someone he had just met in a bar. The

intercom worked only one way; I could not have answered even if I had known what he was saying. The ground voice spoke again, giving brisk orders, and the plane flicked neatly over on a wing and glided steeply downward. The pilot was asking questions, and more orders came from the ground. I could tell that we were hunting and getting close. By now this journey seemed to have gone on for ever; one had sat since the beginning of time on a wobbly crate in the middle of heaven, and there obviously was no end to it. The plane slowed terrifyingly; it felt as if it were standing still in the air, and at the same time the pilot's voice crackled angrily on the radio. Nothing happened. There was some reply from the ground and the pilot said very angrily, 'For God's sake.' The snow-covered land was nearer now and so were the gun flashes.

The pilot spoke again on the intercom. We had been on the trail of an authentic enemy plane, but due to some miscalculation we were brought down on top of the enemy plane instead of under it. We were therefore briefly in the unfortunate position of getting shot at, rather than doing the shooting, but luckily the German did not wish to fight and had streaked off west and lost himself. The pilot was furious.

Now we were going home, as the time limit was nearly up. Suddenly the pilot said, 'See the flak?' I had seen it to the left; I thought it was low and far away and I was sad for the unlucky men who were getting it. This justifies completely the ignorance-is-bliss school of thought. The flak was shooting at us, the distance was too close for comfort, and I imagined that the shells went no higher than the tracers. We did another quick aerial pirouette and roared for home.

We landed as we had taken off, which is to say like a bolt of lightning. We had been out a little over two and a half hours, and the Major was almost blue with cold. He had not been heavily dressed because he could not fly the plane if his body was hampered by all that clothing. So for two and a half hours now and for two and a half hours later that night, and every other night, he would sit in a plane in a temperature of thirty below zero and simply take it. He did say, in passing, 'Gosh, it's cold.'

The Major was depressed about the evening, it had been a boring patrol, nothing happened, there was one good chance of a fight and it had been mucked up, and all in all he felt browned off. So we climbed stiffly into the jeep and went back to the squadron shack. The other planes of this mission were coming in, landing at that soul-shaking speed, and a new mission would be leaving within a few minutes. The radio operator came back to headquarters to report to the interrogating officer and left again immediately, as he was flying with another pilot on the second mission. He had no time for a cup of coffee, or any chance to get warm; I do not think there was a cup of coffee available, for that matter.

But there was much excitement in the headquarters shack; a tall tow-headed boy with a shining face was passing a box of cigars around and getting heavily beaten on the back. His smile was enormous and he couldn't give out cigars fast enough. A cable had just come, announcing the birth of a baby daughter.

'Thank God,' said the Major, 'I've been sweating out that baby for ten days.'

The tow-headed pilot showed his cable and a picture of his wife and offered his cigar box.

'How long is a baby?' he said. He held his hands about three feet apart. 'That long?'

'Hell, no,' said an elderly father of twenty-four. 'About so long.' And he held his hands a foot apart.

There followed a heated argument about the length of babies. No one spoke of the mission completed or of the missions to come; it was after all just another night's work. But people didn't become fathers every night; becoming a father was really something.

The Thunderbolt pilots had invited us to have a drink in their club. They had fixed up a shack as a mess and built a fireplace out of armour plate from a German tank and rigged up a bar, and they had whisky and scrambled-egg sandwiches. We drove along the bad road beside the field and the Major said, 'Let's not talk about Black Widows down there, see? What I mean is, we think those Thunderbolt pilots do a lot tougher job than we do, so let's just not talk about our stuff.' None of the Thunderbolt boys will ride in the

Black Widows for anything, on the grounds that the whole performance is unsound.

The Thunderbolt pilots were all very young and were trying to be gay tonight, because they had lost their squadron leader the day before, and they loved him, and one dare not mourn. He was last seen headed straight down, with his machine-guns still firing ten feet above the ground. His last heard remark was, 'Give 'em hell.' So now everyone was drinking and talking shop. One boy said that he never got used to shooting people, because they rolled so much when they were hit. He just didn't like it, that was all. It was different for the Airborne boys, and such as them, they were real killers; but he just didn't like the way people rolled. The phrase that recurred most was, 'We sure clobbered the Herman.' This means we definitely shot up the Germans. It can mean that they shot up trucks, tanks, command cars or troops; anything German is Herman and 'clobbered' means liquidated. The Major was rather silent and was mainly occupied trying to get warm in front of the curious fireplace. I have never felt better in my life, due to my pleasure in being around at all, and I ate scrambled-egg sandwiches like a starving Armenian. Then the Major had to get back to his headquarters, as he was flying again, so we left with many expressions of mutual esteem and gratitude.

In the jeep, the Major said thoughtfully, 'Those P-47s. I don't hack their talk.'

'Why?' I asked.

'Clobber the Herman,' he said, with a very faint air of contempt. 'What talk is that?'

'What do you say?'

'We say "hose the Hun", of course.'

We dropped him at the door and for a moment we stood there, shivering and shrunken with cold. 'Well, so long,' he said. 'Come and see us again. Give you a ride any time.' In the light from the headquarters shack, he looked tired and cold. You were sure he would not think about being tired or cold or think in any way about himself. They all did their job, that was all. Some men fly by day and others by night, some men work in tanks, others drop out of planes in parachutes, and there is always the infantry. All jobs and all appalling jobs. They do not think of them; they do them; there is nothing else to do.

As we drove away, another sleek sharp plane tore up into the night sky, climbed and headed east toward Germany.

Charles Berlitz

The Bermuda Triangle

The Bermuda Triangle received its name as the result of the disappearance of six navy planes and their crews on 5 December 1945. The first five planes that disappeared, apparently simultaneously, were on a routine training mission with a flight plan designed to follow a triangular flight pattern starting at the Naval Air Station at Fort Lauderdale, Florida, then 160 miles to the east, 40 miles to the north, and then back to their base, following a south-west course. Bermuda has given its name to what has been variously called 'The Devil's Triangle', 'The Triangle of Death', 'The Hoodoo Sea', 'The Graveyard of the Atlantic' and various other appellations, principally because it was noticed at the time that the apex of the triangular flight plan from Fort Lauderdale was in a direct line with Bermuda, and partly because Bermuda seems to be the northern boundary of both earlier and later disappearances of ships and planes in very unusual circumstances. But no incident before or since has been more remarkable than this *total* disappearance of an entire training flight, along with the giant rescue plane, a Martin Mariner with a crew of thirteen, which inexplicably vanished during rescue operations.

Flight 19 was the designation of the group of doomed planes which left their base at Fort Lauderdale on the afternoon of 5 December 1945. They were manned by five officer pilots and nine enlisted crew-members, the latter detailed two to each plane but on this day short one man, who had requested removal from flying status because of a premonition and who had not been replaced. The planes were navy Grumman TBM-3 Avenger torpedo bombers, and each carried enough fuel to enable it to cruise over 1,000 miles. The temperature was 65°, the sun was shining, there were scattered clouds and a moderate north-east wind. Pilots who had flown earlier the same day reported ideal flying weather. Flight time was calculated as two hours for this specific mission. The planes started taking off at 2 p.m. and by 2.10 p.m. they were all airborne. Lieutenant Charles Taylor, with over 2,500 hours' flying time, who was in command, led the planes to Chicken Shoals, north of Bimini, where they were first to make practice runs on a target hulk. Both pilots and crews were experienced airmen and there was no reason to expect anything of an unusual nature to happen during the routine mission of Flight 19.

But something did happen, and with a vengeance. At about 3.15 p.m., after the bombing run had been accomplished and the planes had continued east, the radioman at the Fort Lauderdale Naval Air Station Tower, who had been expecting contact from the planes regarding estimated time of arrival and landing instructions, received an unusual message from the flight leader. The record shows the following:

FLIGHT LEADER (Lieutenant Charles Taylor): Calling Tower. This is an emergency. We seem to be off course. We cannot see land ... Repeat ... We cannot see land.

TOWER: What is your position?

FLIGHT LEADER: We are not sure of our position. We cannot be sure just where we are ... We seem to be lost ...

TOWER: Assume bearing due west.

FLIGHT LEADER: We don't know which way is west. Everything is wrong ... Strange ... We can't be sure of any direction – even the ocean doesn't look as it should ...

At about 3.30 the senior flight instructor at Fort Lauderdale had picked up on his radio a message from someone calling Powers, one of the student flyers, requesting information about his compass readings and heard Powers say, 'I don't know where we are. We must have got lost after that last turn.' The senior flight instructor was able to contact the Flight 19 instructor, who told him, 'Both my compasses are out. I am trying to find Fort Lauderdale ... I am sure I'm in the Keys, but I don't know how far down ...' The senior flight instructor thereupon advised him to fly north – with the sun on the port side – until he reached the Fort Lauderdale Naval Air Station. But he subsequently heard: 'We have just passed over a small island ... No other land in sight ...' – an indication that the instructor's plane was not over the Keys and that the entire flight, since they were unable to see land, which would normally follow a continuation of the Keys, had lost its direction.

It became increasingly difficult to hear messages from Flight 19 because of static. Apparently Flight 19 could no longer hear messages from the tower, but the tower could hear conversations between the planes. Some of these messages referred to possible fuel shortages – fuel for only 75 miles, references to 75 m.p.h. winds, and the unnerving observation that every gyro and magnetic compass in all the planes was off – 'going crazy,' as it was reported at the time – each showing a different reading. During all this time the powerful transmitter at Fort Lauderdale was unable to make any contact with the five planes, although the interplane communications were fairly audible.

By this time the personnel of the base were in an understandable uproar as news spread that Flight 19 had encountered an emergency. All kinds of suppositions concerning enemy attack (although World War II had been over for several months), or even attacks by new enemies, suggested themselves, and rescue craft were dispatched, notably a twin-engined Martin Mariner flying boat patrol plane with a crew of thirteen, from the Banana River Naval Air Station.

At 4 p.m. the tower suddenly heard that Lieutenant Taylor had unexpectedly turned over command to a senior Marine pilot, Captain Stiver. Although obscured by static and strained by tension an understandable message was received from him: 'We are not sure where we are ... We think we must be 225 miles north-east of base ... We must have passed over Florida and we must be in the Gulf of Mexico ... ' The flight leader then apparently decided to turn 180 degrees in the hope of flying back over Florida, but as they made the turn the transmission began to get fainter, indicating that they had made a wrong turn and were flying east, away from the Florida coast over the open sea. Some reports claim that the last words heard from Flight 19 were: 'It looks like we are ...' Although other listeners seem to remember more, such as: 'Entering white water ... We are completely lost ...'

Meanwhile the tower received a message only minutes after take-off from Lieutenant Come, one of the officers of the Martin Mariner, dispatched to the general area where the flight was presumed to be, that there were strong winds above 6,000 feet. This, however, was the last message received from the rescue plane. Shortly after this all search units received an urgent message stating that six planes instead of five were now missing. The rescue plane, with a crew of thirteen, had disappeared as well.

No further message was ever received from the Flight 19 training mission or from the Martin Mariner that was sent to rescue them. Some time after 7 p.m., however, the Opa-Locka Naval Air Station in Miami received a faint message consisting of: 'FT ... FT ...' which was part of the call letters of the planes of Flight 19, the instructor's plane being FT-28. But if this message was really from the 'lost patrol', the time period in which it was received would indicate that the message was sent two hours *after* the planes had presumably run out of fuel.

The original air search, initiated on the day of disappearance, was suspended because of darkness, although Coast Guard vessels continued to look for survivors during the night. The next day, Thursday, an enormous search effort was started at 'first light', i.e. daybreak. But in spite of one of history's most intensive searches, involving 240 planes and 67 additional planes from the aircraft carrier *Solomons*, four destroyers, several submarines, eighteen Coast Guard vessels, search and rescue cutters, hundreds of private planes, yachts and boats, and additional PBMs from the Banana River Naval Air Station and help by RAF and Royal Navy units in the Bahamas, nothing was found.

A daily average of 167 flights, flying about 300 feet above the water from dawn to dusk, a minute inspection of 380,000 square miles of land and sea, including the Atlantic, Caribbean, parts of the Gulf of Mexico and the Florida mainland and neighbouring islands, with air-search time totaling 4,100 hours, revealed no life-rafts, no wreckage and no oil slicks. The beaches of Florida and the Bahamas were checked daily for a period of several weeks for identifiable flotsam from the lost planes, but without success.

All possible leads were investigated. A report that a red flare over land had been seen by a commercial plane on the day of the disappearances was first thought to be the possible explosion of the Martin Mariner, but later denied. Still later a merchant ship reported an explosion in the sky at 7.30 p.m., but if this explosion concerned the five Avengers, it would mean that they were still flying hours after their fuel reserves had been exhausted. Furthermore, to explain in this way the loss without trace of all planes would imply that they crashed together and exploded all at once after having maintained radio silence since the time contact was interrupted. It is further remarkable that no SOS messages were received from Flight 19 or the rescue mission. As far as making forced landings in the sea, the Avengers were capable of making smooth water landings and in any event could stay afloat for ninety seconds, with their crews trained to abandon ship in sixty seconds. Life-rafts were available and were obtained from outside the planes. Therefore, in almost any kind of forced landing the life-rafts would float and would eventually be found. During the early part of the rescue effort, some searchers noted large swells in the sea but the waves were so far apart that the planes could have landed, if necessary, in the troughs between them. The curious reference to 'white water' in the last message received from Flight 19 *may* have had some connection with the thick and confusing white haze which is an occasional feature of the area. This might explain the lack of visual sighting and the report that the sun 'doesn't look right', but this should not have affected the compasses and gyroscopes. In addition, there is a known radio dead spot between Florida and the Bahamas, but the planes' trouble started *before* radio contact was lost.

A Naval Board of Inquiry, after examining all available evidence and incidentally debating the court-martial of the instrument officer (who was later exonerated when it was established that all his instruments had checked out before take-off) ended up as much in the dark as ever as to what had really happened. Part of the report states: 'A radio message intercepted indicated that the planes were lost and that they were experiencing malfunctioning of their compasses.' Captain W. C. Wingard, an information officer, was somewhat more direct in a subsequent press interview: '... Members of the Board of Inquiry were not able to make even a good guess as to what happened.' Another Board member rather dramatically commented: 'They vanished as completely as if they had flown to Mars,' thereby introducing the intriguing elements of space travel and possible UFOs which have since become very much a part of the Bermuda Triangle legend. Serious investigators and oceanographers have offered a variety of opinions as to how these and so many other ships and planes could disappear without trace, and how so many pilots and passengers could completely vanish. Lieutenant Commander R. H. Wirsching, a training officer at the Fort Lauderdale Naval Air Base at the time of the incident, who has considered the case for many years, thinks that the word 'disappear' is an important factor concerning the fate of the crew of Flight 19 as no proof has ever been adduced that they effectively perished. (A mother of one of the lost pilots who attended the naval hearing stated at the time that she had received the impression that her son 'was still alive somewhere in space'.) And Dr Manson Valentine, a scientist who has watched the area for many years from Miami, was quoted in the Miami *News* as saying: 'They are still here, but in a different dimension of a magnetic phenomenon that could have been set up by a UFO.' A Coast Guard officer, a member of the Board of Inquiry, expressed himself with rather refreshing frankness as he observed simply, 'We don't know what the hell is going on out there.' And a final, more formal statement from another officer of the Board expressed the consensus of the investigating officers: '... This unprecedented peacetime loss seems to be a total mystery, the strangest ever investigated in the annals of naval aviation.'

Alexander Frater

Empire Flying Boat

My first love affair began early on the morning of 31 December 1946, a few days before my ninth birthday. It was with an aeroplane – one that has now entered the realms of legend – and was of such intensity that even today, like some incorrigible *boulevardier* giving the eye to every passing woman, I cannot resist looking up whenever I hear the clamour of engines overhead.

The plane was one of the old Empire flying boats and it took me and my family from Rose Bay, Sydney, to the Fiji Islands, where a new job awaited my father; after the rigours and separations of the war this was to be a fresh beginning. Shortly before dawn a motor launch carried us across the dark, calm water to our aircraft, riding at a buoy with its portholes lit. There were lights burning in the cockpit too, high on the upper deck where the captain, a grizzled, white-haired man, sat drinking tea with his officers.

As the launch driver cut the engine I noted the name *Coriolanus* painted on the Empire's massive tugboat nose and, further back, the words 'Qantas Empire Airways'; towards the tail were the registration letters VH-ABG. My mother, keeping her voice low, told us that Coriolanus, the subject of one of Shakespeare's minor plays, had been a famous Roman warrior exiled for haughtiness. We drifted beneath a high, broad wing that hid the paling sky and fading stars. Our wash sucked lazily at the flared keel and giant portside float, secured to the wing-tip by a cat's cradle of wires and struts. Clambering through a low doorway with a curved lintel I sniffed a faint, heady tramp steamer aroma of coffee, grease, paraffin and candlenut which I took to be the smell of the sky itself.

The fuselage was divided, like a ship, into cabins, the one next to ours occupied by a tall, stooped Englishman in a tweed suit, so thin his body seemed to be made from wire; he was taken there by a crew member who called him Sir Brian and treated him with much deference. My father said the Englishman was the Governor of Fiji, returning from a private visit to Sydney, and the chap making the fuss was the ship's clerk. The steward brought us barley sugar and, guessing accurately that we hadn't flown before, said we should suck it during take-off to stop our ears popping.

Then, one by one, the four big supercharged Pegasus engines were started and the clerk hurried forward to the nose mooring hatch and hauled in the line. The Empire began to move, slowly and erratically, turning this way and that, the port float rising a few inches above the water as the wings tilted to starboard then, as they tilted back, splashing down again and cutting a huge creamy furrow in the surface. My father, who had spent the war near a US Navy base in the South Pacific and had daily seen PBY Catalina flying boats manoeuvring in front of his hospital, explained that the sea was too flat to get airborne. The pilot first had to roughen it artificially with his own wake, using the temporary disturbance to break the suction and prise the hull off the water and into the air.

Now, having created a respectable swell, the captain swung towards it and pushed his throttles open. We raced thunderously forward and a high foaming bow wave covered the lower deck portholes, filling the Empire's interior with an eerie green light. Then the nose began to lift and the water level dropped down the windows like a venting tank. I watched the float throwing up a terrific curtain of spray which slowly subsided and ceased altogether as, with a scraping, gravelly sound, the Empire finally rose clear and lumbered into a pink morning sky. I looked down amazed at the toy city, full of shadows and growing tinier by the minute, and marvelled at the fact that it contained millions of sleeping people no larger than sand grains. That extraordinary moment changed a number of my perceptions and made me think that God was perhaps not the good shepherd after all but, rather, a kind of entomologist, the manager and trainer of a giant flea circus.

John J. McDonald

Howard Hughes and the Spruce Goose

The flying boat was the finest example of Howard Hughes's work at its best. This project, as no other, exposes the true genius of this man. Not only is this the world's largest aeroplane, but it was more than twice as big as anything in its day. Its wings are so thick that you can walk upright inside them with another person of average height standing on your shoulders. They are over 11 feet thick. The wings aren't merely the biggest ever built, they are longer than a football field – over 320 feet long and over 11,430 square feet. You could erect average-size homes on top of them. Or place two B-17s under them and never even see them from above.

The fuselage stands 30 feet out of the water and the tail assembly is as tall as an eight-storey building.

What is even more amazing is that this giant plane still is, in many ways, ahead of its time. The flying boat has many systems and innovations that the rest of the aircraft industry has not caught up with to this day.

This one plane also laid the groundwork for modern wide-bodied aircraft. Hughes conceived an aeroplane weighing 400,000 pounds that, with only 24,000 horsepower, could fly some 3,000 miles at speeds of approximately 200 m.p.h. This was a magnificent achievement for the 1940s.

If there is anything about the flying boat more amazing than its pure gargantuan size, it is the construction. While its size dwarfs any aeroplane ever conceived, the construction boggles the imagination of engineers to this very day. There is a small amount of metal used in its farings and the engine mounts are constructed of metal tubing, but basically this 200-ton seaplane is constructed of birch veneer wood.

Contrary to common opinion, there is little or no spruce used in

the ship. Hughes detested the name 'Spruce Goose' given to her by
reporters. The only name he would acknowledge was the 'flying
boat'.

*

On 1 November 1947, preparations were made to float the giant
flying boat out of its dock and moor it in the channel for the next
day's flight. The launching operation took most of the day. A large
tent had been set up for the press conference and for breakfast for
the press as well as other distinguished guests. Over 500 reporters,
photographers and newsreel people were to be on hand. A select
few would be allowed to come aboard and go along for the tests.
Lots were drawn among the press to determine who'd get to go.

On 2 November 1947 it was a cool morning and the mist was
rising off the ocean at the Long Beach Channel. As the sun rose, it
became apparent that this was not just an ordinary day. There were
crowds lined up on both sides of the channel and cars coming in to
park. Everyone seemed to be staring out into the channel as the
early morning sun lifted the mist. In the channel, floating majestic-
ally, was the flying boat. The channel was alive with ships and boats
of all types scurrying about the flying boat at a distance.

Howard Hughes was standing on top of the plane and scanning
the full length of the channel with binoculars. And he was saying a
few words to the Coast Guard ships passing by. Satisfied, Hughes
lowered himself down into the ship. Another roar of the crowd
went up as the engines started. Everyone knew that Hughes was at
the controls. Television cameras trained on the silver bird; photographers scrambled about to get a good picture.

Again the crowd screamed as two of the flying boat's eight
engines revved up and she started to move. There was an air of
excitement with the crowd; the ships at sea and the parked cars all
blew their horns and sirens as the giant silver seabird headed slowly
and gracefully down the channel to get in position for the first taxi
run.

Hughes was talking to Jim McNamara, the radio announcer, who
was recording a running commentary on the flight. Hughes told

him how rough the water was and that the usable area for the tests was somewhat restricted due to the rough seas at the open end of the channel. 'We only have a three-mile run to use,' he said.

Hughes began to call for systems checks from the various stations. There were intercom stations on the ship and he had a mechanic stationed behind each engine in case of trouble. This was a dreadful place to be during the tests – seated in the engine nacelle in the wing – but every mechanic on the project wanted one of those eight spots just to be on board that day. The worst spot was being stuck up in the vertical tail on the rope ladder about 50 feet up inside a hole about 2 feet square. As they reached the Long Beach end of the channel, Howard turned the ship around and took a drink of milk from the carton he always seemed to have with him.

After some last-minute checks, he revved up all eight engines and the first taxi run began. The speed increased gradually up to about 40 m.p.h. and the noise of the water pounding against the hull was loud as she smashed into wave after wave. The waves were really a good size that day. Having moved down the channel about two miles, Hughes cut back on the throttles and slowed her down to turn around to start the second run back toward Long Beach. Everyone was excited about the way the first run went so smooth. Everything handled just exactly as hoped for.

Hughes told everyone to hold on because they were going to really get up some speed on the next run. He pushed the throttles forward a little as the ship began to move out again; then more throttle and the speed was increasing fast to 30, 40 m.p.h. Then he gave more throttle to 50, 60 m.p.h. The noise inside was deafening from the pounding of the waves. More throttle was given, almost half-throttle now, and the speed moved up to 70 m.p.h. The noise almost quit. She was up on the step and planing just like a modern high-speed boat does. The speed reached was between 80 and 90 m.p.h.

It was scary at first, most who were there recall, but it was a thrill. It was, perhaps, only a minute or two that the flying boat was moving at the high speed. Hughes then cut back on the throttles to slow down. Most of the passengers sighed with relief. Everyone was excited, smiling and talking to one another and asking Hughes questions.

Jim McNamara was asking Hughes questions at a rapid rate about everything from the taxi runs to his problems with the Senate Investigating Committee. When the reporters continued to ask him if he might fly, he answered with a casual, 'No, there are too many systems to be checked out first before taking her into the air. We need a lot of taxi runs to make sure of everything.'

Most of the reporters decided they wanted to get off and file their stories and Hughes obliged them by calling for a boat to pick them up and take them back to shore. When they got off, Hughes once again taxied toward the Long Beach end of the channel and turned the ship around, facing San Pedro.

With the two taxi runs completed, the flying boat was ready for a third test run. If Howard Hughes really intended a third taxi run, it is hard to imagine why. Additional taxi runs could tell him no more. But Hughes was moving the flying boat toward the Long Beach end of the channel for a third run.

He picked up his bottle of milk and began to drink. As he continued drinking, he looked around the inside of the great ship's flight deck. His gaze travelled from his co-pilot to one of the flight engineers, to the reporters, the radio man, Coffee, the second flight engineer, and finally to Jucker, his crew chief. Each had nodded to Hughes as he looked at them, but he did not seem to see them. Something else was on his mind at that moment.

Some of the reporters and crew looked at one another. They were puzzled by Howard's apparent daydreaming. Then a few of the reporters began to ask him questions, but again there was no response. Hughes continued to be unaware of anyone's presence. He put his empty milk bottle down and turned back to the controls.

Hughes placed his left hand on the wheel and his right hand loosely on the eight throttles. He sat there motionless for a moment just looking out the windshield. Then without a word to anyone, he pushed the throttles forward. The eight engines roared with the power of 24,000 horses and the flying boat began to move. The crew responded instantly by turning back to their assignments at their individual stations. As the flying boat began moving, Hughes spoke to his copilot, Dave Grant. 'Dave, give me 15° flaps.'

Grant acted at once on Howard's orders. Then, when it had been accomplished, he replied, '15° flaps, Howard.'

Jucker was aware of the results of the wind-tunnel tests and he knew what they indicated would happen with 15° flaps and a speed of about 80 m.p.h. He knew that there would be only one reason to call for 15° flaps. Hughes was intending to fly on this run.

The flying boat was picking up speed now and cutting through those choppy seas at 20, 30, 40 m.p.h. The noise of the waves from the choppy sea pounded against the hull and grew louder and louder as the speed increased. Everything was right for a flight that day. All systems on the ship were functioning perfectly. The flying boat itself appeared to be very sound and there was a slight choppy sea that is so desirable for the take-off in a flying boat.

Everything was just right except that reporters were standing and milling around rather than being in their seats with seat-belts fastened. There were only a few life jackets on board and no parachutes. Besides this, there were eight crewmen out in the wings, one behind each engine, and one up in the vertical stabilizer. These were extremely dangerous conditions if anything went wrong.

In spite of the extensive testing and engineering calculations, Hughes would be risking 28 lives in an aircraft that had never been flown. It was an aircraft that could only be called experimental. These thoughts must have gone through his mind a hundred times and without question weighed heavily. They probably influenced a decision he was to make just moments later.

As the speed increased to 50, 60, 70 m.p.h., Hughes' expression remained unchanged. His eyes were fixed, looking straight through the windshield, right through the horizon finders; the ones he had so carefully laid out and painted on the windshield just a few days before. As the speed increased toward 70 m.p.h., the pounding noise began to disappear. At about 70 m.p.h. the flying boat lifted up off the step and the pounding noise fell off completely. Only the roar of the engines could be heard. Merle Coffee recalls that it was at that moment that he knew they were about to fly. Coffee was monitoring the ship's electrical system and was startled by the rather sudden loss of noise. In spite of the fact that he figured Hughes would fly the plane, he was not quite ready for it just then.

The speed was nearly 80 m.p.h. and everyone on board was aware that something was happening. A quiet had fallen over everyone on board except for the one radio reporter who was recording a running account of what was taking place. Suddenly, at approximately 80 m.p.h., the giant flying boat – without any action on the controls by Hughes – lifted up and out of the water. It did not bounce out of the water and begin to fly as is normally the way seaplanes take off. Instead, the Flying Boat lifted up like a balloon filled with helium.

Both Jucker and Coffee recalled that it was like being in a fast elevator going up. You could actually feel yourself pressing down against the lifting body of the ship. Jucker added that in all his experience of flying, he had never been in a plane that took off in such a manner.

It was as though she was eager to fly and unable to contain herself from this flight. This was a chance to say to the whole world, 'See, I can fly!' Anyone studying the films of the take-off can't help but feel she was like a giant bird from the sea, gracefully reaching for the heavens, a seabird no longer earthbound.

The instant the flying boat lifted off the water, the crowds that lined the shore began to cheer wildly. The many hundreds still in their boats, clear of the channel, stood up and waved things and cheered as she lifted out of the water. There was no less excitement on board the flying boat itself. The radio newsman was almost beside himself with excitement. He repeated over and over, 'I think we're flying, I think we're flying. I don't know if Howard intended this, I don't think so, I think he's surprised.' Reporters and crew alike let out a cheer.

When the flying boat lifted off the water, Hughes had to make the decision as to whether to take it up and over Cabrillo Beach – which was looming up in the distance – or turn and take her out over the open sea. Or he could attempt to put her back down at once. If Hughes had made plans to fly her any distance, no one had any inklings of it. The flyability of the aeroplane certainly does not seem to have played a part. She had performed in every way as the wind-tunnel tests had said she would and all of her systems were working exactly as designed.

As the flying boat was ballooning up to an altitude of some 80 feet and Hughes was pondering his decision, the right wing began to dip down toward the sea. This began to happen almost as soon as she lifted off the water. Chuck Jucker might have been the only other one besides Hughes who was aware of this incident.

As soon as the right wing began to dip, Jucker recalls that Hughes took the controls and swung them all the way to the left. That was an action that on any other ship might have spelled disaster. In this case, however, Hughes knew that the response time of the giant flying boat was so slow that it was the right reaction to what was happening.

As Hughes turned the controls to a full left position, he also made his decision to bring the flight to an end. He pushed the controls forward to bring the ship back down.

Slowly, almost reluctantly, the ship came back down to the water. She landed on the water as gracefully and gently as she had left the water. She landed almost like a feather drifting effortlessly down to rest. She was truly a magnificent sight coming down gently, pressing the water out of her way as she landed.

The flight was over! The one and only flight that she was ever to make.

She had flown approximately 1 mile and 80 feet in the air and had been airborne for approximately 60 seconds.

With the ship down safely in the water, Hughes taxied her over to the mooring buoy and she was tied up. Chaos was breaking loose with the reporters on board and Hughes could hardly get out of his seat for all the questions and microphones being shoved under his nose. The paramount question was, did he intend to fly her or was he taken by surprise? Hughes was grinning as he left the flying boat; he looked back inside of her as he prepared to exit. When he finally stopped to answer the reporters' questions about the flight, he said, 'I like to make surprises.' The reporters didn't quite understand his meaning and asked, 'You mean that you were surprised?' Hughes answered, 'No, I said I like to make the surprises.'

Chuck Yeager and Leo Janos

Breaking the Sound Barrier

First Powered Flight: 29 August 1947

Shivering, you bang your gloved hands together and strap on your oxygen mask inside the coldest aeroplane ever flown. You're being cold-soaked from the hundreds of gallons of liquid oxygen (LOX) fuel stored in the compartment directly behind you at 296°. No heater, no defroster; you'll just have to grit your teeth for the next fifteen minutes until you land and feel that wonderful hot desert sun. But that cold saps your strength: it's like trying to work and concentrate inside a frozen food locker.

That cold will take you on the ride of your life. You watched the X-1 get its 7.00 a.m. feeding in a swirling cloud of vapour fog, saw the frost form under its orange belly. That was an eerie sight; you're carrying 600 gallons of LOX and water alcohol on board that can blow up at the flick of an igniter switch and scatter your pieces over several counties. But if all goes well, the beast will chug-a-lug a ton of fuel a minute.

Anyone with brain cells would have to wonder what in hell he was doing in such a situation – strapped inside a live bomb that's about to be dropped out of a bomb bay. But risks are the spice of life, and this is the kind of moment that a test pilot lives for. The butterflies are fluttering, but you feed off fear as if it's a high-energy candy bar. It keeps you alert and focused.

You accept risk as part of every new challenge; it comes with the territory. So you learn all you can about the ship and its systems, practise flying it on ground runs and glide flights, plan for any possible contingency, until the odds against you seem more friendly. You like the X-1; she's a sound aeroplane, but she's also an experimental machine, and you're a researcher on an experimental flight. You know you can be hammered by something unexpected, but you count on your experience, concentration and instincts to pull you through. And luck. Without luck . . .

You can't watch yourself fly. But you know when you're in sync with the machine, so plugged into its instruments and controls that your mind and your hand become the heart of its operating system. You can make that aeroplane talk, and like a good horse, the machine knows when it's in competent hands. You know what you can get away with. And you can be wrong only once. You smile reading newspaper stories about a pilot in a disabled plane that manoeuvred to miss a schoolyard before he hit the ground. That's crap. In an emergency situation, a pilot thinks only about one thing – survival. You battle to survive right down to the ground; you think about nothing else. Your concentration is riveted on what to try next. You don't say anything on the radio, and you aren't even aware that a schoolyard exists. That's exactly how it is.

There are at least a dozen different ways that the X-1 can kill you, so your concentration is total during the preflight check procedures. You load up nitrogen gas pressures in the manifolds – your life's blood because the nitrogen gas runs all the internal systems as well as the flaps and landing gear. Then you bleed off the liquid oxygen manifold and shut it down. All's in order.

Half an hour ago, we taxied out to take-off in the mother ship. Because of the possibility of crashing with so much volatile fuel, they closed down the base until we were safely off the ground. That's the only acknowledgement from the base commander that we even exist. There's no interest in our flights because practically nobody at Muroc gives us any chance for success.

One minute to drop. Ridley flashes the word from the co-pilot's seat in the mother ship. We're at 25,000 feet as the B-29 noses over and starts its shallow dive. Major Cardenas, the driver, starts counting backwards from ten.

C-r-r-ack. The bomb shackle release jolts you up from your seat, and as you sail out of the dark bomb bay the sun explodes in brightness. You're looking into the sky. *Wrong!* You should be dropped level. The dive speed was too slow, and they dropped you in a nose-up stall. You blink to get your vision, fighting the stall with your control wheel, dropping toward the basement like an elevator whose cable snapped. You're 3,000 pounds heavier than in those glide flights. Down goes that nose and you pick up speed. You level out about 1,000 feet below the mother ship and reach for that rocket igniter switch.

The moment of truth: if you are gonna be blown up, this is likely to be when. You light the first chamber.

Whoosh. Slammed back in your seat, a tremendous kick in the butt. Nose up and hold on. Barely a sound; you can hear your breathing in the oxygen mask – you're out-racing the noise behind you – and for the first time in a powered aeroplane you can hear the air beating against the windshield as the distant dot that is Hoover's high chase P-80 grows ever bigger. You pass him like he's standing still, and he reports seeing diamond-shaped shock waves leaping out of your fiery exhaust. Climbing faster than you can even think, but using only one of four rocket chambers, you turn it off and light another. We're streaking up at .7 Mach; this beast's power is awesome. You've never known such a feeling of speed while pointing up in the sky. At 45,000 feet, where morning resembles the beginning of dusk, you turn on the last of the four chambers. God, what a ride! And you still have nearly half your fuel left.

Until this moment, you obeyed the flight plan to the letter: firing only one chamber at a time, to closely monitor the chamber pressures; if you use two or more, there's too much to watch. If you fire all four, you may accelerate too rapidly, be forced to raise your nose to slow down, and get yourself into a high-speed stall.

Now the flight plan calls for you to jettison remaining fuel and glide down to land. But you're bug-eyed, thrilled to your toes, and the fighter jock takes over from the cautious test pilot. Screw it! You're up there in the dark part of the sky in the most fabulous flying machine ever built, and you're just not ready to go home. The moment calls for a nice slow roll, and you lower your wing, pulling a couple of Gs until you're hanging upside-down in zero Gs and the engine quits. As soon as the X-1 rights itself it starts again, but you've been stupid. At zero Gs the fuel couldn't feed the engine, and you might have been blown up. But the X-1 is forgiving – this time.

You know what you're supposed to do, but you know what you're gonna do. You turn off the engine, but instead of jettisoning the remaining fuel, you roll over and dive for Muroc Air Base. We blister down, shit-heavy, .8 Mach in front of the needle, a dive-glide faster than most jets at full power. You're thinking, 'Let's show those bastards the real X-1.'

Below 10,000 feet is the danger zone, the limit for jettisoning fuel with enough manoeuvre time to glide down to a safe landing. But we're below 5,000, lined up with Muroc's main runway. And we're still in a dive.

We whistle down that main runway, only 300 feet off the ground, until we are parallel with the control tower. You hit the main rocket switch. The four chambers blow a thirty-foot lick of flame. Christ, the impact nearly knocks you back into last week. That nose is pointed so straight up that you can't see the blue sky out the windshield. We are no longer an aeroplane: we're a skyrocket. You're not flying. You're holding on to the tiger's tail. Straight up, you're going .75 Mach! In one minute the fuel is gone. By then you're at 35,000 feet, travelling at .85 Mach. You're so excited, scared and thrilled that you can't say a word until the next day.

But others said plenty. The NACA team thought I was a wild man. Dick Frost chewed me out for doing that slow roll. Even Jack Ridley shook his head. He said, 'Any spectators down there knew damned well that wasn't Slick rattling those dishes. OK, son, you got it all out of your system, but now you're gonna hang tough.' Colonel Boyd fired a rocket of his own. 'Reply by endorsement about why you exceeded .82 Mach in violation of my direct orders.' I asked Ridley to write my reply. 'Bullshit,' he said. 'You did it. You explain it.'

I wrote back: 'The aeroplane felt so good and flew so well that I felt certain we would have no trouble going slightly above the agreed speed. The violation of your direct orders was due to the excited state of the undersigned and will not be repeated.'

A few days later, the old man called me. 'Damn it, I expect you to stick to the programme and do what you are supposed to. Don't get overeager and cocky. Do you want to jeopardize the first air corps research project?'

'No, sir.'

'Well, then, obey the goddamn rules.'

From then on I did. But on that first powered flight I wanted to answer those who said we were doomed in the attempt to go faster than sound. My message was, 'Stick it where the sun don't shine.'

Going out to .85 Mach put the programme out on a limb because it carried us beyond the limits of what was then known about high-speed aerodynamics. Wind tunnels could only measure up to .85 Mach, and as Walt Williams of NACA was quick to point out to me, 'From now on, Chuck, you'll be flying in the realm of the unknown.' Ridley and I called it 'the Ughknown'.

Whatever happened, I figured I was better off than the British test pilots who had attempted supersonic flights in high-powered dives. If they got into trouble, that was it – especially in a tailless aeroplane like the *Swallow*. All my attempts would be made in climbs – the power of the rocket over the jet – and that way, if I encountered a problem, I could quickly slow down. But the price of rocket power was flying with volatile fuel. Running four chambers, my fuel lasted only two and a half minutes; it lasted five minutes on two chambers and ten minutes on one. Each minute of climbing we got lighter and faster, so that by the time we had climbed up and over at 45,000 feet, we were at max speed.

Who would decide the max speed of a particular flight? This was an air corps research project, but the seventeen NACA engineers and technicians used their expertise to try to control these missions. They were there as advisers, with high-speed wind tunnel experience, and were performing the data reduction collected on the X-1 flights, so they tried to dictate the speed in our flight plans. Ridley, Frost and I always wanted to go faster than they did. They would recommend a Mach number, then the three of us would sit down and decide whether or not we wanted to stick with their recommendation. They were so conservative that it would've taken me six months to get to the barrier.

I wanted to be careful, but I also wanted to get it over with.

So I flew in small increments of speed. On 5 October I made my sixth powered flight and experienced shock-wave buffeting for the first time as I reached .86 Mach. It felt like I was driving on bad shock absorbers over uneven paving stones. The right wing suddenly got heavy and began to drop, and when I tried to correct it my controls were sluggish. I increased my speed to .88 Mach to see what would happen. I saw my aileron vibrating with shock waves, and only with effort could I hold my wing level.

The X-1 was built with a high tail to avoid air turbulence off the wings; the tail was also thinner than the wings, so that shock waves would not form simultaneously on both surfaces. Thus far, the shock waves and buffeting had been manageable, and because the ship was stressed for eighteen Gs, I never was concerned about being shaken apart. Also, I was only flying twice a week, to give NACA time to reduce all the flight data and analyse it. Special sensing devices pinpointed the exact location of shock waves on any part of the airframe. The data revealed that the aeroplane was functioning exactly as its designers planned.

But on my very next flight we got knocked on our fannies. I was flying at .94 Mach at 40,000 feet, experiencing the usual buffeting, when I pulled back on the control wheel, and Christ, nothing happened! The aeroplane continued flying with the same attitude and in the same direction.

The control wheel felt as if the cables had snapped. I didn't know what in hell was happening. I turned off the engine and slowed down. I jettisoned my fuel and landed feeling certain that I had taken my last ride in the X-1. Flying at .94, I lost my pitch control. My elevator ceased to function. At the speed of sound, the ship's nose was predicted to go either up or down, and without pitch control, I was in a helluva bind.

I told Ridley I thought we had had it. There was no way I was going faster than .94 Mach without an elevator. He looked sick. So did Dick Frost and the NACA team. We called Colonel Boyd at Wright, and he flew out immediately to confer with us. Meanwhile, NACA analysed the telemetry data from the flight and found that at .94 Mach, a shock wave was slammed right at the hinge point of the elevator on the tail, negating my controls. Colonel Boyd just shook his head. 'Well,' he said, 'it looks to me like we've reached the end of the line.' Everyone seemed to agree except for Jack Ridley.

He sat at a corner of the conference table scribbling little notes and equations. He said, 'Well, maybe Chuck can fly without using the elevator. Maybe he can get by using only the horizontal stabilizer.' The stabilizer was the winglike structure on the tail that stabilized pitch control. Bell's engineers had purposely built into them an extra control authority because they had anticipated elevator ineffectiveness caused by shock waves. This extra authority was a trim switch in the cockpit that would allow a small air motor to pivot the stabilizer up or down, creating a moving tail that could act as an auxiliary elevator by lowering or raising the aeroplane's nose. We were leery about trying it while flying at high speeds; instead, we set the trim on the ground and left it alone.

Jack thought we should spend a day ground testing the hell out of that system, learn everything there was to know about it, then flight test it. No one disagreed. There was no other alternative except to call the whole thing quits, but Jack got a lot of 'what if' questions that spelled out all the risks. What if the motor got stuck in a trim up or trim down position? Answer: Yeager would have a problem. What if the turbulent airflow at high-speed Mach overwhelmed the motor and kept the tail from pivoting? Answer: Yeager would be no worse off than he was during the previous mission. Yeah, but what if that turbulent air ripped off that damned tail as it was pivoting? Answer: Yeager better have paid-up insurance. We were dealing with the Ughknown.

Before returning to Wright, Colonel Boyd approved our ground tests. We were to report the results to him, and then he'd decide whether to proceed with a flight test. Then the old man took me aside. 'Listen', he said, 'I don't want you to be railroaded into this deal by Ridley or anyone else. If you don't feel comfortable with the risks, I want you to tell me so. I'll respect your decision. Please don't play the hero, Chuck. It makes no sense getting you hurt or killed.'

I told him, 'Colonel Boyd, it's my ass on the line. I want us to succeed but I'm not going to get splattered doing it.'

So, Ridley and I ground tested that stabilizer system every which way but loose. It worked fine, and provided just enough control (about a quarter of a degree change in the angle of incidence) so that we both felt I could get by without using the aeroplane's elevator. 'It may not be much,' Ridley said, 'and it may feel ragged to you up there, but it will keep you flying.' I agreed. But would the system work at high Mach speed? Only one way to find out. Colonel Boyd gave us the go-ahead.

No X-1 flight was ever routine. But when I was dropped to repeat the same flight profile that had lost my elevator effectiveness, I admit to being unusually grim. I flew as alert and precisely as I knew how. If the damned Ughknown swallowed me up, there wasn't much I could do about it, but I concentrated on that trim switch. At the slightest indication that something wasn't right, I would break the record for backing off.

Pushing the switch forward opened a solenoid that allowed high-pressure nitrogen gas through the top motor to the stabilizer, changing its angle of attack and stabilizing its upward pitch. If I pulled back, that would start the bottom motor, turning it in the opposite direction. I could just beep it and supposedly make pitch changes. I let the aeroplane accelerate up to .85 Mach before testing the trim switch. I pulled back on the switch, moving the leading edge of the stabilizer down one degree, and her nose rose. I retrimmed it back to where it was, and we levelled out. I climbed and accelerated up to .9 Mach and made the same change, achieving the same result. I retrimmed it and let it go out to .94 Mach, where I had lost my elevator effectiveness, made the same trim change, again raising the nose, just as I had done at the lower Mach numbers. Ridley was right: the stabilizer gave me just enough pitch control to keep me safe. I felt we could probably make it through without the elevator.

I had her out to .96 at 43,000 feet and was about to turn off the engine and begin jettisoning the remaining fuel when the windshield began to frost. Because of the intense cabin cold, fogging was a continual problem, but I was usually able to wipe it away. This time, though, a solid layer of frost quickly formed. I even took off my gloves and used my fingernails, which only gave me frostbite. That windshield was lousy anyway, configured to the bullet-shaped fuselage and affording limited visibility. It was hard to see out during landings, but I had never expected to fly the X-1 on instruments. I radioed Dick Frost, flying low chase, and told him the problem. 'OK, pard,' he said, 'I'll talk you in. You must've done a lot of sweating in that cockpit to ice the damned windshield.' I told him, 'Not as much as I'm gonna do having you talk me in. You better talk good, Frost.' He laughed. 'I know. A dumb bastard like you probably can't read instruments.'

The X-1 wasn't the Space Shuttle. There were no on-board computers to line you up and bring you down. The pilot was the computer. Under normal flight conditions, I'd descend to 5,000 feet above the lakebed and fly over the point where I wanted to touch down, then turn and line up downwind, lowering my landing gear at around 250 m.p.h. The X-1 stalled around 190 m.p.h., so I held my glide speed to around 220 and touched down at around 190. The ship rolled out about three miles if I didn't apply the brakes. Rogers Dry Lake gave me an eight-mile runway, but that didn't make the landing untricky. Coming in nose-high, you couldn't see the ground at all. You had to feel for it. I was sensitive to ground effect, and felt the differences as we lowered down. There was also that depth perception problem, and a lot of pilots bent aeroplanes porpoising in, or flaring high then cracking off their landing gears. My advantage was that I had landed on these lakebeds hundreds of times. Even so, the X-1 was not an easy-landing aeroplane. At the point of touchdown, you had to discipline yourself to do nothing but allow the ship to settle in by itself. Otherwise you'd slam it on its weak landing gear.

So, landing blind was not something you'd ever want to be forced to do. I had survived the Ughknown only to be kicked in the butt by the Unexpected. But that was a test pilot's life, one damned thing after another. Frost was a superb pilot, who knew the X-1's systems and characteristics even better than I did. I had plenty of experience flying on instruments, and in a hairy deal like this, experience really counted. Between the two of us we made it look deceptively easy, although we both knew that it wasn't exactly a routine procedure. Frost told me to turn left 10°, and I followed by using my magnetic compass, monitoring my rate of turn by the needle and ball. I watched the air speed and rate of descent, so I knew how fast I was coming down from that and the feel of the ground effect. I followed his directions moving left or right to line up on the lakebed, which was also five miles wide, allowing him to fly right on my wing and touch down with me.

He greased me right in, but my body sweat added another layer of frost to the windshield. 'Pard,' Dick teased, 'that's the only time you haven't bounced her down. Better let me hold your hand from now on.'

Before my next flight, Jack Russell, my crew chief, applied a coating of Drene Shampoo to the windshield. For some unknown reason it worked as an effective antifrost device, and we continued using it even after the government purchased a special chemical that cost eighteen bucks a bottle.

Despite the frosted windshield, I now had renewed confidence in the X-1. We had licked the elevator problem, and Ridley and I phoned Colonel Boyd and told him we thought we could safely continue the flights. He told us to press on. This was on Thursday afternoon. The next scheduled flight would be on Tuesday. So we sat down with the NACA team to discuss a flight plan. I had gone up to .955 Mach, and they suggested a speed of .97 Mach for the next mission. What we didn't know until the flight data was reduced several days later, was that I had actually flown .988 Mach while testing the stabilizer. In fact, there was a fairly good possibility that I had attained supersonic speed.

Instrumentation revealed that a shock wave was interfering with the air speed gauge on the wing. But we wouldn't learn about this until after my next flight.

All I cared about was that the stabilizer was still in one piece and so was I. We were all exhausted from a long, draining week, and quit early on Friday to start the weekend. I had promised Glennis that I would take her to Elly Anderson's, in Auburn, for a change of scene and to get her away from the kids. As cautiously as we were proceeding on these X-1 flights, I figured that my attempt to break the barrier was a week or two away. So I looked forward to a relaxed few days off. But when I got home, I found Glennis lying down, feeling sick. We cancelled the babysitter and called Elly. By Sunday she was feeling better, so we went over to Pancho's place for dinner. On the way over, I said to Glennis, 'Hey, how about riding horses after we eat?' She was raised around horses and was a beautiful rider.

Pancho's place was a dude ranch, so after dinner we walked over to the corral and had them saddle up a couple of horses. It was a pretty night and we rode for about an hour through the Joshua trees. We decided to race back. Unfortunately there was no moon, otherwise I would have seen that the gate we had gone out of was now closed. I only saw the gate when I was practically on top of it. I was slightly in the lead, and I tried to veer my horse and miss it, but it was too late. We hit the gate and I tumbled through the air. The horse got cut and I was knocked silly. The next thing I remember was Glennis kneeling over me, asking me if I was OK. I was woozy, and she helped me stand up. It took a lot to straighten up, feeling like I had a spear in my side.

Glennis knew immediately. 'You broke a rib,' she said. She was all for driving straight to the base hospital. I said, 'No, the flight surgeon will ground me.' 'Well, you can't fly with broken ribs,' she argued. I told her, 'If I can't, I won't. If I can, I will.'

Monday morning, I struggled out of bed. My shoulder was sore, and I ached generally from bumps and bruises, but my ribs near to killed me. The pain took my breath away. Glennis drove me over to Rosemond, where a local doctor confirmed I had two cracked ribs, and taped me up. He told me to take it easy. The tape job really helped. The pain was at least manageable and I was able to drive myself to the base that afternoon.

I was really low. I felt we were on top of these flights now, and I wanted to get them over with. And as much as I was hurting, I could only imagine what the old man would say if I was grounded for falling off a horse. So, I sat down with Jack Ridley and told him my troubles. I said, 'If this were the first flight, I wouldn't even think about trying it with these busted sumbitches. But, hell, I know every move I've got to make, and most of the major switches are right on the control wheel column.'

He said, 'True, but how in hell are you gonna be able to lock the cockpit door? That takes some lifting and shoving.' So we walked into the hangar to see what we were up against.

We looked at the door and talked it over. Jack said, 'Let's see if we can get a stick or something that you can use in your left hand to raise the handle up on the door to lock it. Get it up at least far enough where you get both hands on it and get a grip on it.' We looked around the hangar and found a broom. Jack sawed off a ten-inch piece of broomstick, and it fit right into the door handle. Then I crawled into the X-1 and we tried it out. He held the door against the frame, and by using that broomstick to raise the door handle, I found I could manage to lock it. We tried it two or three times, and it worked. But finally, Ridley said, 'Jesus, son, how are you gonna get down that ladder?'

I said, 'One rung at a time. Either that or you can piggyback me.'

Jack respected my judgement. 'As long as you really think you can hack it,' he said. We left that piece of broomstick in the X-1 cockpit.

Ninth Powered Flight: 14 October 1947

Glennis drove me to the base at six in the morning. She wasn't happy with my decision to fly, but she knew that Jack would never let me take off if he felt I would get into trouble. Hoover and Jack Russell, the X-1 crew chief, heard I was dumped off a horse at Pancho's, but thought the only damage was to my ego, and hit me with some 'Hi-Ho Silver' crap, as well as a carrot, a pair of glasses and a rope in a brown paper bag – my bucking bronco survival kit.

Around eight, I climbed aboard the mother ship. The flight plan called for me to reach .97 Mach. The way I felt that day, .97 would be enough. On that first rocket ride I had a tiger by the tail; but by this ninth flight, I felt I was in the driver's seat. I knew that aeroplane inside and out. I didn't think it would turn against me. Hell, there wasn't much I could do to hurt it; it was built to withstand three times as much stress as I could survive. I didn't think the sound barrier would destroy her, either. But the only way to prove it was to do it.

That moving tail really bolstered my morale, and I wanted to get to that sound barrier. I suppose there were advantages in creeping up on Mach 1, but my vote was to stop screwing around before we had some stupid accident that could cost us not only a mission, but the entire project. If this mission was successful, I was planning to really push for a sound barrier attempt on the very next flight.

Going down that damned ladder hurt. Jack was right behind me. As usual, I slid feet-first into the cabin. I picked up the broom handle and waited while Ridley pushed the door against the frame, then I slipped it into the door handle and raised it up into lock position. It worked perfectly. Then I settled in to go over my checklist. Bob Cardenas, the B-29 driver, asked if I was ready.

'Hell, yes,' I said. 'Let's get it over with.'

He dropped the X-1 at 20,000 feet, but his dive speed was once again too slow and the X-1 started to stall. I fought it with the control wheel for about 500 feet, and finally got her nose down. The moment we picked up speed I fired all four rocket chambers in rapid sequence. We climbed at .88 Mach and began to buffet, so I flipped the stabilizer switch and changed the setting two degrees. We smoothed right out, and at 36,000 feet, I turned off two rocket chambers. At 40,000 feet, we were still climbing at a speed of .92 Mach. Levelling off at 42,000 feet, I had 30 per cent of my fuel, so I turned on rocket chamber three and immediately reached .96 Mach. I noticed that the faster I got, the smoother the ride.

Suddenly the Mach needle began to fluctuate. It went up to .965 Mach – then tipped right off the scale. I thought I was seeing things! We were flying supersonic! And it was as smooth as a baby's bottom: Grandma could be sitting up there sipping lemonade. I kept the speed off the scale for about twenty seconds, then raised the nose to slow down.

I was thunderstruck. After all the anxiety, breaking the sound barrier turned out to be a perfectly paved speedway. I radioed Jack in the B-29. 'Hey, Ridley, that Machmeter is acting screwy. It just went off the scale on me.'

'Fluctuated off?'

'Yeah, at point nine-six-five.'

'Son, you is imagining things.'

'Must be. I'm still wearing my ears and nothing else fell off, neither.'

The guys in the NACA tracking van interrupted to report that they heard what sounded like a distant rumble of thunder: my sonic boom! The first one by an aeroplane ever heard on earth. The X-1 was supposedly capable of reaching nearly twice the speed of sound, but the Machmeter aboard only registered to 1.0 Mach, which showed how much confidence they had; I estimated I had reached 1.05 Mach. (Later data showed it was 1.07 Mach – 700 m.p.h.)

And that was it. I sat up there feeling kind of numb, but elated. After all the anticipation to achieve this moment, it really was a let-down. It took a damned instrument meter to tell me what I'd done. There should've been a bump on the road, something to let you know you had just punched a nice clean hole through that sonic barrier. The Ughknown was a poke through Jello. Later on, I realized that this mission had to end in a let-down, because the real barrier wasn't in the sky, but in our knowledge and experience of supersonic flight.

And so I was a hero this day. As usual, the fire trucks raced out to where the ship had rolled to a stop on the lakebed. As usual, I hitched a ride back to the hangar with the fire chief. That warm desert sun really felt wonderful. My ribs ached.

Tom Wolfe

The Right Stuff

A young man might go into military flight training believing that he was entering some sort of technical school in which he was simply going to acquire a certain set of skills. Instead, he found himself all at once enclosed in a fraternity. And in this fraternity, even though it was military, men were not rated by their outward rank as ensigns, lieutenants, commanders or whatever. No, herein the world was divided into those who had it and those who did not. This quality, this *it*, was never named, however, nor was it talked about in any way.

As to just what this ineffable quality was ... well, it obviously involved bravery. But it was not bravery in the simple sense of being willing to risk your life. The idea seemed to be that any fool could do that, if that was all that was required, just as any fool could throw away his life in the process. No, the idea here (in the all-enclosing fraternity) seemed to be that a man should have the ability to go up in a hurtling piece of machinery and put his hide on the line and then have the moxie, the reflexes, the experience, the coolness, to pull it back in the last yawning moment – and then to go up again *the next day*, and the next day, and every next day, even if the series should prove infinite – and, ultimately, in its best expression, do so in a cause that means something to thousands, to a people, a nation, to humanity, to God. Nor was there *a test* to show whether or not a pilot had this righteous quality. There was, instead, a seemingly infinite series of tests. A career in flying was like climbing one of those ancient Babylonian pyramids made up of a dizzy progression of steps and ledges, a ziggurat, a pyramid extraordinarily high and steep; and the idea was to prove at every foot of the way up that pyramid that you were one of the elected and anointed ones who had *the right stuff* and could move higher

and higher and even – ultimately, God willing, one day – that you
might be able to join that special few at the very top, that elite who
had the capacity to bring tears to men's eyes, the very Brotherhood
of the Right Stuff itself.

None of this was to be mentioned, and yet it was acted out in a
way that a young man could not fail to understand. When a new
flight (i.e. a class) of trainees arrived at Pensacola, they were
brought into an auditorium for a little lecture. An officer would tell
them: 'Take a look at the man on either side of you.' Quite a few
actually swivelled their heads this way and that, in the interest of
appearing diligent. Then the officer would say: 'One of the three of
you is not going to make it!' – meaning, not get his wings. That was
the opening theme, the *motif* of primary training. We already know
that one-third of you do not have the right stuff – it only remains
to find out who.

Furthermore, that was the way it turned out. At every level in
one's progress up that staggeringly high pyramid, the world was
once more divided into those men who had the right stuff to
continue the climb and those who had to be *left behind* in the most
obvious way. Some were eliminated in the course of the opening
classroom work, as either not smart enough or not hard-working
enough, and were left behind. Then came the basic flight instruction, in single-engine, propeller-driven trainers, and a few more –
even though the military tried to make this stage easy – were
washed out and left behind. Then came more demanding levels,
one after the other, formation flying, instrument flying, jet training,
all-weather flying, gunnery and at each level more were washed out
and left behind. By this point easily a third of the original candidates
had been, indeed, eliminated ... from the ranks of those who might
prove to have the right stuff.

In the navy, in addition to the stages that air force trainees went
through, the neophyte always had waiting for him, out in the ocean,
a certain grim grey slab; namely, the deck of an aircraft carrier; and
with it perhaps the most difficult routine in military flying, carrier
landings. He was shown films about it, he heard lectures about it
and he knew that carrier landings were hazardous. He first practised

touching down on the shape of a flight deck painted on an airfield. He was instructed to touch down and gun right off. This was safe enough – the shape didn't move, at least – but it could do terrible things to, let us say, the gyroscope of the soul. *That shape! – It's so damned small!* And more candidates were washed out and left behind. Then came the day, without warning, when those who remained were sent out over the ocean for the first of many days of reckoning with the slab. The first day was always a clear day with little wind and a calm sea. The carrier was so steady that it seemed, from up there in the air, to be resting on pilings, and the candidate usually made his first carrier landing successfully, with relief and even *élan*. Many young candidates looked like terrific aviators up to that very point – and it was not until they were actually standing on the carrier deck that they first began to wonder if they had the proper stuff, after all. In the training film the flight deck was a grand piece of grey geometry, perilous, to be sure, but an amazing abstract shape as one looks down upon it on the screen. And yet once the newcomer's two feet were on it ... *Geometry* – my God, man, this is a ... skillet! It *heaved*, it moved up and down underneath his feet, it pitched up, it pitched down, it rolled to port (this great beast *rolled*!) and it rolled to starboard, as the ship moved into the wind and, therefore, into the waves, and the wind kept sweeping across, sixty feet up in the air out in the open sea, and there were no railings whatsoever. This was a *skillet*! – a frying pan! – a short-order grill! – not grey but black, smeared with skid marks from one end to the other and glistening with pools of hydraulic fluid and the occasional jet-fuel slick, all of it still hot, sticky, greasy, runny, virulent from God knows what traumas – still ablaze! – consumed in detonations, explosions, flames, combustion, roars, shrieks, whines, blasts, horrible shudders, fracturing impacts, as little men in screaming red and yellow and purple and green shirts with black Mickey Mouse helmets over their ears skittered about on the surface as if for their very lives (you've said it now!), hooking fighter planes onto the catapult shuttles so that they can explode their afterburners and be slung off the deck in a red-mad fury with a *kaboom!* that pounds through the entire deck – a procedure that seems absolutely controlled, orderly, sublime, however, compared to what he is about to watch as aircraft return to the ship for what is known in the engineering stoicisms of the military as 'recovery and arrest'. To say that an F-4 was coming back onto this heaving barbecue from out of the sky at a speed of 135 knots ... that might have been the truth in the training lecture, but it did not begin to get across the idea of what the newcomer saw from the deck itself, because it created the notion that perhaps the plane was gliding in. On the deck one knew differently! As the aircraft came closer and the carrier heaved on into the waves and the plane's speed did not diminish and the deck did not grow steady – indeed, it pitched up and down five or ten feet per greasy heave – one experienced a neural alarm that no lecture could have prepared him for: This is not an *aeroplane* coming toward me, it is a brick with some poor sonofabitch riding it (*someone much like myself!*), and it is not *gliding*, it is *falling*, a 30,000 pound brick, headed not for a stripe on the deck but for *me* – and with a horrible *smash!* it hits the skillet, and with a blur of momentum as big as a freight train's it hurtles toward the far end of the deck – another blinding storm! – another roar as the pilot pushes the throttle up to full military power and another smear of rubber screams out over the skillet – and this is nominal! – quite OK! – for a wire stretched across the deck has grabbed the hook on the end of the plane as it hit the deck tail down, and the smash was the rest of the fifteen-ton brute slamming onto the deck, as it tripped up, so that it is now straining against the wire at full throttle, in case it hadn't held and the plane had 'boltered' off the end of the deck and had to struggle up into the air again. And already the Mickey Mouse helmets are running toward the fiery monster ...

And the candidate, looking on, begins to *feel* that great heaving sun-blazing deathboard of a deck wallowing in his own vestibular system – and suddenly he finds himself backed up against his own limits. He ends up going to the flight surgeon with so-called conversion symptoms. Overnight he develops blurred vision or numbness in his hands and feet or sinusitis so severe that he cannot tolerate changes in altitude. On one level the symptom is real. He really cannot see too well or use his fingers or stand the pain. But somewhere in his subconscious he knows it is a plea and a beg-off; he shows not the slightest concern (the flight surgeon notes) that the condition might be permanent and affect him in whatever life awaits him outside the arena of the right stuff.

Those who remained, those who qualified for carrier duty – and even more so those who later on qualified for *night* carrier duty – began to feel a bit like Gideon's warriors. *So many have been left behind!* The young warriors were now treated to a deathly sweet and quite unmentionable sight. They could gaze at length upon the crushed and wilted pariahs who had washed out. They could inspect those who did not have that righteous stuff.

The military did not have very merciful instincts. Rather than packing up these poor souls and sending them home, the navy, like the air force and the marines, would try to make use of them in some other role, such as flight controller. So the wash-out has to keep taking classes with the rest of his group, even though he can no longer touch an aeroplane. He sits there in the classes staring at sheets of paper with cataracts of sheer human mortification over his eyes while the rest steal looks at him ... this man reduced to an ant, this untouchable, this poor sonofabitch. And in what test had he been found wanting? Why, it seemed to be nothing less than *manhood* itself. Naturally, this was never mentioned, either. Yet there it was. *Manliness, manhood, manly courage* ... there was something ancient, primordial, irresistible about the challenge of this stuff, no matter what a sophisticated and rational age one might think he lived in.

Perhaps because it could not be talked about, the subject began to take on superstitious and even mystical outlines. A man either had it or he didn't! There was no such thing as having *most* of it. Moreover, it could blow at any seam. One day a man would be ascending the pyramid at a terrific clip, and the next – bingo! – he would reach his own limits in the most unexpected way. This man had been the budding ace of the training class; he had flown the hottest fighter-style trainer, the T-38, like a dream; and then he began the routine step of being checked out in the T-33. The T-33 was not nearly as hot an aircraft as the T-38; it was essentially the old P-80 jet fighter. It had an exceedingly small cockpit. The pilot could barely move his shoulders. It was the sort of aeroplane of which everybody said, 'You don't get into it, you *wear* it.' Once inside a T-33 cockpit this man, this budding ace, developed claustrophobia of the most paralysing sort. He tried everything to overcome it. He even went to a psychiatrist, which was a serious mistake for a military officer if his superiors learned of it. But nothing worked. He was shifted over to flying jet transports, such as the C-135. Very demanding and necessary aircraft they were, too, and he was still spoken of as an excellent pilot. But as everyone knew – and, again, it was never explained in so many words – only those who were assigned to fighter squadrons, the 'fighter jocks', as they called each other with a self-satisfied irony, remained in the true fraternity. Those assigned to transports were not humiliated like wash-outs – *somebody* had to fly those planes – nevertheless, they, too, had been *left behind* for lack of the right stuff.

Or a man could go for a routine physical one fine day, feeling like a million dollars, and be grounded for *fallen arches*. It happened – just like that! (And try raising them.) Or for breaking his wrist and losing only *part* of its mobility. Or for a minor deterioration of eyesight, or for any of hundreds of reasons that would make no difference to a man in an ordinary occupation. As a result all fighter jocks began looking upon doctors as their natural enemies. Going to see a flight surgeon was a no-gain proposition; a pilot could only hold his own or lose in the doctor's office. To be grounded for a medical reason was no humiliation, looked at objectively. But it was a humiliation, nonetheless! – for it meant you no longer had that indefinable, unutterable, integral stuff. (It could blow at *any* seam.)

All the hot young fighter jocks began trying to test the limits themselves in a superstitious way. They were like believing Presbyterians of a century before who used to probe their own experience to see if they were truly among *the elect*. When a fighter pilot was in training, whether in the navy or the air force, his superiors were continually spelling out strict rules for him, about the use of the aircraft and conduct in the sky. They repeatedly forbade so-called hot-dog stunts, such as outside loops, buzzing, flat-hatting, hedge-hopping and flying under bridges. But somehow one got the message that the man who truly *had* it could ignore those rules – not that he should make a point of it, but that he *could* – and that after all there was only one way to find out – and that in some strange unofficial way, peeking through his fingers, his instructor halfway expected him to challenge all the limits. They would give a lecture about how a pilot should never fly without a good solid breakfast – eggs, bacon, toast, and so forth – because if he tried to fly with his blood-sugar level too low, it could impair his alertness. Naturally, the next day every hot dog in the unit would get up and have a breakfast consisting of one cup of black coffee and take off and go up into a vertical climb until the weight of the ship exactly cancelled out the upward thrust of the engine and his air speed was zero, and he would hang there for one thick adrenal instant – and then fall like a rock, until one of three things happened: he keeled over nose first and regained his aerodynamics and all was well, he went into a spin and fought his way out of it or he went into a spin and had to eject or crunch it, which was always supremely possible.

Likewise, 'hassling' – mock dogfighting – was strictly forbidden, and so naturally young fighter jocks could hardly wait to go up in, say, a pair of F-100s and start the duel by making a pass at each other at 800 m.p.h., the winner being the pilot who could slip in behind the other one and get locked in on his tail ('wax his tail'), and it was not uncommon for some eager jock to try too tight an outside turn and have his engine flame out, whereupon, unable to restart it, he has to eject ... and he shakes his fist at the victor as he floats down by parachute and his million-dollar aircraft goes *kaboom!* on the palmetto grass or the desert floor, and he starts thinking about how he can get together with the other guy back at the base in time for the two of them to get their stories straight before the investigation: 'I don't know what happened, sir. I was pulling up after a target run, and it just flamed out on me.' Hassling was forbidden, and hassling that led to the destruction of an aircraft was a serious court-martial offence, and the man's superiors knew that the engine hadn't *just flamed out*, but every unofficial impulse

on the base seemed to be saying: 'Hell, we wouldn't give you a
nickel for a pilot who hasn't done some crazy rat-racing like that.
It's all part of the right stuff.'

The other side of this impulse showed up in the reluctance of
the young jocks to admit it when they had manoeuvred themselves
into a bad corner they couldn't get out of. There were two reasons
why a fighter pilot hated to declare an emergency. First, it triggered
a complex and very public chain of events at the field: all other
incoming flights were held up, including many of one's comrades
who were probably low on fuel; the fire trucks came trundling out
to the runway like yellow toys (as seen from way up there), the
better to illustrate one's hapless state; and the bureaucracy began to
crank up the paper monster for the investigation that always
followed. And second, to declare an emergency, one first had to
reach that conclusion in his own mind, which to the young pilot
was the same as saying: 'A minute ago I still *had* it – now I need
your help!' To have a bunch of young fighter pilots up in the air
thinking this way used to drive flight controllers crazy. They would
see a ship beginning to drift off the radar, and they couldn't rouse
the pilot on the microphone for anything other than a few
meaningless mumbles, and they would know he was probably out
there with engine failure at a low altitude, trying to reignite by
lowering his auxiliary generator rig, which had a little propeller that
was supposed to spin in the slipstream like a child's pinwheel.

'Whiskey Kilo Two Eight, do you want to declare an emergency?'

This would rouse him! – to say: 'Negative, negative, Whiskey
Kilo Two Eight is not declaring an emergency.'

Kaboom. Believers in the right stuff would rather crash and
burn.

One fine day, after he had joined a fighter squadron, it would
dawn on the young pilot exactly how the losers in the great fraternal
competition were now being left behind. Which is to say, not by
instructors or other superiors or by failures at prescribed levels of
competence, but by death. At this point the essence of the enterprise
would begin to dawn on him. Slowly, step by step, the ante had
been raised until he was now involved in what was surely the

grimmest and grandest gamble of manhood. Being a fighter pilot –
for that matter, simply taking off in a single-engine jet fighter of the
Century series, such as an F-102, or any of the military's other
marvellous bricks with fins on them – presented a man, on a
perfectly sunny day, with more ways to get himself killed than his
wife and children could imagine in their wildest fears. If he was
barrelling down the runway at 200 m.p.h., completing the take-off
run, and the board started lighting up red, should he (a) abort the
take-off (and try to wrestle with the monster, which was gorged
with jet fuel, out in the sand beyond the end of the runway) or (b)
eject (and hope that the goddamned human cannonball trick works
at zero altitude and he doesn't shatter an elbow or a kneecap on the
way out) or (c) continue the take-off and deal with the problem
aloft (knowing full well that the ship may be on fire and therefore
seconds away from exploding)? He would have one second to sort
out the options and act, and this kind of little workaday decision
came up all the time. Occasionally a man would look coldly at the
binary problem he was now confronting every day – Right Stuff/
Death – and decide it wasn't worth it and voluntarily shift over to
transports or reconnaissance or whatever. And his comrades would
wonder, for a day or so, what evil virus had invaded his soul ... as
they left him behind. More often, however, the reverse would
happen. Some college graduate would enter navy aviation through
the reserves, simply as an alternative to the army draft, fully
intending to return to civilian life, to some waiting profession or
family business; would become involved in the obsessive business of
ascending the ziggurat pyramid of flying; and, at the end of his
enlistment, would astound everyone back home and very likely
himself as well by signing up for another one. What on earth got
into him? He couldn't explain it. After all, the very words for it had
been amputated. A navy study showed that two-thirds of the fighter
pilots who were rated in the top rungs of their groups – i.e. the
hottest young pilots – reenlisted when the time came, and practically all were college graduates. By this point, a young fighter jock
was like the preacher in *Moby Dick* who climbs up into the pulpit
on a rope ladder and then pulls the ladder up behind him; except

the pilot could not use the words necessary to express the vital lessons. Civilian life, and even home and hearth, now seemed not only far away but far *below*, back down many levels of the pyramid of the right stuff.

A fighter pilot soon found he wanted to associate only with other fighter pilots. Who else could understand the nature of the little proposition (right stuff/death) they were all dealing with? And what other subject could compare with it? It was riveting! To talk about it in so many words was forbidden, of course. The very words *death, danger, bravery, fear* were not to be uttered except in the occasional specific instance or for ironic effect. Nevertheless, the subject could be adumbrated in *code* or *by example*. Hence the endless evenings of pilots huddled together talking about flying. On these long and drunken evenings (the bane of their family life) certain theorems would be propounded and demonstrated – and all by *code* and *example*. One theorem was: there are no *accidents* and no fatal flaws in the machines; there are only pilots with the wrong stuff. (I.e., blind Fate can't kill me.) When Bud Jennings crashed and burned in the swamps at Jacksonville, the other pilots in Pete Conrad's squadron said: *How could he have been so stupid?* It turned out that Jennings had gone up in the SNJ with his cockpit canopy opened in a way that was expressly forbidden in the manual, and carbon monoxide had been sucked in from the exhaust, and he passed out and crashed. All agreed that Bud Jennings was a good guy and a good pilot, but his epitaph on the ziggurat was: *How could he have been so stupid?* This seemed shocking at first, but by the time Conrad had reached the end of that bad string at Pax River, he was capable of his own corollary to the theorem: viz., no single factor ever killed a pilot; there was always a chain of mistakes. But what about Ted Whelan, who fell like a rock from 8,100 feet when his parachute failed? Well, the parachute was merely part of the chain: first, someone should have caught the structural defect that resulted in the hydraulic leak that triggered the emergency; second, Whelan did not check out his seat-parachute rig, and the drogue failed to separate the main parachute from the seat; but even after those two mistakes, Whelan had fifteen or twenty seconds, as he fell, to disengage himself from the seat and open the parachute manually. Why just stare at the scenery coming up to smack you in the face! And everyone nodded. (He failed – but I wouldn't have!) Once the theorem and the corollary were understood, the navy's statistics about one in every four navy aviators dying meant nothing. The figures were averages, and averages applied to those with average stuff.

A riveting subject, especially if it were one's own hide that was on the line. Every evening at bases all over America, there were military pilots huddled in officers' clubs eagerly cutting the right stuff up in coded slices so they could talk about it. What more compelling topic of conversation was there in the world? In the air force there were even pilots who would ask the tower for priority landing clearance so that they could make the beer call on time, at 4 p.m. sharp, at the officers' club. They would come right out and state the reason. The drunken rambles began at four and sometimes went on for ten or twelve hours. Such conversations! They diced that righteous stuff up into little bits, bowed ironically to it, stumbled blindfolded around it, groped, lurched, belched, staggered, bawled, sang, roared and feinted at it with self-deprecating humour. Nevertheless! – they never mentioned it by name. No, they used the approved codes, such as: 'Like a jerk I got myself into a hell of a corner today.' They told of how they 'lucked out of it'. To get across the extreme peril of his exploit, one would use certain oblique cues. He would say, 'I looked over at Robinson' – who would be known to the listeners as a non-com who sometimes rode back seat to read radar – 'and he wasn't talking any more, he was just staring at the radar, like this, giving it that *zombie* look. Then I *knew* I was in trouble!' Beautiful! Just right! For it would also be known to the listeners that the non-coms advised one another: '*Never* fly with a lieutenant. *Avoid* captains and majors. Hell, man, do yourself a favour: don't fly with anybody below colonel.' Which in turn said: 'Those young bucks shoot dice with death!' And yet once in the air the non-com had his own standards. He was determined to remain as outwardly cool as the pilot, so that when the pilot did something that truly petrified him, he would say nothing; instead, he would turn silent, catatonic, like a zombie. Perfect! *Zombie*. There you had it, compressed into a single word, all of the foregoing. I'm a hell of a pilot! I shoot dice with death! And now all you fellows know it! And I haven't spoken of that unspoken stuff even once!

The talking and drinking began at the beer call, and then the boys would break for dinner and come back afterward and get more wasted and more garrulous or else more quietly fried, drinking good cheap PX booze until 2 a.m. The night was young! Why not get the cars and go out for a little proficiency run? It seemed that every fighter jock thought himself an ace driver, and he would do anything to obtain a hot car, especially a sports car, and the drunker he was, the more convinced he would be about his driving skills, as if the right stuff, being indivisible, carried over into any enterprise whatsoever, under any conditions. A little proficiency run, boys! (There's only one way to find out!) And they would roar off in close formation from, say, Nellis Air Force Base, down Route 15, into Las Vegas, barrelling down the highway, rat-racing, sometimes four abreast, jockeying for position, piling into the most listless curve in the desert flats as if they were trying to root each other out of the groove at the Rebel 500 – and then bursting into downtown Las Vegas with a rude fraternal roar like the Hell's Angels – and the natives chalked it up to youth and drink and the bad element that the air force attracted. They knew nothing about the right stuff, of course.

More fighter pilots died in automobiles than in aeroplanes. Fortunately, there was always some kindly soul up the chain to certify the papers 'line of duty', so that the widow could get a better break on the insurance. That was OK and only proper because somehow the system itself had long ago said *Skol!* and *Quite right!* to the military cycle of Flying & Drinking and Drinking & Driving, as if there were no other way. Every young fighter jock knew the feeling of getting two or three hours' sleep and then waking up at 5.30 a.m. and having a few cups of coffee, a few cigarettes, and then carting his poor quivering liver out to the field for another day of flying. There were those who arrived not merely hungover but still drunk, slapping oxygen tank cones over their faces and trying to burn the alcohol out of their systems, and then going up, remarking later: 'I don't *advise* it, you understand, but it *can* be done.' (Provided you have the right stuff, you miserable pudknocker.)

*

Air force and navy airfields were usually on barren or marginal stretches of land and would have looked especially bleak and Low Rent to an ordinary individual in the chilly light of dawn. But to a young pilot there was an inexplicable bliss to coming out to the flight line while the sun was just beginning to cook up behind the rim of the horizon, so that the whole field was still in shadow and the ridges in the distance were in silhouette and the flight line was a monochrome of Exhaust Fume Blue, and every little red light on top of the water towers or power stanchions looked dull, shrivelled, congealed, and the runway lights, which were still on, looked faded, and even the landing lights on a fighter that had just landed and was taxiing in were no longer dazzling, as they would be at night, and looked instead like shrivelled gobs of candlepower out there – and yet it was beautiful, exhilarating – for he was revved up with adrenalin, anxious to take off before the day broke, to burst up into the sunlight over the ridges before all those thousands of comatose souls down there, still dead to the world, snug in home and hearth, even came to their senses. To take off in an F-100 at dawn and cut in the afterburner and hurtle 25,000 feet up into the sky so suddenly that you felt not like a bird but like a trajectory, yet with full control, full control of *five tons* of thrust, all of which flowed from your will and through your fingertips, with the huge engine right beneath you, so close that it was as if you were riding it bareback, until you levelled out and went supersonic, an event registered on earth by a tremendous cracking boom that shook windows, but up here only by the fact that you now felt utterly free of the earth – to describe it, even to wife, child, near ones and dear ones, seemed impossible. So the pilot kept it to himself, along with an even more indescribable ... an even more sinfully inconfessable ... feeling of superiority, appropriate to him and to his kind, lone bearers of the right stuff.

From *up here* at dawn the pilot looked down upon poor hopeless Las Vegas (or Yuma, Corpus Christi, Meridian, San Bernardino or Dayton) and began to wonder: how can all of them down there, those poor souls who will soon be waking up and trudging out of their minute rectangles and inching along their little noodle highways toward whatever slots and grooves make up their everyday lives – how could they live like that, with such earnestness, if they had the faintest idea of what it was like up here in this righteous zone?

But of course! Not only the washed-out, grounded and dead pilots had been left behind – but also all of those millions of sleepwalking souls who never even attempted the great gamble. The entire world below ... *left behind*. Only at this point can one begin to understand just how big, how titanic, the ego of the military pilot could be. The world was used to enormous egos in artists, actors, entertainers of all sorts, in politicians, sports figures and even journalists, because they had such familiar and convenient ways to show them off. But that slim young man over there in uniform, with the enormous watch on his wrist and the withdrawn look on his face, that young officer who is so shy that he can't even open his mouth unless the subject is flying – that young pilot – well, my friends, his ego is even *bigger*! – so big, it's *breathtaking*! Even in the 1950s it was difficult for civilians to comprehend such a thing, but *all* military officers and many enlisted men tended to feel superior to civilians. It was really quite ironic, given the fact that for a good thirty years the rising business classes in the cities had been steering their sons away from the military, as if from a bad smell, and the officer corps had never been held in lower esteem. Well, career officers returned the contempt in trumps. They looked upon themselves as men who lived by higher standards of behaviour than civilians, as men who were the bearers and protectors of the most important values of American life, who maintained a sense of discipline while civilians abandoned themselves to hedonism, who maintained a sense of honour while civilians lived by opportunism and greed. Opportunism and greed: there you had your much-vaunted corporate business world. Khrushchev was right about one thing: when it came time to hang the capitalist West, an American businessman would sell him the rope. When the showdown came – and the showdowns always came – not all the wealth in the world or all the sophisticated nuclear weapons and radar and missile systems it could buy would take the place of those who had the uncritical willingness to face danger, those who, in short, had the right stuff.

Ann and John Tusa

The Berlin Airlift

On 6 July the three Western allies handed versions of the same note to Soviet ambassadors in their capitals. These laid out protests against the blockade of Berlin, a city which they insisted was not part of the Soviet zone but an international area of occupation where all four Powers were present as a result of agreed and established right and to which the Western allies had access in consequence of their withdrawal to the zonal frontiers in 1945. The Western Powers would not be induced by threats or pressure to forgo their rights in Berlin. They were willing to negotiate on outstanding problems if and when free communications with the city were restored.

There was not the slightest chance that the Soviet Union would ever reply to any letter by return of post. The Western allies would have to wait for a response to their notes, and Berliners would have to endure more uncertainty and more privation. It was likely that the Russians would want to negotiate before lifting the blockade – any talks, however amicable, would take yet more time and involve still more suffering in Berlin. The only palliative for the stress of time was the airlift.

Yet when Robert Murphy, Eisenhower's Political Adviser on German Affairs, reviewed the condition of Berlin on 9 July, he had to report that 'time is working against us'. The situation in the city had 'deteriorated with alarming rapidity within the last two weeks and, more particularly, within the last few days'. Faced with the coal crisis the authorities had slashed power supplies further. Domestic consumers were limited to four hours of electricity a day, on a rota which sometimes meant they had to cook in the middle of the night. Electric trains, trolley buses and the U-bahn (underground railway) started at six in the morning and ended at six in the evening. Buses could not take over: most were off the road waiting in vain for delivery of spare parts or tyres. Generators were being flown in for hospitals, telephone exchanges and a few vital offices, but industry must lose 80 per cent of its electricity. Since power cuts meant breakdown in radio services, the British and American military were going to send round broadcasting vans to relay the latest news. It was painful to see a city which had struggled for three years to restore normal life reverting so quickly to misery. No wonder the British Embassy in Moscow reported that the Russians were confident the airlift could not supply Berlin and the Western Powers must soon leave.

*

Fortunately Murphy's report of 9 July dealt with the past not the present. He recorded the early results of the airlift which had been cobbled together on the spur of the moment with puny resources of aircraft, crews and ground staff, with no existing logistical organization, and totally inadequate airfields and traffic-control methods. During the last week in June, when only C-47s and RAF Dakotas were flown, the combined Anglo-American airlift had carried a mere 1,404 tons into Berlin. In the first week in July thirty-five USAF C-54s and the first RAF Yorks arrived in Germany, but the total tonnage did not reflect the increased number and capacity of aircraft. There were neither systems nor facilities to use them properly.

Extracts from a diary kept by Group Captain Noel Hyde, appointed on 29 June as Officer Commanding Transport Wing at Wunstorf, give some idea of the confusion and limitations which hamstrung the early operation. 1 July: 'Well behind schedule chiefly owing to loading difficulties.... P[etrol] and F[uel] section completely overworked and in a muddle ...' 'Yorks going to be difficult to handle with present congestion on airfield. Insufficient oil and petrol bowser ...' 3 July: 'Gatow asked if we could speed up rate of flow at night to one every ten minutes. P and F could not cope ... Plumbers behind with serviceable a/c [aircraft], chiefly rectifications ... It appears that night flying under present conditions costs us more than we gain because of difficulties of loading, servicing

etc. at night ... Big gap of over an hour in flow due to unservice-
ability and P and F loading u/s [unserviceable] aircraft.'

In those first two vital, chaotic weeks the British and Americans
had to scour their records for men of every expertise: air-traffic
controllers, mechanics, electricians, drivers, staff experienced in
loading. They rummaged stores for spare parts, PSP, radios, fuel
lines, marshalling bats, flares, cords for lashing down freight. They
rounded up lorries, jeeps, cars; signed on thousands of Germans
and Displaced Persons as labourers and loaders; found stoves, pots
and pans to feed the sudden influx on to the airfields.

As if manpower, equipment and organization did not present
problem enough, the airlift faced truly appalling weather. In what
was supposed to be the height of summer there were thunderstorms,
snow and heavy icing, fog if the wind dropped, continuous low
cloud which was often below 200 feet and incessant driving rain.
For three weeks and more, aircraft struggled to and from Berlin
against conditions in which, as a British officer admitted, crews
would not normally be asked to fly. Some American pilots encountered such icing that they had to maintain full power just to stay in
the air; when they used their de-icing equipment, great lumps of ice
would crack off the wings and thud down the fuselage. The RAF
could seldom meet its target of 160 sorties a day because of poor
visibility which prevented landings or because Gatow was closed
while sheets of water were swept from the runway. Tempelhof was
unusable for hours at a stretch thanks to dense cloud or violent
tailwinds. Everyone on the ground was soaked to the skin – little or
no protective clothing could be found. Rain seeped into the aircraft
and engines would not start – on 2 July twenty-six Dakotas were
out of service because of electrical faults caused by damp. Aircraft
and motor vehicles churned the airfields into quagmires, then
skidded and bogged down. Bulldozers laboured night and day to
flatten the fields; PSP, rubble and bricks were thrown down to give
some solid-standing. Crews waded to their aircraft through heavy,
glutinous sludge, then flew in caked wellingtons or boots which
glued or even froze to the rudder. Wunstorf was encapsulated by
the RAF's pet cartoonist, 'Frosty' Winterbottom: a lake across which

a crew had just been rowed by dinghy to a half-submerged aircraft, where they perched on the fuselage reading their manual 'All Weather Flying'.

The only thing not dampened was morale. Men worked round the clock without grumbling or slacking. Pilots flew every hour the weather would let them and took frightening risks to land in minimal visibility. A flying control officer at Wunstorf was on duty for fourteen hours nonstop. Drivers worked for twenty-four hours without a break. Ground staff put in regular sixteen-hour shifts. High-ranking officers stood in the pouring rain and marshalled aircraft or exchanged their warm offices for a freezing aircraft packed with flour for Berlin. US airmen gave up their Independence Day holiday and kept flying – the *New York Times* commented: 'We were proud of our Air Force during the war. We're prouder of it today.' Even when there was some time off, there was little rest. Aircraft and motor vehicles kept up an incessant din. American aircrews lay in rows as Nissen huts were hammered together around them and men clattered in and out, on and off duty at all hours; RAF pilots climbed ladders into attics at Wunstorf to sleep on the floor and be trampled on by people looking for a space to lie down. Other ranks, American and British, settled into sodden tents and tried to rest on the soggy ground. Everyone kept going on adrenalin. Old hands recognized 'a flap' and responded to it as they had in the war; young recruits were excited and keen to show how good they were. On paper the odds against the airlift being able to feed Berlin were impossible; the results of the first few weeks were paltry. The people involved saw only a challenge and leapt at it. Never mind the problems: 'Do your best,' 'Every little pound helps.' Men who only three years before would have set out to bomb Berlin were now using all their skill and energy to feed it. It was a target into which they put their hearts.

And by the second week in July the airlift began to show signs of coming to grips with its problems, even though they were far from solved. Systems for handling freight had been developed, staffs of all kinds expanded, air-traffic control improved, equipment scrounged or indented for. The C-54s and Yorks were being integrated into the operation. On 4 July half a dozen Sunderland flying boats landed at Finkenwerde on the Elbe and next day made their first trips to the Havel. The Russians protested at their use of the lake and claimed to control all Berlin waterways (and they were right), but they were ignored. Sunderlands could carry 10,000 pounds in their lower decks and bomb compartments. Their primary use would be to transport salt – they were anodized against salt water and their controls were tucked up out of reach of cargo so that, unlike other aircraft, they would not be corroded. They soon settled to taking other freight as well: meat, cigarettes, sanitary towels. The Havel made a natural flying-boat base: calm, thanks to the shelter of low hills on all sides, with a long take-off run (often afflicted with crosswinds) and deep moorings close to the shore. Finkenwerde, on the other hand, was not ideal. The Elbe was choppy and strewn with wrecks and rubble. There were no facilities for refuelling, and the job had to be done by hand from 40-gallon drums until REME mechanics brought out a barge with a pipeline floating on jerrycans. Objectively the Sunderland itself was something of a liability – slow and ponderous, it presented scheduling problems because its run had to be slotted between those for Gatow and Tempelhof. Yet it did much to cheer the Germans, who saw it as a sign that efforts were being made and that resources were available. The ten daily Sunderland landings on the Havel attracted crowds of delighted spectators, and children especially were enchanted by this new monster duck.

With more and bigger aircraft and better back-up, Allied tonnage figures started to rise. On 8 July 1,117 tons were flown into Berlin; next day the total dropped to 819; but on 11 July it was 1,264 and by 15 July 1,480. Obviously this was still short of the 2,000 tons of food needed every day, let alone the 12,000 tons of goods in all. Even so, measured against the 1,404 tons brought in during the whole of June, it was quite an achievement.

As the airlift grew, so did ambitions. The Allies were no longer satisfied with just trying to feed Berlin. At the beginning of July Yorks carried 100 emergency generators. Pilots watched with horror as two of these 6,000 pound machines were swung by crane into their holds without the slightest regard for the standard load factor or the usual rules for distribution of weight, and they wondered if they would get off the ground without the cargo dropping through the floor. The Americans and British flew in petrol – a dangerous, volatile consignment which had to be carried in heavy metal drums taking up valuable space and difficult to load and secure. The backlog of letters and parcels from Berlin was cleared and more industrial goods were brought out, though the British drew the line at transporting an upright piano and a baby grand destined for export to South Africa.

Most dramatically, the decision was taken early in July to fly in coal. The Americans had practised in their zone dropping it from the bomb bays of B-29s, but faced at the receiving end with piles of dust they soon gave up the scheme. The first coal landed at Tempelhof on 7 July packed in old service duffle bags. Nobody, two weeks before, had dreamed of bringing fuel to Berlin. Even now no one imagined that they could ever meet minimal needs. Nevertheless, coal was a new demonstration to the Russians of Allied determination and capability, a new offer of hope to Berliners, another way of giving time to the politicians and diplomats to get the blockade lifted.

By October most of the organizational difficulties in the coal lift had been ironed out – but just in time for delivery targets to be hit by the first fog and the grim news that ice had formed on the Rhine near Wiesbaden. How could Berlin conceivably be kept warm in winter, or given even a few hours of electric light? The airlift had barely kept up with summer demand for fuel; it had proved incapable of building up winter stocks. During the bitter cold of 1946–7 Berliners had been rationed to 4 hundredweight of brown coal and 3.5 hundredweight of wood; several hundred people had frozen to death. Next year the coal ration had risen to 5 hundredweight and Berliners shivered though the weather was unusually mild. For the winter of 1948–9 Hamburg (warmer than Berlin) was promised 17.5 hundredweight of fuel per household. Southern Britain (very much warmer) would get 34 hundredweight. The most optimistic British estimate suggested that the Western sectors could only be supplied with a mere tenth of that – 3 hundredweight a family – and the Americans feared that no domestic fuel could be provided at all. And coal supply was not just a matter of health and comfort. It had political consequences too: it could sustain morale which was already vulnerable to the lure of superior Russian rations and would limit the fear which was bound to grow in the dark.

People could, of course, burn wood. It was rationed, though scavenging for fallen branches and twigs might help to kindle a few brief fires. On 7 October the occupation authorities recommended the Magistrat to cut 200,000 cubic metres of wood from the city's forests and another 150,000 from the streets, parks and gardens. According to British forestry experts this proposal would reduce Berlin's woodland by two-thirds and the rest of its timber by a half. Magistrat officials were appalled and the population outraged. Berliners had always loved their trees, been agonized to see so many destroyed during the war and in the battle for survival which followed; the trees which remained were particularly cherished. Everyone preferred to freeze rather than fell. The Magistrat beat down the target: they would agree to cut 125,000 cubic metres of timber but no more. The Western allies accepted the decision: it was not worth arguing when they well knew that even if every tree and shrub were chopped down, the heat provided would be little enough and no electricity or gas could be made. Coal was the irreplaceable commodity. And unless the airlift got more planes Berlin would get no coal. As Washington delayed sending the extra C-54s, weeks of flying weather were wasted and the coal depot stayed empty.

Then, as hopes of Berlin surviving the winter tottered, the situation was transformed more or less overnight. On 14 October the National Security Council advised President Truman that sixty-six more C-54s should be sent to Germany. General Lucius Clay, Military Governor of the Ameican zone, went to Washington a few days later and told the Council how vital they would be, that the airlift was no longer an experiment, that even bad weather would not prevent the supply of Berlin as long as there were enough aircraft. Truman authorized the increase of C-54s on 22 October, and as a first step two naval squadrons, twenty-four aircraft in all, were ordered to prepare to leave. Clay, on his return to Germany, triumphantly announced: 'The airlift will be continued until the blockade is lifted'; winter supply was guaranteed. Even a less euphoric RAF report estimated that the extra C-54s would boost the lift from the previously expected 3,000 tons a day to something nearer 5,000. That was dangerously little, in all conscience, and the report warned: 'At least until January the airlift will be unable to fulfil the hopes placed in it.' But at least it was now possible to have hopes. There had been very few recently.

*

In the early days of the blockade there would have been little point in throwing more aircraft into the sky: the organization could not make effective use of them. By fortunate coincidence, the airlift was ready in October to exploit its new capacity properly. It had evolved from an improvised expedient running on luck and nervous energy into a sophisticated transport operation for unprecedented volume and complexity of traffic over a limitless period.

Sheer experience over three months had, of course, polished flying and navigation skills. Practice had made air-traffic control more efficient and given everyone greater confidence in bad weather flying. The number of controllers had increased, cutting the strain of the work and the risk of mistakes from tiredness, and their burdens had been eased in mid-September by the loan of eighteen experienced men from the American Civil Aeronautics Administration. Everyone engaged in the airlift now had regular shifts and periods of leave in requisitioned hotels for proper rest and real nights' sleep from time to time. New crews from Britain were better briefed than their predecessors who had had to learn on the job. In October the USAF opened a school in Great Falls, Montana, to teach up to a hundred crews a month instrument flying along a 'Little Corridor'. There was even a trained team of RAF falcons at Gatow to keep the local bird population in order.

A much greater hazard to the airlift than the feathered kind had been eradicated, thanks to a frightening experience on, of all days,

Friday 13 August. During those twenty-four hours Berlin had its worst storms for thirty years; there were sheets of rain and cloud down to 200 feet, and in eight hours of daylight only eight aircraft managed to land at Gatow. General Tunner had left Wiesbaden that morning in reasonable weather, but he flew to Berlin in conditions of which he remembered Bob Hope once saying, 'Soup I can take but this stuff's got noodles in it.' He reached Tempelhof in a cloudburst. Radar had been washed out. One C-54 had tried to land, overshot the runway and caught fire in a ditch (the crew had mercifully escaped); another had braked hard to avoid the blaze, blown out its tyres and blocked more of the runway; a third could not find any runway at all in the murk and had touched down on a construction site for a new one. While everyone struggled to sort out the mess on the ground, air-traffic control stacked incoming aircraft from 3,000 to 12,000 feet. The air was packed with machines milling about in dense cloud and radio traffic was jammed with pilots trying to find out what on earth (in both senses) was going on. No one dared take off into the chaos. Tunner exploded: 'This is no way to run a railroad.' He grabbed the radio: 'This is Tunner talking and you listen. Send every plane in the stack back to its home base.' There was silence from the tower, then an aghast, 'Please repeat.' Tunner repeated, in no uncertain terms. Everyone else was sent home, Tunner landed and told his two co-pilots: 'Stay in Berlin until you've figured out a way to eliminate any possibility of this mess ever happening again – ever.'

One thing was immediately apparent: stacking had to be abolished. From now on, if the weather closed unexpectedly and ground control could not cope, aircraft had to turn round and take their cargoes back. Furthermore, any aircraft having trouble over Tempelhof or Gatow was asked to go and have it somewhere else: there was no time for complicated landings or room for pranged machines. Overshooting then circling round to have another go at landing was prohibited too: airspace could not be wasted on second attempts. As traffic built up in the zones, landing disciplines were tightened there as well. Tunner issued a threat: 'I would reduce to co-pilot status any pilot who failed to land with ceiling and visibility greater than 400 feet and a mile'; and if conditions were worse, 'I would court-martial any pilot who did land.'

It was not enough to keep the airspace tidy at either end of the lift. The whole pattern of dispatch, flight, landing and turn round had to be regular and clear. After the dreadful Friday the 13th Tunner incarcerated his two co-pilots in one room, gave them a navigator and artist, and told them to stay put until they had devised a proper traffic system. They looped cat's cradles of string from the ceiling, dangled model planes from them on coat hangers and played until they and their toys were practically worn out, but they found a tight and rhythmic system. Within it each airlift station was allocated a block of time for its aircraft to be over the Frohnau beacon at the end of the corridors: six blocks a day for each dispatching airfield into which as many flights as possible could be crammed. Each pilot had to arrive at Frohnau with a thirty-second margin of accuracy. There was a safety gap of six minutes between the last aircraft of one block and the first of the next, and a separation of three minutes between the planes in each wave when flying by VFR (Visible Flight Rules) and five minutes under IFR (Instrument Flying Rules). One-way traffic was introduced. Aircraft from the British zone flew into Berlin by the northern corridor, those from the American zone by the southern, then both sets went home along the central corridor. Aircraft from each base were given their own operating heights and maintained vertical separation of 500 feet in the northern and central corridors and 1,000 in the southern.

The RAF never really liked the system: it was designed for the natural cycle of the C-54 and did not suit the non-standard loads the British often carried or accommodate the different cruising speeds of British aircraft and the various lengths of journey from British bases. The RAF had to lump it: it was clearly the best way to get the best use out of the best load carrier, and it simplified the integration of USAF aircraft into northern airfields.

For all the precision of the air-traffic pattern and the care with which it was maintained, accidents happened. Some of them were fatal. After the two American crashes in July there was a third on 24 August, when two C-47s collided in midair over their zone and four men were killed. The first RAF disaster came on the night of 19 September, when a York crashed at Wunstorf after engine failure and all five crew-members died. In October a C-54, three minutes from Rhein Main, hit a tree in low cloud and rain and burst into flames killing three aircrew. Next month an RAF Dakota crashed on approach to Lübeck in bad weather. A survivor was rushed to the nearest hospital, which was in the Russian zone, but died some days later; one of those already dead was reported to have been an army sergeant hitching a lift to see his wife who was expecting a baby.

Whatever the Allies did to improve flying safety, the Russians did something else to threaten it. In September their air force staged mock battles over Berlin and held three and a half hours of anti-aircraft practice in the northern corridor, announcing the exercise an hour after it started. At the same time they demanded that the Air Safety Centre be given an hour's notice of each Allied flight, with exact detail of the route, altitude and radio frequency, the type, number and load of the aircraft, and the pilot's name. The airlift authorities were already supplying information on time, type and altitude and had no intention of giving more, not least because they themselves often did not have further details until aircraft were ready to take off. Russian anti-aircraft firing went on through October, one day so heavily that all the windows at Gatow were rattled by the shelling. There were mock attacks on Allied planes, large scale manoeuvres and aerial target practices in the corridors. Western protests were met by Soviet accusations of 'mass violations' of air-safety rules and the claim that the air agreements were no longer valid thanks to Western infringements. In the meantime, though many Allied pilots never ran into any trouble, a few came to regard buzzing, towed drogues and exploding shells as all in a day's work.

*

The airlift had begun in June 1948 with three supplying airfields: Rhein Main and Wiesbaden in the American zone, and Wunstorf in the British. By the end of the year there were nine. The six new bases were all in the British zone to cut the length of the journey to Berlin.

While new airfields were built old ones had to be repaired: terrible damage had been inflicted by the incessant landings of laden aircraft on runways meant for traffic light in every sense. The runways at Tempelhof and Gatow began to crack up in August thanks to heavy loads and heavy rain; repairs were carried out in patches and slotted in between blocks of arrivals so that most of the track could be kept in use. The surface at Tempelhof was strengthened and waterproofed with coarse sand, grit, hot tar and asphalt. Construction machinery was hacked into transportable chunks in the zone and welded together on site. A new parallel runway was planned. At Gatow (now the busiest airfield in the world, handling three times the traffic of La Guardia, the old record holder), extra hardstanding and administrative offices were built in August. To make sure the runway would be serviceable in winter, aircraft were diverted on to the extended PSP track while it was reconstructed with Berlin brick rubble and ballast from railways which had helpfully been torn up by the Russians. A surface was made from old tarmacadam ripped from local streets and boiled up with 5 per cent of flown-in tar and bitumen to give it body. Legend has it that the work was greatly helped when a man trundled over from the Soviet sector with his steamroller and that the occasional barrel of tar toppled across in the night.

Gatow had a heart-stopping reminder of how precarious its existence was when its electricity supply was suddenly threatened. Startlingly, the airfield's electricity came from a power station in the Russian sector. Providentially, there had been intermittent faults in the supply (which is hardly surprising if one considers the overloading) and the cables had been modified to allow the system to be switched to a Western source if need be. At 2 a.m. on 2 October the chief load distributor at the Soviet-controlled power station telephoned to say that supply would be discontinued, probably 'permanently'. Four minutes later, all the electricity went off; ten minutes after that a rather flickery current arrived from the Western sector by cables known to be incapable of sustaining the load for long. Gatow officials had one trick up their sleeve: they pointed out to the SMA that British-controlled power stations supplied the Russian airfield at Staaken as well as the Radio Berlin building and some of its transmitters. By noon the regular Gatow supply had resumed. The Russians never pulled out the Gatow plugs again.

*

New airfields, sophisticated traffic-control and all the aircraft in the world would have been wasted if they had been unable to respond to the complex needs of the two and a half million people in the western sectors of Berlin. The airlift had to cater for a variety of everyday needs but also fit in one-off essentials; change cargoes when demand altered; compensate for shortages; and foresee future requirements. All this involved alert assessment, intricate planning and continual sensitive adjustment.

The balance of basic supplies was easily upset. By November, for instance, there was such anxiety about providing winter fuel for the city that the airlift authorities conscientiously piled in coal until there was a panic in the city because food stocks had dropped alarmingly. Even when the exact requirement for a particular commodity was known it could not always be met: for a week in October only 6 tons of sugar arrived in Berlin each day whereas the order was for a steady 86 – refiners had failed to supply enough. Some needs took time to discover. Only in November did anyone realize that Berlin's remnant Jewish population could not eat the tinned meat being flown in whereas there was no great problem in lifting kosher meat. Planners never seemed to bring themselves to make the relatively simple calculation of how many sanitary towels Berlin women required. Other needs had to be insisted on: many people wanted or, if diabetic, needed saccharine rather than sugar (which was a light, convenient cargo), but they had to plead for three months before the zonal authorities would send it. Everyone knew that a low, monotonous ration sustained life but did little for morale; providing variety and the occasional treat caused problems, however. Suppliers of smoked fish were hard to come by and worked slowly; the fish itself was a smelly and unpopular payload, and the day a Hastings crew flew in a consignment and forgot to turn off the hold heating the Russians must have thought the Allies were starting gas warfare. Honey sounded delicious but was packed in containers which oozed all over Lübeck. It took nearly four months of scrounging ingredients and negotiating with manufacturers before anyone could be certain that Berlin children would get a little chocolate for Christmas.

Some necessities would never have occurred to the male bureaucrats and military men: how, for example, Berliners could 'Make do and Mend'. An air commodore suddenly had the bright but very masculine idea that 'it would help to keep German women occupied during the winter if they can be given facilities for making clothes', and then the airlift planners went mad and put in a monthly order for endless cotton thread, 40,000 packets of machine needles, 30,000 sewing and darning needles, 400 kilograms of steel pins and 150,000 gross of safety pins. It all sounds excessively enthusiastic, but who knows off the cuff exactly how many pins and needles are needed every month by two and a half million people? These were light, easily obtained items. Even so they involved a policy decision: priorities, like cargoes, always had to be weighed. It was simple common sense to allocate 9 tons of wholewheat flour for use by rat exterminators in November. It was much more complicated to decide to fly in everything for the renovation of Berlin West power station – each girder had to be justified in terms of a couple of loads of food or coal lost. It was either humane, silly or neither here nor there to satisfy the pining 1st Battalion Welch Fusiliers by bringing them a new mascot goat.

Stanley Williamson

The Munich Air Disaster

On 4 December 1957 Manchester United travelled to Prague to play Dukla, the Czech football champions, in the second leg of a European Cup tie. They lost 1–0, which wasn't disastrous because having already beaten Dukla 3–0 at Old Trafford they were the winners on aggregate, and therefore qualified to meet Red Star, the Yugoslav side, in the quarter-finals of the competition.

The journey home from Prague was muddled and frustrating. Fog delayed the normal BEA service on which the party was booked, and there was some doubt as to whether United would arrive in time to play their next League fixture. Seats were found for the team in due course on a KLM flight via Amsterdam. The pressmen who had covered the match finally reached Manchester by way of Zurich and Birmingham. This kind of confusion, it was apparently decided, should not happen again. For the match against Red Star in Belgrade on 5 February a plane would be chartered and the whole party would travel together and in its own time.

The first leg of the quarter-finals, played in Manchester on 14 January 1958, offered less reassurance than was hoped for. Red Star were beaten, but only by 2 goals to 1, a margin too narrow for comfort when they came to be faced on their own soil, in the presence of their own loyal cohorts, in February. At Old Trafford the mood was outwardly calm and buoyant, although perhaps a little more tense behind the scenes. On the terraces, of course, talk of failure was, as always, a form of treason.

To Captain James Thain, of BEA, none of this was of great moment. A southerner, and no football fan, he could hardly have told you the first thing about Manchester United, except possibly, after a good deal of thought, the name of their manager. So he was far less enthusiastic than he was presumably expected to be when he was rung up towards the end of January by the Administrative Officer of the Elizabethan Flight and offered a 'plum trip' – commanding the Elizabethan which United had chartered for their forthcoming visit to Belgrade.

*

When Thain reported for duty at London Airport, he found that his co-pilot in RMA 'Lord Burleigh', officially known as G-ALZU AS 57, was to be not First Officer Hughes, as the roster stated, but Captain Rayment.

The first leg of the trip was from London to Manchester, on Sunday 2 February, to pick up the passengers. The following morning the party, consisting of footballers, officials and pressmen, assembled at the airport for the flight to Belgrade. To Rayment they were not wholly strangers because in 1957 he had been pilot of a BEA service flight which had taken many of them to Spain on a similar mission. Thain was making the acquaintance for the first time of the world-famous and enormously valuable 'Busby Babes', as they were tired of being called, not a man of them over thirty years of age, a surprisingly large number of them home-grown talent, and according to some reckonings, the greatest representatives yet of the most consistently successful club in post-war British football. Roger Byrne, the captain, Manchester born, recently married and at twenty-eight one of the veterans of the side; Duncan Edwards, twenty-three, a Midlander, once the youngest footballer ever to play for England; Jackie Blanchflower, brother of Tottenham Hotspurs' Danny, and an Irish international; Eddie Colman, twenty-one, discovered as a schoolboy in Salford, just across the Irwell; Mark Jones, twenty-four, another schoolboy discovery, from Barnsley; David Pegg, twenty-two, an international and son of a Doncaster miner; Bill Foulkes, formerly a miner himself; Harry Gregg, goalkeeper, recently acquired from Doncaster for £23,000, in place of the injured Wood; Tommy Taylor, newly engaged to be married, transferred four years ago from Barnsley for £29,999, the most costly member of the side; Dennis Viollet, Bobby Charlton, Bill Whelan, Geoff Bent ... the 'Busby Babes', alternatively and incongruously known as the 'Red Devils', represented an investment in playing ability and box-office appeal almost unprecedented in British football, and valued currently at around £350,000.

They were accompanied on this trip, as always, by the small group of experts who had moulded their combined talents into the superbly fit and cohesive force which had carried the club so far along the road: Walter Crickmer, secretary to the club for over thirty years; Bert Whalley, twenty-five years with the club, now its chief coach and developer of young talent; Tom Curry, its trainer since the 1930s; and of course Matt Busby, the quiet-spoken, immensely respected Scot whom Manchester was to honour in 1967 with the freedom of the city for having done as much as any man living or dead to send its name ringing round the world. A former Scottish international, Busby had crowned a brilliant playing career, spent chiefly with Liverpool and Manchester City, by joining the rival establishment at Old Trafford as manager in 1945. At that time the club was in debt and its ground unusable because of severe bomb damage. From the day of his arrival United, formerly a good but unpredictable side, had been transformed. In eleven seasons under his management they had won ten distinctions, including the FA Cup and three League championships, an achievement approached only by the great pre-war Arsenal side. With the present youthful team and the skill and experience of Matt Busby to count on for some years to come, there were no heights which United could not aspire to; and whatever rivalries might confront and harass them on the domestic scene their international exploits assured them of the backing and goodwill of most English football lovers.

As was only to be expected the Manchester press had sent a strong contingent to cover the match in Belgrade. Some, like Tom Jackson of the *Manchester Evening News* and Alf Clarke of the *Evening Chronicle*, reported every United match, home and away. Others were senior soccer reporters of their papers in the north of England. Dominant among them in every way was the huge, irrepressible, popular Frank Swift, a star in his own right when he kept goal for Manchester City, now writing for the *News of the*

World. Henry Rose of the *Daily Express*, equally genial, generous, often wildly wrong in his forecasts but a first-class journalist and editor of one of the most widely read daily columns in northern journalism; George Follows of the *Daily Herald*, Frank Taylor of the *News Chronicle*, Archie Ledbrooke of the *Daily Mirror*, Eric Thompson of the *Daily Mail* and the only non-professional present, Donnie Davies, 'Old International' of the *Guardian*, a schoolteacher on the staff of a great Manchester engineering works, who described himself humorously as 'a camp follower of United', and was one of the few men to bring to the art of writing on soccer something of the wit and descriptive power of the outstanding cricket correspondents; however well or badly it was played, the Manchester United–Red Star encounter would be well reported. The press party also included Peter Howard, the *Daily Mail* photographer, and his telegraphist Ted Ellyard.

*

Belgrade was in the grip of vile weather and raging football fever. The army stadium pitch was, in the words of one reporter, 'a real snow heap', on which it seemed only barely possible for the match to be played. On the other hand, the excitement and tension in the city made a postponement almost unthinkable. 'No international match has ever created ... such a mad scramble for tickets in Belgrade. Soccer chiefs from all the Balkan countries have gathered here in force, and officials of the European Cup Committee, whose headquarters are in Paris, have also made special journeys to see the game.' United's unofficial status as diplomatic visitors was underlined by a cocktail party held on the evening of the match at the British Embassy.

The match itself justified all the furore, and most of the forebodings of those who had held United's one-goal lead to be inadequate in the circumstances.

A remarkable improvement in the weather had brought warm sunshine and melted all but a few flecks of snow from the pitch. By half-time United were leading 3–0, but after the interval, in 'a battle of wits, guts and rugged tackling' (*Guardian*), Red Star ruthlessly and inexorably reduced the gap until they drew level at 3–3. Opinion in the British sector of the press box was almost unanimous in blaming the near debacle on the referee, Karl Kajner ('pronounced mud in touring circles' – *Daily Mail*). Red Star's first goal came from a penalty awarded against Foulkes, 'which I am sure nine out of ten referees wouldn't have given' (*Manchester Evening News*). The whole second half appeared to Henry Rose 'a rough, tough tale of tempers and crazy decisions'. Eric Thompson felt that the referee 'would have been howled off an English ground for his niggling, anti-tackling phobia'. Donny Davies, mindful as ever of the *Guardian*'s philosophy in the matter of fact and comment, strove to achieve a balanced view: 'the referee's performance on the whistle assumed the proportions of a flute obbligato, due to the frequency with which fouls were committed on both sides'.

And in spite of the drawn game, Manchester United were once again home and dry, by virtue of their aggregate score in the two legs of the tie; through for the second year running to the semifinals of the European Cup, and free to concentrate on their next hurdle, a match in three days' time against the current leaders in Division One, Wolverhampton Wanderers. In the meantime, for all except the crew of G-ALZU, who had a job to do on the following day, there was time for a banquet and other forms of celebration. United were a team of high-spirited young men, always, in the words of one of them, 'laughing and clowning and playing practical jokes on each other'. In Belgrade, Bill Foulkes recalled later, 'we had great larks messing up Bill Whelan's hotel room and arranging a birthday party for Eddie Colman'.

Captain Thain, who had watched the match and then spent the evening with his friend Captain Rayment, was also looking forward to a quiet celebration. February 7, the day after they reached home, would be his thirty-seventh birthday.

*

The party which assembled at Belgrade airport on the morning of 6 February was slightly larger than the one which had flown out from

Manchester. In addition to the team, the officials, the press contingent and Mr Satinoff, a Manchester business man and United supporter, who had come for the ride, there were now Mr Miklos, a travel agent, and his wife, Mrs Vera Lukic, wife of the Yugoslav air attaché in London, and her baby daughter, and a Mr Tomasevic. The crew of the aircraft of course remained the same: Captains Thain and Rayment, Radio Officer William Rodgers, and a cabin staff of three, William Cable, Margaret Bellis and Rosemary Cheverton.

The Elizabethan, as operated by BEA, could carry forty-seven passengers, so there was plenty of room for the party of thirty-eight to dispose themselves. There were ten rows of seats, of which the four nearest the cockpit faced aft and the remaining six faced forward.

Mr Tomasevic settled himself in the far right-hand corner of the cabin. Behind him was the small galley separating the cabin from the cockpit. The seat beside him remained vacant. The two in front of him were occupied by the *Daily Mail* photographic team, Peter Howard and Ted Ellyard.

Frank Taylor, of the *News Chronicle*, normally sat with the rest of his cronies, who favoured the rear of the plane, but this morning, weighing up the situation, he came to the conclusion that the tail wasn't the best place for him. The combination of February weather and a crossing of the Alps didn't augur well for a smooth flight, at least on the way up and the way down. So Taylor worked his way forward and plumped down on the port side, in the middle of the foremost row of aft-facing seats. Behind him were two rows of seats in pairs, then the luggage compartment, corresponding to the galley on the starboard side of the plane, and beyond that, on the flight deck, Bill Rodgers and all his radio gear.

To Taylor's left, in the same row but on the other side of the gangway, was Harry Gregg, spread out across both seats. Immediately in front was Bobby Charlton and to *his* right, next to the window, Denis Viollet.

Most of the rest of the team were grouped in the middle of the cabin. Looking down his own side, Taylor could see Johnny Berry,

Roger Byrne and Jackie Blanchflower, all set for the game of cards that usually whiled away a plane journey. Not far from him was Bill Foulkes with David Pegg. Somewhere on the starboard side, about half way down, were Matt Busby and Bert Whalley. Passing by them on the way to his own seat Taylor had noticed how tired and drawn Busby looked, and no wonder. It was barely a month since he had left hospital after an operation, and the midwinter journey to Belgrade must be putting a severe strain on him.

The press men were congregated in the rear seats, where Taylor thought he might join them, once the trials of the take-off were over. Some of them were planning to put in an appearance that evening at the annual Manchester Press Ball, where Frank Swift was to be the MC; others would be glad of a quiet time at home with their wives and families. Swift, as usual, was in hilarious form.

As they took off from Belgrade on the morning of 6 February the weather was a mixture of snow and sunshine, but radio reports from Munich weren't encouraging. The cloud base was low, 'practically down to the deck', and with a lot of traffic using the airport, where they must make another stop for fuel, they were plainly in for another landing with full let-down procedure.

The cloud over Munich was thick from 18,500 feet down to something like 500 feet. As the aircraft nosed into it Rayment switched on the de-icing equipment – air heated up to 170°F by fuel burners in the wings and circulating under pressure through special ducting built into the leading edges of the wings, the tailplane and the rudder. They caught their first glimpse of the airfield as they emerged below the cloud to find, stretching before them, a plain of white streaked with the dark lines of the runway. They landed safely, sending great bow-waves of spray high above the cabin windows, and taxied to the airport buildings. The engines were switched off at 13.11.

The tarmac was a morass of water and slush, 'like a jelly not set', Taylor noted. Rain which had continued from the small hours until nearly midday, had then slowly turned to snow, which was still falling. The temperature was still above freezing point, but the air was raw enough, after the pleasant fug of the cabin, to send all but the hardiest of the athletes, to say nothing of out-of-condition newsmen, scurrying for shelter and the promised light refreshments.

*

The passengers, clutching parcels of the usual duty free bric-a-brac, trooped back on board. At 14.19 Captain Rayment, still at the controls and sitting in the left-hand seat, requested permission to taxi. Eleven minutes later, having given clearance for take-off, the airport control tower heard the voice of Rodgers, the radio officer, informing them that 609 Zulu Uniform was 'rolling'.

The throttles were on the central column between the two pilots. As Rayment gradually opened them with his right hand Thain followed with his left, one of his routine duties as co-pilot. When they were fully opened Thain lightly tapped Rayment's hand, which was removed, and held the levers in position with his own hand. Rayment called, 'Full power,' Thain confirmed, 'Full power,' and then, monitoring the instruments in front of him, called, 'Temperature and pressures OK, warning lights out.' The aircraft accelerated, with Thain calling out the speed in knots. An uneven note in the engine noise caught his attention, and he had just time to see the indicators on the pressure gauges fluctuating when he felt a stinging blow on the knuckles of his left hand. Rayment had whipped the throttles back, calling, 'Abandon take-off.' Thain asked no questions but gripped the control column and helped to hold it fully forward while Rayment applied the brakes. Forty seconds after the start of the take-off the aircraft had slowed almost to a halt. Thain ruefully sucked his bruised knuckles and swore mildly. Rayment apologized. There hadn't been time to shout a warning. He too had heard the uneven engine note, seen the needle wobbling and taken the split-second decision to shut off the power and slow the aircraft down while there was still time.

Inside the cabin there was consternation but no panic. Cable, the steward, caught on his feet in the galley when he should have been in the tail, had slipped into the vacant seat by Mr Tomasevic. The inevitable questions and theories were flying to and fro. Why hadn't the plane taken off?

The answer, in two words, was 'power surging', colloquially known as 'boost surging', a fault to which the Elizabethan was much prone when first operated by BEA. According to the official explanation, 'the surging is due to over-rich mixture which affects the full distribution characteristics of the engine, causing certain cylinders to operate in an over-rich state. This naturally creates uneven engine running, causing boost pressure surge and sometimes r.p.m. fluctuation.' The surging, it was reassuringly stated, should not cause much reduction of overall take-off power, but because of its nature it gave the impression of unsatisfactory engine perform- ance – and no pilot launching himself, forty or so other people and several tons of metal and machinery into the sky is happy with the suspicion, however unfounded, that the engines are not doing their job. This was why Rayment had prudently decided to abandon the take-off. Thain fully supported the decision, and agreed that with the permission of Air Traffic Control, which was immediately given, they should back-track down the runway and try again. Both pilots knew that boost surging could be caused by, among other things, opening the throttles too quickly. On the way back to the take-off point Rayment told Thain that at the start of the next attempt he proposed to open the throttles a little before releasing the brakes and then continue opening them more slowly.

At 14.34, having once again been given clearance for take-off, Rayment opened the throttles to 28 inches of boost and released the brakes. G-ALZU began rolling.

Forty seconds later the plane shuddered almost to a halt again, halfway down the runway. This time it was Thain who took the decision to abandon take-off. With the throttles fully open he had seen the starboard engine pressure steady itself at 57½ inches, but the port pressure continued 'off the clock', to 60 inches and beyond.

The accepted remedial action – slower opening of the throttles – apparently hadn't worked, and Thain wasn't happy. With the permission of Traffic Control he decided to return to the tarmac for a consultation with Black, the BEA Station Engineer. When they were clear of the runway he took over the controls, finding difficulty in identifying the edge of the perimeter track because of the snowfall, while Rayment for the first time gave his bewildered passengers some reassurance over the public address system. There was, he explained, 'a technical fault' and he would let them know as soon as possible what the outcome was likely to be. Then he resumed control himself and brought the aircraft to a halt outside the airport buildings twenty minutes, almost to the second, after he had asked permission to leave it. The prospect of reaching Manchester that afternoon appeared to be unexpectedly receding.

*

A technical fault, as most air travellers discover at some stage, is a convenient euphemism to cover every conceivable mishap or piece of mismanagement which can prevent them from taking off on time. Manchester United and the pressmen had, collectively and individually, met a wide variety. In Bilbao a year earlier their plane, a scheduled BEA flight, had been unable to leave for home until the whole team had turned out to clear ice and snow from it. Harry Gregg, returning from an Irish international, had flown in a plane which lost a propeller in flight. Alf Clarke had experienced his share of thrills in the 1914–18 war, as a pilot in the RFC. Frank Taylor had served in the RAF during the recent war, and wasn't unduly alarmed by the latest turn of events. As the party trooped off the plane again he told Frank Swift, 'It's probably ice on the wing. We might be here for two or three hours.'

Back in the airport lounge any feelings of apprehension were masked by an outbreak of the inevitable wisecracks and tomfoolery. Swift, over six feet tall, swapped overcoats with Thompson, five-foot-odd. Coffee was ordered, and there was considerable astonishment when, before it could be drunk, the call came for a return to the aircraft.

On its arrival at the terminal building the BEA Station Engineer, William Black, had immediately gone to the cockpit to find out what the trouble was. The pilots explained about the boost surging, and Black replied that it was a fairly common feature at airports such as Munich, because of their height above sea level. Rayment, who had flown into Munich on previous occasions, was aware of this; Thain had landed at Munich before but only in Vikings. Black described the recommended procedures for overcoming the trouble, and was told that they had been tried, with partial success. The only other course he had to propose was that he should retune the engines, which would mean a night stop. Thain rejected this as unnecessary. On the last run the starboard engine had behaved itself, and there was some discussion now about the possibility of opening the throttles even more slowly.

Finally, after consultation with Rayment, Thain announced that a third attempt to take off would be made, and then discovered that he had no passengers aboard. Black was sent to instruct the Traffic Officer to summon everybody, while Thain and Rayment, neither of whom had left the cockpit since shortly after two o'clock, held another important discussion.

'I talked to Captain Rayment about the snow. We looked at the wings and agreed that we had lost the thin film which we had observed before our initial departure, and again considered that there was no necessity to have the wings swept.'

This conversation was overheard by no one, and the decision was imparted to no one, but the implications were soon evident, and caused a certain amount of comment around the tarmac. G-ALZU was by now a focus of some attention. In his first-floor office in the terminal building the Airport Director, preparing for the expected arrival later in the day of Chancellor Erhardt, took time off to stand by the window and watch developments. On the floor above some young trainees looked down on the plane and speculated about the amount of snow they thought they detected on the wings, and why it hadn't been removed. Someone took a photograph of the rather bleak scene outside. An army officer, on a sightseeing tour of the airport installations, had watched the first two abandoned attempts from the control tower, and now took up a strategic position with a colleague, near the baggage ramp on the apron, and waited.

A Volkswagen, carrying two members of the airport staff, travelled down the runway to check that the German Chancellor would run no risk in landing on it. A Convair took off, almost submerged in waves of spray and slush. The routine of a moderately busy airport on any bleak, damp, winter afternoon, except for the slightly disquieting presence, on the centre of the stage, of an aircraft with which all was apparently not well.

As the passengers shuffled up the steps to the door of the plane Peter Howard, the *Daily Mail* photographer, took a picture. 'Another scoop,' said Duncan Edwards, and disappeared inside, where the badinage continued, but with appropriately macabre inflections. 'You are now asked to fasten your seat-belts *very* tightly,' said a voice from the press area. Harry Gregg, sliding deep down into his seat, grinned at Roger Byrne. 'I don't want to die in Germany, I don't speak German.' Bill Foulkes also slid as far down into the seat as his big frame would allow. The stewardess, counting heads, found one short, and a quick roll call identified the missing man as Alf Clarke of the *Evening Chronicle*. A few minutes later he panted out to the aircraft and climbed aboard amid a good deal of banter. The prospect of United's being marooned in Munich overnight had alerted the reporter in him: he had been on the phone, passing the warning to the paper in Manchester. It could have been another scoop.

The door was fastened, Rayment broadcast to the cabin an estimated time of arrival, a stewardess announced that lunch would be served immediately after take-off.

In one respect the events of the next four minutes or so are accurately documented. The interchanges between aircraft and control tower were recorded on tape, as a matter of routine.

At 14.56.30 Rayment asked and received permission to taxi out to the runway.

'Six zero nine Zulu Uniform – München Tower – wind two nine zero – eight knots – cleared to runway two five – QNH one zero zero four – over.'

Two minutes or so to taxi to the east end of the runway, and then the next request: 'Are we cleared to line up?'

'München Control clears B-Line to the Manchester Airport via the route as filed – maintain one seven thousand feet – right turn after take-off – climb on south course inbound Freising Range and maintain four thousand feet until further advised – over.'

A complete power check, routine cockpit checks and then, at 40 seconds past 3 o'clock, '609 Zulu Uniform is ready for take-off.'

At 15.03.06 Wireless Operator Rodgers once again informed the tower that Zulu Uniform was 'rolling'. The tower acknowledged.

15.04.00. 'Munich – from B-Line Zulu Unif—' Rodgers did not succeed in completing his call. 'The last message,' says the official record, 'starts with a howling-whistling noise and ends with a loud background noise after the message was broken off.' This lucid and accurate description of what was heard in the control tower and recorded on tape set a standard which certain other official accounts would have done well to aim at. But they, of course, were concerned not with a physical record, which could be played back time and time again, but with something seen or lived through once, in a matter of seconds, and thereafter to be sought and pinned down only in recollection – hazy, distorted, bewildered, appalled, apprehensive recollection, depending on the station and status of the witness. The recovery, assembly and interpretation of these recollections took years, and is still not completed to everyone's satisfaction.

Probably no one in the passenger seats had been looking forward to a smooth take-off, although they might have been hard put to it to say what they were expecting. For most of them the desire to get the journey over conflicted with an edgy suspicion that it was tempting Providence to try for a third time. 'I felt,' Foulkes recalled, 'that this was it, or nothing.'

Outwardly there was calm. The tables were cleared for the promised meal. The card game was set up again, and David Pegg, who had spent the first two runs sitting near Foulkes, chose to go aft this time and join it. Frank Taylor once again resisted the temptation to swap seats, but unobtrusively slipped his dentures out.

As the plane moved off the immense sprays of slush arched from the wheels again, streaming past the cabin windows and blotting out the view. The speed and roar of the engines built up but not, to the sensitive ear, as fast or as smoothly as they should have done. The starboard engine seemed to Gregg to be 'straining'; others thought they heard the engine note drop.

After clearance was given Rayment had opened the throttles to about 28 inches with the brakes on. The readings for both engines were quite steady. He released the brakes and the aircraft began to roll forward. He continued to open the throttles and Thain followed the movement with his left hand until the levers were in a fully open position. 'I tapped his hand, which he removed. He called, "Full power" and having checked the instrument readings I replied, "Full power."' Temperature and pressures were satisfactory and the warning lights were put out, but at about 85 knots the old trouble began to manifest itself. 'I called "Port surging slightly" and pulled the port throttle lever back until the surging was arrested – the reading was about 54 inches – and then advanced the lever again until it was fully open, indicating 57½ throughout. I called "Full power" again and glanced at the temperatures and pressures. I then looked at the air speed indicator [which registered] 105 knots.' The recommended procedure had worked, but satisfaction over the solution of one problem was rapidly replaced by a new anxiety.

'The needle of the air speed indicator was flickering, and when it indicated 117 knots I called, "V I" and waited for a positive indication of more speed. Captain Rayment was adjusting the trim of the aircraft. Up to this point, although I had not looked out of the cockpit, I had not experienced any feeling that the acceleration had been other than normal under the circumstances. The needle wavered at 117 knots and then dropped 4 or 5 knots. I was conscious of the lack of acceleration. The needle dropped further to about 105 knots and wavered at this speed. Suddenly Captain Rayment called out, "Christ, we won't make it."'

In the cabin at least one alarmed passenger had reached the same conclusion. For several seconds Frank Taylor had been catching glimpses of the port wheel churning through the slush, and wondering why it was taking so long to lift. The feeling that they had passed the point of no return became a shattering certainty when he glanced over his shoulder – he was facing aft – and saw through the window behind him a line of wooden poles – the perimeter fence.

They were already more than 200 yards beyond the end of the runway.

Until Rayment called out his warning Thain's eyes had not left his instruments. Now he glanced ahead and saw directly in their path a house and a tree. 'All this time my left hand had been behind the throttle levers. I raised it and banged the throttles but they were fully forward. I believe Captain Rayment was pulling the control column back. He hurriedly called, "Undercarriage up" and I selected up and then gripped the ledge in front with both hands and looked forward. The aircraft's passage was smooth as if we had become airborne, and it looked as if we were slowly turning to starboard. I remember thinking that we couldn't get between the house and the tree. I lowered my head and then the aircraft crashed.'

Frank Taylor, still bewildered by his glimpse of the boundary fence, felt a sudden stunning blow behind the ear. A playful tap from an overenthusiastic Frank Swift? No, he was sitting yards away. Harry Gregg perhaps? He fought to retain consciousness. 'Now there was a fierce bucking and a tremendous rending of metal with the machine shaking like a wild thing,' he later wrote in his book, *The Day a Team Died*. 'Was that the port wheel coming through the side of the fuselage at me? ... Confused noises, a fearful ripping and tearing and grinding of metal like a giant hammering the side with a sledge hammer.' Then he passed out.

Foulkes felt 'a sickening thud ... and then another one, and then another one, and then a terrific crash, and then we were spinning all over the place'. He saw 'sky, and then blackness'.

To Harry Gregg, bracing himself with his feet against the seat in front of him, 'the plane seemed to start going up, then I felt the undercarriage going up ... there were bumps and then darkness'.

After crashing through the fence the aircraft had crossed a minor road and struck a house standing on the other side. The port wing and part of the tail unit were torn off, and the house caught fire. It was occupied at the time by Mrs Anna Winkler, the mother of four children. Her husband was away, her eldest daughter was at a neighbour's house, two others were asleep and she was busy sewing.

As the flames spread she threw the two sleeping children into the snow and four-year-old Anna crawled out through a window.

Spinning and lurching completely out of control the remains of the aircraft hurtled on. A tree just beyond the house stove in the port side of the flight deck. A lorry driver saw a wheel come off the undercarriage and shoot towards him. One hundred metres beyond the house was a wooden shed housing a lorry filled with petrol and oil. The starboard side of the fuselage struck it and was ripped open. The petrol exploded, setting fire to the hut. Still the wrecked plane slithered on for a further 70 metres before coming to rest.

'The whole aircraft was enveloped with flame, we seemed to be spinning all over the place, there was a tremendous noise and then quite suddenly no noise at all – absolute quiet – most uncanny.' (Thain.)

'No one cried out, no one spoke – just a deadly silence.' (Howard.)

But not for long. Thain, alarmed by the encroaching flames, gave the order to abandon aircraft. Rodgers, the wireless operator, stopping long enough to put off the battery master switch and trip a couple of circuit breakers, left through the emergency window of the galley door, which had sprung out during the crash. The door to the passenger cabin was jammed with piled luggage. Rayment, on the wrecked side of the cockpit, tried to leave his seat, and called out that his foot was jammed. Thain urged him to try – 'Come on; man, get out' – but he couldn't move, so Thain had to leave him and follow Rodgers through the emergency exit to deal with the fire risk. 'There were seven or eight small fires, some of them at the end of what was left of the port wing, and some under the starboard wing which of course was full of petrol.' The stewardesses had already left by the crew door, and Thain, 'expecting the plane to go up any minute', ordered them to get well away, and climbed back into the cockpit with Rodgers to fetch the two fire extinguishers, telling Rayment to hold on until the fires had been put out. Then together they attacked the flames at the end of the port wing. The small extinguishers, quite inadequate for a blaze on this scale, were soon exhausted and thrown away.

In the silence following the last of the plane's mad gyrations passengers nearest the flight deck had heard the cry, 'Get clear, run for it,' and obeyed as best they could. Howard was so dazed that he just 'scrambled about' until he found a hole in the wreckage and crawled out on his hands and knees. His assistant, Ellyard, followed him, drenched in plum brandy bought as a present in Belgrade.

Gregg pushed some bits of broken metal aside and scrambled out, sure that he was the only one left alive. His nose was bleeding and he had a sore back, but he was otherwise intact, apart from the loss of both shoes. Running around barefoot in the snow he found one and picked up the other later.

Foulkes, dazed by the impact, was still sitting in his seat when he became aware through the window of Thain attacking the flames with a fire extinguisher and telling him 'in no uncertain terms' to get clear. 'I tried to get out of my seat and I couldn't. I was a little bit panic-stricken, but I suddenly remembered it was my safety belt. I took it off quickly and felt my legs to see if they were all there ... The plane had broken underneath my feet, leaving a big gaping hole. I made my way through it and I didn't stop. I just ran. I remembered films I'd seen of engines exploding, and this passed through my mind and I ran. I must have run about 200 yards before I stopped to look round.'

Gregg, Howard, Ellyard, the radio officer and the stewardesses, braving the risk of explosion, had re-entered the wreckage and were trying to free survivors. Foulkes, recovering from his momentary panic, joined them. Blanchflower had a gash on his elbow which Foulkes bound up with his tie – the most immediately apparent of his serious injuries. 'I remember seeing Mr Busby sitting up on one arm and holding his side. I ran across to help him, and we put a coat under him. Bobby Charlton was sitting close by, still strapped in his seat. He seemed to be slumped over, and I thought he'd had it, but suddenly, just as if he was waking up out of sleep, he took his safety belt off, stood up and walked over to us. Dennis Viollet, who was also sitting in his seat, did exactly the same thing, and I began to think that everyone was all right . . .'

He was soon disillusioned. In the confusion of that moment no one knew the extent of the casualties, but in fact of forty-four occupants of the aircraft twenty were already dead, killed instantly by the impact with the house, the tree and the hut, their bodies either flung clear of the rent and whirling fuselage like stones from a catapult, or pinned under a chaos of twisted metal, luggage, football gear and churned up mud and slush. They included seven members of the team – Byrne, the captain, Bent, Colman, Jones, Pegg, Taylor and Whelan; three club officials – Crickmer, Curry and Whalley; seven pressmen – Clarke, Davies, Follows, Jackson, Ledbrooke, Rose and Thompson; one crew-member, Cable; and two other passengers, Satinoff and Miklos. The official report gives the number of dead as twenty-one, apparently including Frank Swift among them; an independent account implies that he died in hospital, from burns, later that evening.

A British inquiry presided over by Mr Justice Fay in 1969 exonerated Captain Thain, the pilot of the Manchester United flight, from any responsiblility for the accident at Munich. – S. W.

Peter George

Dr Strangelove

Leper Colony

Aesthetically the exterior shape of the aeroplane was pleasing. The swept wings gave an impression of arrow swiftness; the shining body, of brightness and cleanness; the eight great engines, of power and pure functional efficiency. Effortlessly, matter-of-factly, *Leper Colony* was putting nearly 700 airborne miles behind her each hour, scorning distance and reducing the globe to a few hours' flying time.

Inside the aeroplane the six men of the crew were looking forward now to turning at their Fail-Safe point. They would have to stick around the general area a little longer, it was true, but at least when they turned they were past the worst. These were men who had to pay the price of vigilance. Dedicated men. Their motto: *Peace is our profession.*

The layout of the bomber was essentially simple for so complex an aeroplane. In front sat the pilot and co-pilot. Behind them and facing to the rear were the defence-systems officer and the radar/radio officer with all their complicated, ingenious apparatus. On a lower deck were the navigator and the bombardier, each with his complicated devices at finger's touch. Below them again and a little aft was the bomb bay. Here were stored two thermonuclear bombs, each of twenty megatons yield. Most SAC crews had given affectionate names to the bombs they carried, and these names were usually chalked on the bomb itself.

In *Leper Colony* the bombs had been given female faces of a sort. Their names were *Hi-There* and *Lolita*.

*

Lieutenant Goldberg's attention was suddenly and unpleasantly disturbed by a clicking from the CWIE. He watched with vague interest while letters and numerals clicked into place on the dials, reached for his code book and began decoding. When he had finished, he frowned in puzzlement, tapped the defence-systems officer, Lieutenant Dietrich, lightly on the shoulder to draw his attention and showed him the message pad.

'Some screwy joker,' Dietrich said briefly and returned to the new card trick he was trying to perfect.

Goldberg frowned again, thought for a moment, then switched on his intercom. He said, 'Hey, King, get a load of this off the CWIE. Just come through. It says, "Attack using Ultech."'

King considered the matter. He repeated the message musingly. 'Now what the hell they talkin' about?'

'Attack using Ultech,' Goldberg repeated. 'That's exactly what it says.'

Captain Ace Owens lowered his magazine. He looked across at King. 'Is he kidding?'

King said firmly, 'Well, check your code again, that just can't be right.'

'I *have* checked it again,' Goldberg said.

King gestured to Ace, indicating that he was in executive command of the flight deck. He stood up slowly, then said, 'Goldy, you must have made a mistake, Goldy.'

'I'm telling you, goddammit,' Goldberg said irately, 'that's how it decodes. You don't believe me, you come and see for yourself.'

The whole crew had heard this interchange. From the lower deck Lothar Zogg and Sweets Kivel emerged and crowded with King around Goldberg and Dietrich. Ace Owens, leaving the plane to cruise on autopilot, went back to join the group.

Goldberg held out the code book to King. 'Here,' he said, 'you want to check it yourself?'

King looked at the book briefly, then he said, 'All right, git a confirmation on that, Goldberg. Don't you mention the message, you hear, jest ask fer confirmation.'

Goldberg manipulated various switches on the machine. The

whole crew watched as first the letters and numerals disappeared, then reappeared exactly as before. There were a few moments of absolute silence while they thought about the unthinkable.

King scratched his head. He said, 'You know, I'm beginnin' to work to certain conclusions.'

In the silence of the next few moments, while they thought about it, the expressions of the crew became grim. Slowly they all turned toward King, waiting for him to say the definitive word.

When King spoke, it was with quiet dignity. 'Well, boys, I reckon this is it.'

'What?' Ace Owens said.

'*Com*-bat.'

'But we're carrying hydrogen bombs,' Lothar Zogg muttered.

King nodded gravely in assent. 'That's right, *nuclear com*-bat! Toe-to-toe with the Russkies.'

The War Room

The room was vast, cavernous, with sloping concrete walls that came together at the apex of the triangle they formed with the black, shining floor.

One of these walls was decorated by a series of displays which gave vital information on all aspects of the national defence to those who were privileged to see it. The displays were presented in a series of illuminated charts, and at a glance it was possible to view the situation as it changed.

On the extreme left was a display showing a polar projection of the United States and Russia. This was linked to the Ballistic Missile Early Warning System, two bases in the US and one in the UK. It would give visual indication of any rocket trajectories detected by them.

Next was a display showing the number of SAC bombers available, and their readiness state. It also showed the number of US missiles and how long it would take to make them ready to go.

On the right of this indicator there was a projection of the

United States, extending north as far as the Arctic. On this could be seen any build-up of Russian bomber forces in the north, and also the submarines which were within missile range of the American coast.

Next came the biggest display – a projection of Russia and its surrounding territory and sea. Here would be shown the pre-computed tracks of SAC bombers as they headed toward their assigned targets. The targets could also be shown. Primary targets were represented by triangles, and secondary targets by squares. These targets were mostly missile and bomber bases, with a few radar positions and defensive missile complexes. Some were near big centres of population, some were not. But it was impossible to tell from the display. Centres of population were not shown.

There were also other displays showing global weather conditions, fallout possibilities and the disposition of NATO and Russian forces, land, sea and air, in Europe and the Mediterranean.

The series of displays was known affectionately to those who conducted global strategy as the 'Big Board'.

These men were now seated round a huge circular table covered with green cloth and with recessed telephones built into it. Above them a suspended ring of lights shone down on each man's position. The air was thick with cigarette smoke.

They waited expectantly for the sound of the trapdoor and the appearance of the President's balding head and thick spectacles.

As the President's chair rose into the one vacant position at the table, twenty-two men who were already seated round it rose to their feet. One did not, because he was seated in a wheelchair, which he could not leave without assistance. However, he jerked his head as a mark of respect. His name was Dr Strangelove. President Muffley blew his nose vigorously then said, 'Good morning, gentlemen. Please sit down. Is everyone here?'

Staines, one of the presidential aides, said, 'Mister President, the Secretary of State is in Vietnam, the Secretary of Defense is in Laos and the Vice President is in Mexico City. We can establish contact with them at any time if it is necessary.'

'Fine, fine,' the President said absently, then looked toward

General Buck Turgidson, the Air Force Chief of the Joint Chiefs of Staff. 'Now, Buck, what the hell's going on here?'

General Turgidson rose smartly to his feet. As usual, there was a slight smile on his face. Those who knew him well were not deceived by it. He was dressed now in full uniform and on his shoulders the four stars of his rank gleamed under the overhead light. He said, 'Well now, Mr President, there appears to be a bit of a problem.'

The President said, 'Obviously. I don't expect to be got out of my bed at this hour unless there is a problem. Just what is the nature of this problem?'

Turgidson said, 'Mr President, it appears that over thirty bombers of one of our airborne alert wings have been ordered to attack their targets inside Russia. The planes are fully loaded with nuclear weapons with an average load of forty megatons each. The central display of Russia will indicate the planes' positions – the triangles are their primary targets, the squares are their secondary targets. The aircraft will begin penetrating Russian radar cover inside twenty-five minutes from now.'

Nicholas Tomalin

The General Goes Zapping Charlie Cong

After a light lunch last Wednesday, General James F. Hollingsworth, of Big Red One, took off in his personal helicopter and killed more Vietnamese than all the troops he commanded.

The story of the General's feat begins in the divisional office, at Ki-Na, twenty miles north of Saigon, where a Medical Corps colonel is telling me that when they collect enemy casualties they find themselves with more than four injured civilians for every wounded Viet Cong – unavoidable in this kind of war.

The General strides in, pins two medals for outstanding gallantry to the chest of one of the colonel's combat doctors. Then he strides off again to his helicopter, and spreads out a polythene-covered map to explain our afternoon's trip.

The General has a big, real American face, reminiscent of every movie general you have seen. He comes from Texas, and is forty-eight. His present rank is Brigadier General, Assistant Division Commander, 1st Infantry Division, United States Army (which is what the big red figure one on his shoulder flash means).

'Our mission today,' says the General, 'is to push those goddam VCs right off Routes 13 and 16. Now you see Routes 13 and 16 running north from Saigon toward the town of Phuoc Vinh, where we keep our artillery. When we got here first we prettied up those roads, and cleared Charlie Cong right out so we could run supplies up.

'I guess we've been hither and thither with all our operations since, an' the ol' VC he's reckoned he could creep back. He's been puttin' out propaganda he's goin' to interdict our right of passage along those routes. So this day we aim to zapp him, and zapp him, and zapp him again till we've zapped him right back where he came from. Yes, sir. Let's go.'

The General's UH18 helicopter carries two pilots, two 60-calibre machine-gunners, and his aide, Dennis Gillman, an apple-cheeked subaltern from California. It also carries the General's own M16 carbine (hanging on a strut), two dozen smoke-bombs, and a couple of CS anti-personnel gas-bombs, each as big as a small dustbin. Just beside the General is a radio console where he can tune in on orders issued by battalion commanders flying helicopters just beneath him, and company commanders in helicopters just below them.

Under this interlacing of helicopters lies the apparently peaceful landscape beside Routes 13 and 16, filled with farmhouses and peasants hoeing rice and paddy fields.

So far today, things haven't gone too well. Companies Alpha, Bravo and Charlie have assaulted a suspected Viet Cong HQ, found a few tunnels but no enemy.

The General sits at the helicopter's open door, knees apart, his shiny black toecaps jutting out into space, rolls a filtertip cigarette to-and-fro in his teeth, and thinks.

'Put me down at Battalion HQ,' he calls to the pilot.

'There's sniper fire reported on choppers in that area, General.'

'Goddam the snipers, just put me down.'

Battalion HQ at the moment is a defoliated area of four acres packed with tents, personnel carriers, helicopters and milling GIs. We settle into the smell of crushed grass. The General leaps out and strides through his troops.

'Why, General, excuse us, we didn't expect you here,' says a sweating major.

'You killed any Cong yet?'

'Well, no, General, I guess he's just too scared of us today. Down the road a piece we've hit trouble, a bulldozer's fallen through a bridge, and trucks coming through a village knocked the canopy off a Buddhist pagoda. Saigon radioed us to repair that temple before proceeding – in the way of civic action, General. That put us back an hour ...'

'Yeah. Well, Major, you spread out your perimeter here a bit, then get to killin' VCs, will you?'

Back through the crushed grass to the helicopter.

'I don't know how you think about war. The way I see it, I'm just like any other company boss, gingering up the boys all the time, except I don't make money. I just kill people, and save lives.'

In the air the General chews two more filter-tips and looks increasingly forlorn. No action on Route 16, and another Big Red One general has got his helicopter in to inspect the collapsed bridge before ours.

'Swing us back along again,' says the General.

'Reports of fire on choppers ahead, sir. Smoke flare near spot. Strike coming in.'

'Go find that smoke.'

A plume of white rises in the midst of dense tropical forest, with a Bird Dog spotter plane in attendance. Route 16 is to the right; beyond it a large settlement of red-tiled houses.

'Strike coming in, sir.'

Two F-105 jets appear over the horizon in formation, split, then one passes over the smoke, dropping a trail of silver, fish-shaped canisters. After four seconds' silence, light orange fire explodes in patches along an area fifty yards wide by three-quarters of a mile long. Napalm.

The trees and bushes burn, pouring dark oily smoke into the sky. The second plane dives and fire covers the entire strip of dense forest. 'Aaaaah,' cries the General. 'Nice. Nice. Very neat. Come in low, let's see who's left down there.'

'How do you know for sure the Viet Cong snipers were in that strip you burned?'

'We don't. The smoke position was a guess. That's why we zapp the whole forest.'

'But what if there was someone, a civilian, walking through there?'

'Aw, come on, you think there's folks just sniffing flowers in tropical vegetation like that? With a big operation on hereabouts? Anyone left down there, he's Charlie Cong all right.'

I point at a paddy field full of peasants less than half a mile away.

'That's different, son. We know they're genuine.'

The pilot shouts: 'General, half right, two running for that bush.'

'I see them. Down, down, goddam you.'

In one movement he yanks his M16 off the hanger, slams in a clip of cartridges and leans right out of the door, hanging on his seat belt to fire one long burst in the general direction of the bush.

'General, there's a hole, maybe a bunker, down there.'

'Smoke bomb, circle, shift it.'

'But, General, how do you know those aren't just frightened peasants?'

'Running? Like that? Don't give me a pain. The clips, the clips, where in hell are the cartridges in this ship?'

The aide drops a smoke canister, the General finds his ammunition and the starboard machine-gunner fires rapid bursts into the bush, his tracers bouncing up off the ground round it.

We turn clockwise in ever tighter, lower circles, everyone firing. A shower of spent cartridge cases leaps from the General's carbine to drop, lukewarm, on my arm.

'I ... WANT ... YOU ... TO ... SHOOT ... RIGHT ... UP ... THE ... ASS ... OF ... THAT ... HOLE ... GUNNER.'

Fourth time round the tracers flow right inside the tiny sandbagged opening, tearing the bags, filling it with sand and smoke.

The General falls back off his seatbelt into his chair, suddenly relaxed, and lets out an oddly feminine, gentle laugh. 'That's it,' he says, and turns to me, squeezing his thumb and finger into the sign of a French chef's ecstasy.

We circle now above a single-storey building made of dried reeds. The first burst of fire tears the roof open, shatters one wall into fragments of scattered straw, and blasts the farmyard full of chickens into dismembered feathers.

'Zapp, zapp, zapp,' cries the General. He is now using semi-automatic fire, the carbine bucking in his hands.

Pow, pow, pow, sounds the gun. All the noises of this war have an unaccountably Texan ring.

'Gas bomb.'

Lieutenant Gillman leans his canister out of the door. As the pilot calls, he drops it. An explosion of white vapour spreads across the wood a full hundred yards downwind.

'Jesus wept, Lootenant, that's no good.'

Lieutenant Gillman immediately clambers across me to get the second gas bomb, pushing me sideways into his own port-side seat. In considerable panic I fumble with an unfamiliar seat belt as the helicopter banks round at an angle of fifty degrees. The second gas bomb explodes perfectly, beside the house, covering it with vapour.

'There's nothing alive in there,' says the General. 'Or they'd be skedaddling. Yes there is, by golly.'

For the first time I see the running figure, bobbing and sprinting across the farmyard towards a clump of trees dressed in black pyjamas. No hat. No shoes.

'Now hit the tree.'

We circle five times. Branches drop off the tree, leaves fly, its trunk is enveloped with dust and tracer flares. Gillman and the General are now firing carbines side by side in the doorway. Gillman offers me his gun: no thanks.

Then a man runs from the tree, in each hand a bright red flag which he waves desperately above his head.

'Stop, stop, he's quit,' shouts the General, knocking the machine-gun so tracers erupt into the sky.

'I'm going down to take him. Now watch it, everyone, keep firing round about, this may be an ambush.'

We sink swiftly into the field beside the tree, each gunner firing cautionary bursts into the bushes. The figure walks towards us.

'That's a Cong for sure,' cries the General in triumph and with one deft movement grabs the man's short black hair and yanks him off his feet, inboard. The prisoner falls across Lieutenant Gillman and into the seat beside me.

The red flags I spotted from the air are his hands, bathed solidly in blood. Further blood is pouring from under his shirt, over his trousers.

Now we are safely in the air again. Our captive cannot be more than sixteen years old, his head comes just about up to the white name patch – Hollingsworth – on the General's chest. He is dazed, in shock. His eyes calmly look first at the General, then at the Lieutenant, then at me. He resembles a tiny, fine-boned wild animal. I have to keep my hand firmly pressed against his shoulder to hold him upright. He is quivering. Sometimes his left foot, from some nervous impulse, bangs hard against the helicopter wall. The Lieutenant applies a tourniquet to his right arm.

'Radio base for an ambulance. Get the information officer with a camera. I want this Commie bastard alive till we get back ... just stay with us till we talk to you, baby.'

The General pokes with his carbine first at the prisoner's cheek to keep his head upright, then at the base of his shirt.

'Look at that now,' he says, turning to me. 'You still thinking about innocent peasants? Look at the weaponry.'

Around the prisoner's waist is a webbing belt, with four clips of ammunition, a water bottle (without stopper), a tiny roll of bandages and a propaganda leaflet which later turns out to be a set of Viet Cong songs, with a twenty-piastre note (about 1s. 6d.) folded in it.

Lieutenant Gillman looks concerned. 'It's OK, you're OK,' he mouths at the prisoner, who at that moment turns to me and with a surprisingly vigorous gesture waves his arm at my seat. He wants to lie down.

By the time I have fastened myself into yet another seat we are back at the landing pad. Ambulance orderlies come aboard, administer morphine, and rip open his shirt. Obviously a burst of fire has shattered his right arm up at the shoulder. The cut shirt now allows a large bulge of blue-red tissue to fall forward, its surface streaked with white nerve fibres and chips of bone (how did he ever manage to wave that arm in surrender?).

When the ambulance has driven off the General gets us all posed round the nose of the chopper for a group photograph like a gang of successful fishermen, then clambers up into the cabin again, at my request, for a picture to show just how he zapped those VCs. He is euphoric.

'Jeez, I'm so glad you was along, that worked out just dandy. I've been written up time and time again back in the States for shootin' up VCs, but no one's been along with me like you before.'

We even find a bullet hole in one of the helicopter rotor blades. 'That's proof positive they was firin' at us all the time. An' firin' on us first, boy. So much for your fellers smellin' flowers.'

He gives me the Viet Cong's water bottle as souvenir and proof. 'That's a Chicom bottle, that one. All the way from Peking.'

Later that evening the General calls me to his office to tell me the prisoner had to have his arm amputated, and is now in the hands of the Vietnamese authorities, as regulations dictate. Before he went under, he told the General's interpreters that he was part of a hard-core regular VC company whose mission was to mine Route 16, cut it up, and fire at helicopters.

The General is magnanimous in his victory over my squeamish civilian worries.

'You see, son, I saw rifles on that first pair of running men. Didn't I tell you that at the time. And, by the way, you mustn't imagine there could have been ordinary farm folk in that house, when you're as old a veteran as I am you get to know about those things by instinct. I agree there was chickens for food with them, strung up on a pole. You didn't see anything bigger, like a pig or a cow, did yuh? Well, then.'

The General wasn't certain whether further troops would go to the farmhouse that night to check who died, although patrols would be near there.

It wasn't safe moving along Route 16 at night, there was another big operation elsewhere the next day. Big Red One is always on the move.

'But when them VC come back harassin' that Route 16, why, we'll zapp them again. And when they come back after that we'll zapp them again.'

'Wouldn't it be easier just to stay there all the time?'

'Why, son, we haven't enough troops as it is.'

'The Koreans manage it.'

'Yeah, but they've got a smaller area to protect. Why, Big Red One ranges right over – I mean up to the Cambodian border. There ain't no place on that map we ain't been.

'I'll say perhaps your English generals wouldn't think my way of war is all that conventional, would they? Well, this is a new kind of war, flexible, quick-moving. Us generals must be on the spot to direct our troops. The helicopter adds a new dimension to battle.

'There's no better way to fight than goin' out to shoot VCs. An' there's nothing I love better than killin' Cong. No, sir.'

Frank Snepp

The Fall of Saigon

29 April 1975

From the moment the first military chopper had landed in the Saigon Embassy courtyard around midafternoon, the United States Ambassador, Graham Martin, had insisted that evacuation be carried out on a first-come, first-served basis; the Americans were to receive no preferential treatment. But as with practically every aspect of the airlift, the Ambassador's dictates finally counted for little against the pressure of events. Throughout the late afternoon and early evening well-meaning Embassy officers had persisted in helping whomever they chose in whatever manner they could. Some slipped Vietnamese friends to the head of the waiting lines; others like the CIA Station Chief, Thomas Polgar, shadowed the gates, demanding that the Marines open up whenever they spotted a friend or colleague in the crowds outside.

Finally, one of the Mission Warden officers had all he could tolerate, and stormed up to the third floor of the Embassy to register his concerns. In the midst of his harangue Martin walked in. 'I'm not aware that anyone is being given priority in terms of seat space,' the Ambassador declared serenely. 'Everybody is supposed to be an equal here.' The Mission Warden officer was so stunned by the remark he could not restrain himself. 'Well, sir,' he said, 'obviously you don't know what's happening out there. Every rule is breaking down.' Then, without waiting for a reply, he stalked out. Martin clearly was out of touch, he thought angrily to himself as he waded back into the crowds in the courtyard. The evacuation had become a free-for-all.

*

As I walked past the door of Polgar's office I saw him kneeling on a suitcase, trying to press it closed. 'We're near the end,' he said softly as he struggled with the latch. I asked him if I could help. He said no; he could manage. He was ready to leave.

Polgar sat down at his typewriter a few minutes later and pounded out a message to Washington, explaining he was ready to close shop, since there was no longer any role for intelligence officers here. He then took the message down to the third floor to clear it with the Ambassador. When he returned he said nothing, but merely picked up his suitcase. That served as a cue for the rest of us. I reached under the receptionist's desk for two small attaché cases I had managed to liberate from the litter of my own office earlier in the day. The Air America officer, T. D. Latz, a former U-2 pilot with an Arkansas twang, walked in with two Zenith transoceanic radios under his arm. 'Want one?' he said to me. 'It's a shame to leave them for the Commies.'

'Yes, take everything you can,' Polgar murmured as he booted a small $700 General Electric two-way radio across the floor. 'The agency has already lost over five million dollars' worth of equipment in this place over the past two months.' That jolted even the most anaesthetized among the dozen of us still in the anteroom – the last of the CIA's once proud three hundred man contingent in South Vietnam.

The last I saw of Polgar that night, he was ambling back down the hall toward his office with one of the Marines at his side. He was pleading with the young officer to help him liberate a carton of Heineken beer that was locked in one of the storerooms downstairs.

*

The roof of the Embassy was a vision out of a nightmare. In the centre of the dimly lit helo-pad a CH-47 was already waiting for us, its engines setting up a roar like a primeval scream. The crew and controllers all wore what looked like oversized football helmets, and in the blinking under-light of the landing signals they reminded me of grotesque insects rearing on their hindquarters. Out beyond the edge of the building a Phantom jet streaked across the horizon as tracers darted up here and there into the night sky.

I stumbled up the stubby ladder to the cabin of the helicopter, reaching back to help Polgar's Vietnamese friends. CIA officer General Charles Timmes sat down next to me on the starboard side, along with Bob Kantor, the administrative officer. Bill Johnson, the old experienced CIA hand who had spent his morning chauffeuring the Hungarians and the Poles to safety, slumped down in a sling bunk opposite us, his flop-brimmed fishing hat still shading his eyes.

Almost imperceptibly the chopper began rising straight up. Through the open exterior door, where the tail-gunner was now crouching over his weapon, I watched numbly as the edge of the pad sank slowly out of sight. Then the cabin lights dimmed, and the chopper banked and arched up over the centre of the city. For one brief moment I saw, framed in the porthole over my shoulder, the old Kim Do Hotel on Nguyen Hue Boulevard, my first home in Vietnam, across the street from Mimi's Flamboyant. The street-lamps cast splotches of light along the deserted sidewalks.

The chopper set a course along the highway I had so often driven on those Sunday trips to Vung Tau. As we veered eastward, past Bien Hoa City, the ammunition dump at nearby Long Binh was going up in a succession of miniature atomic explosions, and along the spiderweb of highways leading in from Xuan Loc, I could see literally thousands of trucks and tanks, presumably North Vietnamese, inching their way forward, their headlights blazing.

The Vietnamese woman seated across from me pulled her child closer, wrapping her arms around his head to muffle the ear-splitting whine of the engines. Out of the rear door of the cabin, the lights of Saigon became flickering ciphers as the city receded in the distance.

Just outside the small town of Ba Ria, north of Vung Tau, they opened up on us. At first I thought the fiery stitching in the plastic window across from me was merely the reflection of some interior cabin light, but as I watched, the scattering of yellow and red

semaphore formed itself into a perfect replica of a radar screen. I
elbowed Timmes. 'We're taking ground fire!' I screamed in his ear
over the engine. He fairly bolted out of his seat. 'Why, it's almost
like Normandy!' he bellowed back at me, his eyes glistening.
Timmes had been a distinguished Airborne commander at Normandy in 1944, one of the first of the paratroopers to drop in
behind the lines, and the old soldier stared at the tattoo outside the
port window as if it were some fond acquaintance out of his past.
The chopper groped for altitude as the motors wailed in protest. A
small radar screen behind the pilot's seat began pulsing with a pale-
green glow, converting the navigator's face into a ghoulish mask.

For three or four minutes the tracers continued reaching up for
us, slowly burning out as they fell short. Then there was another
burst off to the right, and I thought to myself, How absurd. To be
shot down on the way out. I tried to divert myself by harking back
to a little game I used to play as a kid while waiting in the doctor's
office for a hypodermic needle. It will be all over in a few minutes,
I repeated to myself again and again, and then you'll be so relieved,
the fear and pain won't make any difference at all.

Sometime after 10 p.m. the chopper began its descent toward
the fleet in the South China Sea. There was a stirring in the cabin
as several of my fellow passengers strained at the windows for a
glimpse of the ships. Suddenly one swung into full view, frozen in
the open exterior doorway. The landing lights were brightly lit and
I could see choppers hovering to the port and starboard. Gradually
we were enveloped by the light, the dull-grey superstructure of the
USS *Denver* folding in around us like a metallic cocoon. A wave of
sadness swept over me. I did not even feel the shudder of the
touchdown.

*

Slightly before midnight Graham Martin, his face chalk white,
strode out into the Embassy courtyard, and with several of his
aides, began hustling the remaining Americans into the chancery.
No one gave any explanation for the move, but rumour had it
among the Marines that a Communist radio message foreshadowing

a massive NVA thrust into the city had been intercepted a few minutes before.

Over the walkie-talkie in his office Martin could eavesdrop on the radio chatter between the Marines in the recreation compound and those in the courtyard.

'Hey, there's another gook climbing over the wall. Shoot him!' a caller exclaimed at one point.

'I can't shoot him,' came the reply. 'For Chrissakes, let him over.'

Given the growing impatience in Washington, Martin knew he would have to put a stop to such generosity. If the airlift was to end within any reasonable time frame, the steady trickle of additional bodies into the Embassy complex could not continue. He therefore instructed Major Kean, the commander of the Marine detachment, to seal off the recreation compound and move all remaining evacuees into the Embassy courtyard itself. That, at least, would make it easier for the Marines to keep other Vietnamese from coming in over the walls.

It was a laborious process. There was little room around the chopper pad itself for all the passengers they counted off – a total of 1,200, far more than Martin had reported to Washington. Some of the Vietnamese had to be crowded onto the roof of the small firehouse on one side of the courtyard. Others were stuffed into the vest-pocket parking lot alongside the Mission Wardens' office. Only after much pushing and tussling was the recreation compound emptied and sealed off. And all the while Colonels Madison and Summers and Captain Herrington, the three officers charged with marshalling the passengers, circulated through the crowds, trying to reassure them, promising over and over: 'You will not be abandoned.'

*

Shortly before 3 a.m. there was another brief lull in the helo-lift from the courtyard. Ambassador Martin, fearful that the US military had finally reached the end of its tether, pleaded for at least six more big CH-53s – a number which, he insisted, would finally accommodate all the civilians in the compound. Within the next forty minutes the half-dozen choppers landed in quick succession. In the meantime, the Embassy's remaining communications officers smashed what was left of their radio gear and joined the diminishing passenger lines on the sixth floor.

At 3.45 a.m., on the stroke of the White House deadline for the evacuation, Martin walked out into the Embassy courtyard, scanned the crowds, then motioned to Colonel Madison. All remaining Vietnamese, he told the army officer, would be lifted out by CH-53. Those still waiting inside the Embassy were to be herded out into the courtyard. The helo-lift off the roof was now to be reserved for Americans only.

With the Embassy's radio transmitter now off the air, Martin's only link to the outside world was the walkie-talkie system which the Marines were using to communicate with the helicopters. By relaying messages through the pilots, he could still communicate with the fleet, and vice versa. But it was a long, roundabout process, and Martin reasoned that by the time Admiral Whitmire on USS *Blueridge*, or Secretary of State Kissinger in Washington could get word to him, protesting his failure to end the evacuation on schedule, the last of the evacuees at the Embassy would be airborne.

As the remaining Vietnamese in the chancery building stumbled into the courtyard, Madison and the Marines were already breaking the crowd down into chopper-sized loads. Minutes later Madison sent word to the Ambassador's office: six *more* CH-53s would be sufficient to evacuate everybody. The entire operation could be completed within twenty minutes.

In that case, replied the office, the necessary lift would be provided.

At 4.20 a.m. another CH-53 came in. Madison and his team flung passengers aboard and quickly sent it off, then waited anxiously for the next scheduled chopper.

They waited in vain. On the other end of the chain of command, the admirals had finally decided to call Martin's bluff. Convinced that he was still trying to stall off a shutdown, they refused to accept his protestations that there were only a few more Vietnamese still to be evacuated. In accordance with White House instructions, the helo-lift was to be terminated forthwith, as soon as Martin himself could be pulled out.

*

Major Kean came roaring in to the Ambassador's office. Bellowing at the top of his voice, the young Marine officer reeled off his message from the White House. President Ford had directed that the Ambassador leave by the next chopper from the roof!

Martin merely nodded and picked up his suitcase. 'Looks like this is it,' he said to the others, and walked out to the elevators.

'I was lying down on the roof near the stairwell, waiting for the next chopper,' the Ambassador's aide, Ken Moorefield, recalled later.

'I crouched down at the entrance and counted off twenty-five passengers. Unfortunately, as luck would have it, the Ambassador was not among them. A few minutes later, as a chopper set down, I rushed that first group across the roof to begin boarding. But then there was one hell of a row, the Marines and the pilots shouting at each other over the prop blast. Apparently the White House had directed that the Ambassador be on this very chopper, and I had screwed things up by leaving him out of the passenger load. I went back to the stairwell to talk to him. I don't think he understood me. He looked at me quizzically – you know, the way he could look at you – and then nodded his head. He didn't understand, but I guess he was deferring to me.

'The helicopter stayed put for several minutes as the pilot talked to the fleet. Finally somebody said to me, "Orders are orders. The Ambassador will have to get aboard – and as soon as possible, since there's a chance the ARVN down in the streets may get pissed off and start taking shots at us if this chopper sits up here too long." At that point I went back to the stairwell and escorted the Ambassador to the ramp. As I lifted him through the door of the helicopter, he seemed ... frail, so terribly frail.'

Out in the courtyard Summers was puzzled. Where were those promised choppers? At last Major Kean walked out and gave him an answer: there were to be no more, he said, except for the ones

for the Marines and the few remaining Embassy and army personnel. When Madison heard that, he could scarcely restrain himself.
There were six more passenger loads, he rasped. He would not leave
without them. Where was the Ambassador? He would take the
matter up with him.

Kean shook his head. 'The Ambassador just left,' he sighed. All
the Americans were leaving.

Madison, shocked and incredulous, looked Kean square in the
eye. *Neither he nor his team,* he said carefully, *would leave until the
rest of the Vietnamese had been evacuated. Kean and his men were to
hold the perimeters until that was accomplished.*

But again Kean shook his head. The President had ordered the
Ambassador's departure and an end to the airlift, he insisted. He
would not defy the President. Nor would he put his own men in
any further jeopardy. With that, he turned and directed his Marines
to begin pulling back into the Embassy.

When Madison, Colonel Summers and the rest of the army team
reached the top of the Embassy stairwell, Moorefield was waiting at
the pad to help them board.

'After putting them all on the chopper', Ken Moorefield recalled,
'I went back to the stairwell. No one else was coming. I turned
around and walked back to the helicopter and got on. As the
chopper spiralled up off the roof I looked at my watch: 5.24 in the
morning, 30 April. From the cabin window I could see those
Vietnamese evacuees still waiting in the courtyard below.

'We flew out over Saigon and I strained to capture a last
impression of the city in my mind's eye. I remember thinking it
could have been a surburban community in the United States. All
was calm and peaceful, except for the fires burning in the distance.'

*

At approximately 5.30 a.m., local time, NVA Tank Brigade 203
crossed the Newport bridge and inched its way into Saigon, as the
squadron commander pored over his maps, trying to locate his
primary objective, the Presidential Palace.

At 7.30 a.m., Saigon time, Major Kean's men slammed the

Embassy's huge oaken doors, barred them and ran into the stairwells. On the first and fourth floors they threw gas grenades into the elevator shafts and pulled the steel shutters closed behind them on the landings. But even as they leaped up the last few steps to the rooftop pad, the panic-stricken Vietnamese from the courtyard were smashing through the doors on the ground floor and surging up after them.

At the top of the stairwell the Marines managed to lock and bar the small door leading to the pad, buying themselves a few precious moments to clamber aboard the waiting chopper. But by the time the last of them shinnied into the cabin, several Vietnamese were already scrambling up over the edge of the pad. Just as those in the lead dove for the wheels, the helicopter pulled off.

Julian Barnes

Fear of Flying

Aeroplanes never frightened Jean. She didn't need to cram music into her ears through a plastic tube, order stout little bottles of spirits or probe a heel beneath her seat for the life jacket. Once she had dropped several thousand feet over the Mediterranean; once her aeroplane had turned back to Madrid and circlingly burnt up fuel for two hours; once, landing from the sea at Hong Kong, they had bounced along the runway like a skimming stone – as if they really had put down on water. But on each occasion Jean had merely withdrawn into thought.

Gregory – studious, melancholy, methodical Gregory – did the worrying for her. When he took Jean to the airport he would smell the kerosene and imagine charred flesh; he would listen to the engines at take-off and hear only the pure voice of hysteria. In the old days, it had been hell, not death, that was feared, and artists had elaborated such fears in panoramas of pain. Now there was no hell, fear was known to be finite, and the engineers had taken over. There had been no deliberate plan, but in elaborating the aeroplane, and in doing all they could to calm those who flew in it, they had created, it seemed to Gregory, the most infernal conditions in which to die.

Ignorance, that was the first aspect of the engineers' modern form of death. It was well known that if anything went wrong with an aeroplane, the passengers were told no more than they needed to know. If a wing fell off, the calm-voiced Scottish captain would tell you that the soft-drinks dispenser was malfunctioning, and this was why he had decided to lose height in a spin without first warning his cargo to put on their seat-belts. You would be lied to even as you died.

Ignorance, but also certainty. As you fell 30,000 feet, whether towards land or water (though water, from that height, would be the same as concrete), you knew that when you hit the ground you would die: you would die, in fact, several hundred times over. Even before the nuclear bomb, the aeroplane had introduced the concept of overkill: as you struck the ground, the jolt from your seat-belt would induce a fatal heart-attack; then fire would burn you to death all over again; then an explosion would scatter you over some forlorn hillside; and then, as rescue teams searched ploddingly for you beneath a mocking sky, the million burnt, exploded, cardiac-arrested bits of you would die once more from exposure. This was normal; this was certain. Certainty ought to cancel out ignorance, but it didn't; indeed, the aeroplane had reversed the established relation between these two concepts. In a traditional death, the doctor at your bedside could tell you what was wrong, but would rarely predict the final outcome: even the most sceptical sawbones had seen a few miracle recoveries. So you were certain of the cause but ignorant of the outcome. Now you were ignorant of the cause but certain of the outcome. This didn't strike Gregory as progress.

Next, enclosure. Do we not all fear the claustrophobia of the coffin? The aeroplane recognized and magnified this image. Gregory thought of pilots in the First World War, the wind playing tunes as it whistled through their struts; of pilots in the Second World War, doing a victory roll and embracing as they did both the skies and the earth. Those fliers touched nature as they moved; and when the plywood biplane peeled apart under sudden air pressure, when the Hurricane, excreting the black smoke of its own obituary, wailed down into some damp cornfield, there was a chance – just a chance – that these endings were in some degree appropriate: the flier had left the earth, and was now being called back. But in a passenger plane with mean windows? How could you feel the dulcet consolation of nature's cycle as you sat there with your shoes off, unable to see out, with your frightened eye everywhere assailed by garish seat-covers? The surroundings were simply not up to it.

And the surroundings included the fourth thing, the company. How would we most like to die? It is not an easy question, but to

Gregory there seemed various possibilities: surrounded by your family, with or without a priest – this was the traditional posture, death as a kind of supreme Christmas dinner. Or surrounded by gentle, quiet, attentive medical staff, a surrogate family who knew about relieving pain and could be counted on not to make a fuss. Third, perhaps, if your family failed and you had not merited hospital, you might prefer to die at home, in a favourite chair, with an animal for company, or a fire, or a collection of photographs or a strong drink. But who would choose to die in the company of three hundred and fifty strangers, not all of whom might behave well? A soldier might charge to a certain death – across the mud, across the veld – but he would die with those he knew, three hundred and fifty men whose presence would induce stoicism as he was sliced in half by machine-gun fire. But these strangers? There would be screaming, that much you could rely on. To die listening to your own screams was bad enough; to die listening to the screams of others was part of this new engineers' hell. Gregory imagined himself in a field with a buzzing dot high above. They could all be screaming inside, all three hundred and fifty of them; yet the normal hysteria of the engines would drown everything.

Screaming, enclosed, ignorant and certain. And in addition, it was all so domestic. This was the fifth and final element in the triumph of the engineers. You died with a headrest and an antimacassar. You died with a little plastic fold-down table whose surface bore a circular indentation so that your coffee cup would be held safely. You died with overhead luggage racks and little plastic blinds to pull down over the mean windows. You died with supermarket girls waiting on you. You died with soft furnishings designed to make you feel jolly. You died stubbing out your cigarette in the ashtray on your armrest. You died watching a film from which most of the sexual content had been deleted. You died with the razor towel you had stolen still in your sponge-bag. You died after being told that you had made good time thanks to following winds and were now ahead of schedule. You were indeed: way ahead of schedule. You died with your neighbour's drink spilling over you. You died domestically; yet not in your own home, in someone else's, someone whom you had never met before and who had invited a load of strangers round. How, in such circumstances, could you see your own extinction as something tragic, or even important, or even relevant? It would be a death which mocked you.

Craig Raine

'Flying to Belfast, 1977'

It was possible to laugh
as the engines whistled to the boil,

and wonder what the clouds looked like –
shovelled snow, Apple Charlotte,

Tufty Tails . . . I enjoyed
the Irish Sea, the ships were faults

in a dark expanse of linen.
And then Belfast below, a radio

with its back ripped off,
among the agricultural abstract

of the fields. Intricate,
neat and orderly. The windows

gleamed like drops of solder –
everything was wired up.

I thought of wedding presents,
white tea things

grouped on a dresser,
as we entered the cloud

and were nowhere –
a bride in a veil, laughing

at the sense of event, only
half afraid of an empty house

with its curtains boiling
from the bedroom window.

Brian Calvert

Concorde at Mach 2

'How do you like your coffee, Captain – cream and sugar?'

We are at Thirty West, the halfway point between the European and North American continents, and the stewardess in charge of the forward galley is looking after her aircrew during a pause in serving the passengers' meals.

Mach 2. On autopilot, 11 miles high, moving at 23 miles a minute. Nearly twice as high as Mount Everest, faster than a rifle bullet leaving its barrel. The side windows are hot to the touch, from the friction of the passing air. Despite the speed, we can talk without raising our voices.

'Milk, please, and no sugar.'

Through the windscreen, between the sloping bars of the transparent visor, the horizon 300 miles away is whitish and indistinct – an oblique view of the tops of the clouds ahead. Nevertheless the earth's curvature is detectable. As the eye travels down towards the sea, the clouds appear to form up into the familiar patterns of North Atlantic weather: a series of anticlockwise swirls of low pressure, with warm and cold fronts spoking out from them. Patches of unstable air lie between, scattered with thunder clouds which, when seen from so far above, look surprisingly benign. That's what Britain will be getting, the day after tomorrow.

Upwards from the horizon, the sky darkens, becoming space-purple above – pure colour, with nothing for the eye to focus on. There is no sense of movement. No rushing of air. No turbulence. We seem to be stopped, fixed in the stratosphere, while the earth rotates beneath. Magical. Somewhere in the back of the mind lurks the wish that this was really so, that we didn't have to come down again – but there is work to do, and the three white-shirted figures on the flight deck get on with it.

No zippered flying suits here, no bulbous helmets, no terse commands. Calm and unhurried, the two pilots and the flight engineer are quietly busy, attending to the aeroplane: scanning the instruments, programming the flight path, assessing the remaining fuel and range, checking each other's actions. The coffee, moving a mile every 2.7 seconds, doesn't even ripple.

Colonel Jim Wadkins

Lockheed SR-71 'Blackbird': The World's Fastest Plane

'I had 600 hours piloting Blackbird, and my last flight was just as big a thrill as my first. At 85,000 feet and Mach 3, it was almost a religious experience. My first flight out of Beale in '67, I took off late on a winter afternoon, heading east where it was already dark, and it was one of the most amazing and frightening moments going from daylight into a dark curtain of night that seemed to be hung across half of the continent. There was nothing in between – you streaked from bright day and flew into utter black, like being swallowed up into an abyss. My God, even now, I get goosebumps remembering. We flew to the east coast then turned around and headed back to California and saw the sun rising in the west as we re-entered daylight. We were actually out-speeding the earth's rotation!

'Nothing had prepared me to fly that fast. A typical training flight, we'd take off from Beale, then head east. I'd look out and see the Great Salt Lake – hell of a landmark. Then look back in the cockpit to be sure everything was OK. Then look out again and the Great Salt Lake had vanished. In its place, the Rockies. Then you scribbled on your flight plan and looked out again – this time at the Mississippi River. You were gobbling up huge hunks of geography by the minute. Hell, *you're flying three thousand feet a second*! We flew coast to coast and border to border in three hours fifty-nine minutes with two air-to-air refuelings. One day I heard another SR-71 pilot calling Albuquerque Center. I recognized his voice and knew he was flying lower than me but in the vicinity, so I called and said, "Tony, dump some fuel so I can see you." In only a couple of blinks of an eye, fuel streaked by underneath my airplane. He was like 150 miles ahead of me.

'One day our automatic navigation system failed. Ordinarily that's an automatic abort situation, but I decided to try to fly without the automatic navigation. I advised the FAA I was going to try this and to monitor us and let us know where we were if we got lost. I quickly learned that if we started a turn one second late, we were already off course, and if my bank angle wasn't exact, I was off by a long shot. I started a turn just below LA and wound up over Mexico! I realized right then that we couldn't navigate by the seat of our pants. Not at those incredible speeds.

'I remember when a new pilot flying the SR-71 for the first time out of Beale began shouting, "Mayday, Mayday!" over Salt Lake City. "My nose is coming off!" My God, we all panicked and cranked out all the emergency vehicles. The guy aborted, staggered back to Beale. All that really happened was that the airplane's nose wrinkled from the heat. The skin always did that. The crew smoothed it out using a blowtorch. It was just like ironing a shirt.

'My favourite route was to refuel over the Pacific right after take-off, then come in over northern California going supersonic, flying just north of Grand Forks, North Dakota, then turn to avoid Chicago, swing over Georgia, then coast out over the Atlantic, then refuel over Florida, west of Miami, then head straight back to Beale. Total elapsed time: three hours twenty-two minutes. Take off at nine or ten in the morning and land before two in the afternoon, in time to play tennis before cocktail hour.'

V. S. Naipaul

Little Bits of Africa on Me

I had never travelled on an aeroplane before. I half remembered what Indar had said about aeroplane travel; he had said, more or less, that the aeroplane had helped him to adjust to his homelessness. I began to understand what he meant.

I was in Africa one day; I was in Europe the next morning. It was more than travelling fast. It was like being in two places at once. I woke up in London with little bits of Africa on me – like the airport tax ticket, given me by an official I knew, in the middle of another kind of crowd, in another kind of building, in another climate. Both places were real; both places were unreal. You could play off one against the other; and you had no feeling of having made a final decision, a great last journey.

Bill Buford

Turin Soccer Charter

By the time I arrived, Mick was well into an eight-litre bottle of red wine. I have since seen eight-litre bottles of wine – they are called Methuselahs – but I hadn't seen one at the time. It was gigantic and unwieldy but, according to Mick, extremely good value. You had to admire his strength; his stomach must have been made of bricks.

I spotted Clayton. He had not brought a change of clothing and was wrestling with the same pair of trousers, now colourfully stained. I hadn't seen him the night before: having passed out early in the afternoon, he had missed the match and had woken up this morning inside a cardboard box.

By eleven o'clock, most of the supporters had surfaced, and it was evident that, although our flight back was early in the afternoon, the day was not going to be very different from the one before. This was a prospect that was difficult to contemplate, but the fact was everyone had had a head start. The quantity of alcohol already in the bloodstream *before* anyone started drinking again was considerable: a few hours' sleep wasn't about to undo yesterday's good work. And by the time the supporters reached the airport, they were spectacularly drunk – again. They came crashing out of the coaches, tripping over each other, singing loudly, zigzagging as they roared into the terminal.

I was tired. I had seen enough. But I didn't have a choice: I was going to see more.

When we finally got outside the terminal, one of the supporters passed out. He had just about reached the bus that was to take us to the plane when he dropped to his knees and fell on to his face, unconscious. The temptation must have been to leave him there. It didn't seem sensible that, in his state, he should be allowed to fly: he was bound to get sick; he might have been very ill. None of this was as dangerous as allowing him to remain behind. Four soldiers lifted him up and heaved him onto the bus.

Meanwhile, Mick had started to act up. I don't know what had happened to his eight-litre bottle of red wine. I fear that he had drunk it. He was on to lager now, ordinary can size.

Once outside, Mick had thought it would be amusing if he made a dash for the runway. He sprinted – a sight in itself – into the open territory of the landing strip, and the airport was thrown into a panic. Someone started shouting in Italian, and ten or twelve soldiers bolted across the tarmac in pursuit of one very large English supporter in a state of dangerous intoxication. Mick stopped just short of the runway and waited for the soldiers, giggling and hooting and pointing his finger. He thought it would be more amusing if, once the soldiers had caught up with him, he then ran off in another direction. More panic, more urgent shouting, as Mick – from our vantage place by the terminal, a large dot in the distance – ran round in circles frantically chased by smaller dots in uniforms. When I returned to England, Mick was to send me a package of photographs that someone had taken after he had been apprehended by the soldiers. 'I don't remember', Mick wrote, 'any of it happening. Isn't that funny?'

*

On reflection, I can see now that there had been more people there than expected. I had recognized some of the nine-year-olds from the night before, and I did not think that they had been on the plane from London. I had spotted Roy, who I knew had not been on the plane. But I didn't think much of it. I had other concerns.

My first one had been retrieving my passport. One of the younger supporters had been staring at it uncomprehendingly when it, along with his own British passport, was inexplicably delivered into his hands. The reason why it was in his possession and not mine was because of the perplexing pandemonium at passport control.

Once the supporters had passed into the terminal from the buses outside, they all made straight for the immigration desks. They were weaving and bobbing and swaying from side to side from the drink, but were nevertheless so purposeful that it made me think that the flight was about to leave. But this was not likely: we were early, and, besides, the flight was a charter: what was the hurry? There were cries for order, but they were ignored. Two officials were in charge of immigration and passports, and the normal procedure was to pass one by one between their desks. The supporters passed through them, but it wasn't one by one: it was in packs of twenty. Turin is not a busy airport, and the two men would have never been confronted by such a crowd. There was a terrible crush, with people squeezing through sideways and pressed on top of each other. I saw younger supporters crawling on the floor on their hands and knees. One slipped through by going underneath one of the desks.

Once on the other side of passport control, the surge continued: the pack headed straight for the gate. The attendants collecting tickets for Monarch Airways were less protected than the immigration officers, who had desks to hide behind.

The stewardess standing in the door of the plane was next.

It was only when I found my place – suspecting that I was one of the few passengers sober enough to discover the correspondence between the number printed on his boarding pass and the one displayed above his seat – that I understood what had happened. It wasn't simply the case that, once again, English supporters were behaving in a drunk and disorderly way. They were drunk and disorderly for a reason: I had just seen what it was to be on the jib.

I reached down to put my bag away and noticed that there was no room for it: there were two feet. I bent down and confirmed what I felt: there were indeed two feet. The two feet were attached to two legs, which were, as I bent down a little further, attached to an ordinary human body at the far end of which was a human face, a familiar one, that, with his forefinger brought to his lips, was telling me not to say anything.

I looked around the plane, which had grown exceptionally quiet: not, I then appreciated, because it was about to take off but because it was about to take off filled with stowaways: they were all crushed

underneath the window seats. I didn't know how many there were.
I started counting them – I got up to ten – when I realized who was
in the seat next to me.

It was Roy, elegantly dressed in a light-blue cotton suit, a white
waistcoat, Italian canvas shoes and a diamond earring. I thought
afterwards that I should have asked him how he got on the
aeroplane – had he managed to get the Mercedes on board as well?
– but I was so taken aback by the fact that he was sitting next to me
that I couldn't think of anything to say. For the duration of the
flight I couldn't think of anything to say. My luck, it seemed, had
changed, and Roy, who couldn't bear to look at me before, had also
concluded, I learned later, that I wasn't such a bad sort after all.
Roy, too, had decided that I was a good geezer.

Matters on the flight, meanwhile, had become strange. The
stewardesses were not supplying anyone with food or drink because
they were refusing to walk down the aisle: the last one who tried
was still shaken up following a wrestling match she had with Mick,
who was now on to vodka, drinking it from a large two-litre duty-
free bottle. The wrestling match had ended up with the stewardess
suddenly disappearing behind one of the seats, with her feet, rising
above the headrest, kicking in the air.

Matters had also become confused because there were so many
people. Now that the plane had become airborne, the feet I found
underneath my seat were no longer there, and the young man to
whom they were attached was looking around for a place to sit. He
was joined in this by many others. He explained to me that, with
no way of getting back to England, he and his friends had decided
to join us on our return flight. Although they didn't have a ticket
or a boarding pass, they had succeeded in sneaking on board, but
then realized that as the flight was fully booked they would have to
hide underneath the seats. It seemed fairly ingenious, but it raised
doubts in my mind about the measures taken to stop hijackers. I
was unable to express these doubts because by this time Roy was
creating a bit of a stir. He had emptied one of his trouser pockets.
In it there were three things: a large roll of twenty-pound notes; a
key-ring, with a small silver knife attached to it (was the Mercedes

on board after all?); and a brown envelope containing a large quantity of white powder that Roy proceeded to chop up. Many people had gathered around, with whom Roy, being a generous fellow, was sharing his white powder, now disappearing rapidly up one of the tightly rolled twenty-pound notes.

When our plane was about to land, there was another problem. No one, from that wayward group of ten, really wanted to climb back underneath the seats, and thus, with a cavalier disregard for international flight regulations, many people were wandering up and down the aisle unable to find a place to sit as the plane descended. One person who was not wandering up and down the aisle was Mick. And that was because he was lying in the middle of it. Mick had abandoned his duty-free bottle of vodka, because Mick had become copiously ill.

Mick's stomach was not made of bricks after all.

Nicholson Baker

Ventilation Nozzles

And on the flight to my sister's wedding, the Bug gestured upward toward the personal ventilation jets above our seats, already as captivated by this trio of motorized nostrils as I had been on BOAC trips to Bermuda when I was five.

I held her up so that she could feel the air streaming from the aeroplane ventilators, and I showed her how they pivoted in their plastic sockets, and how they could be screwed one way or another to vary their amplitude. She made the inhaling seagull cry that at that period signified sudden joy. Our actual vibrating rush down the runway and our lift into flight and the clunk of the withdrawn landing gear did not distract her from her rapt appreciation of the interior invention: a participatory jet engine for each passenger, with a cream-coloured pointed cone of plastic in its centre similar to the metallic cones at the rear of the impossibly heavy GE engines outside, whose turbines ground slowly in and out of phase. It was a calming bit of self-paced instruction in the behaviour of compressible fluids; it was even a useful deception of sorts, since after an hour of feeling that spotlight of air playing over your face, your thoughts full of the remembered sight of contrails in a blue sky as seen from earth – the way they first appear like narrow staves of music a little way behind a very high plane, and gradually fatten into shaving-cream crudities before fading – or of cold rides in the back of pick-up trucks, when your cheek nerves grew deadened to the insistent flapping of a lock of hair that now doesn't exist, or of the print ad for Maxell tape in which a man sits in an armchair and experiences a blast of *La Mer* from his speakers that sinks him deep into the cushions and flings his tie over his shoulder and tips the shade of the standing lamp, you began to think that if the real jet engines were to fail, the plane would float to earth on the output of these tame little verniers alone, as in the parlour trick in which ten guests each use one finger to lift a heavy volunteer – and as the plane lost altitude and the captain flipped desperately through the technical manuals muttering, 'It's *got* to be a bad chip!' one alert hero would jump up and say, 'Turn your air vents to full, people!' and Ernest Borgnine would passionately chime in, 'The man's right! Do as he says!' and every arm would extend, so that from the smoking section you had the impression of an elephant herd reaching their prehensile noses for leafy leftovers on higher branches, and the plane's descent would slow to a pilotable rate, and as we drifted lower and lower over the water, like the brave Frenchmen who crouched in the wicker passenger basket of the damaged and half-empty balloon as it ladled through enormous wavetops in a terrifying illustration for *Mysterious Island* (the nineteenth-century use of wicker is part of what gives ballooning such a Fragonardian, picnicky feel), or like the later Frenchmen who belly-landed on the beach in *Tintin and the Red Sea Sharks*, when we finally slapped down onto the ocean, nobody would be dead: saved yet again by cooperative action and by our own cabin pressure system.

These air nozzles were in fact one of a number of details you could control or adjust from your seat that offered you the illusion that you were actually in charge of the aircraft: the tray tables were landing gear to be stowed and unstowed, the Phillips head screws were buttons that activated various wing lights and radar antennae, the forbidden stewardess-call button released a very big bomb, the tilt-adjustment button kicked in powerful afterburners that threw you backward in your seat, the opaque portshades that slid down from inside the wall of the plane (like the either-or eyelids of one of my sister's dolls that descended with unrealistic slowness because of a cantilevered weight inside the doll's head which I discovered by cutting through the moulded contours of its rubber hair) were heat shields that you deployed as the craft plunged directly into the rice-grain ferment of the sun; and when you were safely through the centre of the solar system, and you coolly flipped up the top on the armrest ashtray, an airfoil flap would unsheath itself out on the patchwork wing, where there were even more beautiful mid-tone varieties of grey than in the nail and screw bins in smaller hardware stores, a platinum-process print of the fields below, and where each rivet had a shadow from years in the airstream; and the pitch of your banked, rib-crushing turn toward home would be at exactly the angle at which you had set the ashtray's lid.

Only much later did I begin to realize that all that childish poking and seat adjustment had been irritating to the strangers in front of and behind me: that (at least on short flights) we were not really meant ever to push the seat to its extreme restful tilt, and that in tilting it way back solely for the purpose of taking possession of a window that had been only halfway in our seat area (the seats and the windows were puzzlingly out of synchronization), we were being rude to the woman behind us, and especially that any rough treatment of our tray-table latches during flight simulation exercises was transmitted straight through seat foam to the back of the person ahead. We were taught the Golden Rule in first and second grades, but it was only after I had begun reviewing TV commercials for a new arts magazine and was flying back from a stormy punctuational session with a copy-editor there – a time when I thought I had lost all sensitivity to the physical interiors of aeroplanes and wanted, instead of thinking about the design of air nozzles, to continue reading Pattison's life of Isaac Casaubon – that I noticed and was first bothered by a rough stowage of the tray table behind me (by an adult!), and even then I initially thought not with irritation but with surprise and interest that my absorption in a piece of learned intellectual biography could be interrupted simply by some dufe closing a latch at my back, and I went on to wonder whether in twenty years, when Boeing was begging for loan guarantees and sleek airships by Daewoo and Honda with perfect safety records were taxied on every runway, the humble latches on the tray table would be one of the first things in the new non-US planes to announce their instant superiority, despite the fact that once our tray tables had exemplified the state-of-the-art Murphy-bed modernism of a design sense energized by the war; and I felt pity and shame for American plane engineers who had failed to see that thirty years of improvements in the on/off switch, the suitcase closure, the cassette ejection system, the umbrella lock, the calculator button – refinements almost entirely of Asian origin, without which we would still be lost in a stamped-steel twilight of toggle switches, too powerful springs and rough metal-to-metal frictive contact – that all these parallel novelties were demanding that we dig deeper and find some subtler sort of click or even a clickless but convincing thumplet, like the final leg of the closing of a mason jar, that would remain undetectable even by a sleeping princess in the seat ahead. And later in that same plane ride, instead of feeling hate for this man behind me who in his late forties had not yet learned to stow his tray table without interrupting the reading of a fellow passenger, this man who was too coarse apparently ever to have been bothered by a rough stowage behind *him*, though he looked to have logged tens of thousands of flight miles a year, I simply used extreme care in closing my own table after dinner: I painstakingly clutched the top of the seat ahead of me and, thus stably based, used that thumb to squeeze the table under the fastener before I allowed it to slide into place, imagining as I did so that I was closing the coffin on the US tradition of industrial design.

And yet, if the Japanese designers did get rid of personal air outlets, murmuring contemptuously among themselves about 'barbaric holdovers from the infancy of cabin pressurization', I expected to feel, the first time I noticed their absence, the same sort of long-awaited jolt of grief I felt when in the early seventies, intent on being a composer, I came across horrifying articles in the Arts and Leisure section with titles like 'Is the Symphony Orchestra Dead?'. Like a reporter assigned the obituary page, I gathered my envoical emotions together ahead of time to be ready for the loss: I recalled how I once tried to stretch a balloon around an air nozzle but was ordered to sit down before I found out whether it would inflate; and how, while my sister was occupied with a connect-the-dot book, I very stealthily stole her air and aimed it so that I could revel in a twin convergence; and how, pretending to study the stewardess-call button, I pointed my mother's, my sister's, and my own nozzles toward my sister and turned them all on full, so that the corner of her half-connected rabbit page flapped out of control. As soon as I was sure she was going to cry, I returned nonchalantly to *The Family of Man*, feigning interest in the shots of dust bowls and calloused hands, but in fact fixing in my mind the straining images of the childbirth sequence – the incredible full-lipped ugly powerful arousing frown of the woman pushing amid the hospital sheets – for it, along with a pen-and-ink drawing in a Dover book of Heinrich Kley's drawings, showing a tribal woman giving suck to a foot-and-a-half-tall baby elephant at each full breast, their squeezed mammalian yieldingness beautifully captured by repeatedly sinuous pen strokes, was my pornography between the ages of seven and nine. But despite hundreds of examples of calculated meanness to my sister, on aeroplanes, on car rides, at dinner tables, she still loved me enough to invite me to her wedding; indeed, she wanted me to be one of the people who read a little biblical something at the ceremony; and it was only on the way to this wedding, holding my Bug, the product of my own marriage, up to the air vent above us and seeing how entranced she was by it, that my appreciation of it and the screws and the footrest and the tufted-cloud design on the wall that separated us from first-class passengers, and the portshades and the ashtrays, all returned; and I wondered for the first time whether the shape of the nozzle's inner cone was in fact more than decorative, whether it functioned aerodynamically to focus the outflow into a coherent column and allowed it to continue, even at the hissiest stage near shutoff, to offer a palpable incumbency of coolness – unlike the gun-sprayers on garden hoses, which just before the flow of water was completely cut off created instead a Panamanian circular fan of mist on a plane perpendicular to the direction you were pointing the hose, so that you couldn't mist the delicate poppy three feet in front of you unless you aimed away from it and misted yourself as well, or else strengthened your grip on the sprayer's handle so that the flow became injuriously direct. In the hectic last months of design, had the same engineer who had just finished putting the final touches on the turbine's taper been hired away from GE and assigned the cabin details, and had he miniaturized the same principle, smiling to himself?

Participating in my sister's wedding made my own marriage more fixed and comprehensible; I had to be jostled from behind before I took care with the tray table myself; I had to see my Bug love the air nozzle before my own curiosity about it revived. And in holding the Bug up until my arms trembled, I thought I felt the force of some wider, more emotional golden rule that stated that only after having experienced something from both sides – breaking up with someone and being yourself broken up with, and even being born and later assisting at a birth were other examples – did you stand any chance of understanding the event fully. But then, immediately afterward, I was embarrassed, because I realized that this 'both sides' idea, which I thought was the outcome of an upsurge of personal feeling at travelling to my sister's wedding and showing the Bug the air vent, was due mainly to the Joni Mitchell song about clouds and dual perspectives that I must have heard (since I now discovered that I had been humming it to myself for over an hour) on the airport Muzak while we were waiting to board.

Permission acknowledgements

The editor and publisher have made every effort to trace copyright holders. If any have been inadvertently overlooked, we shall be pleased to make restitution at the earliest opportunity.

'Mr Butteridge's First Flight' from *The War in the Air*. Originally published by George Bell and Sons, London 1908. Copyright © The Literary Executors of the Estate of H. G. Wells. Reprinted by permission of A. P. Watt Ltd. on behalf of the Literary Executors of the Estate of H. G. Wells.

'Alcock and Brown over the Atlantic' from *The Flight of Alcock and Brown*. Originally published by Putnam, London 1955. Now o/p.

'Rumpties' from *Winged Victory*. Originally published by Jonathan Cape, London 1934. Now published by Ashford, Buchan and Enright.

'Air Observer at Amiens' from *Sagittarius Rising*. Originally published by Peter Davies, London 1936. Now published by Greenhill Books (h/b) and Warner Books (p/b). Copyright © Cecil Lewis 1936. Reprinted with the permission of Greenhill Books.

'An Irish Airman Foresees His Death' from *The Collected Poems of W. B. Yeats* (Second Edition). Originally published by Macmillan, London 1950. Now published by Macmillan. Reprinted with the permission of A. P. Watt Ltd. on behalf of Michael Yeats.

'Happy Landing on Helvellyn' originally published by the *Guardian*, December 1986.

'Biggles Shoots the Falls' from *Biggles and the Cruise of the Condor*. Originally published by John Hamilton, London 1933. Now published by

'The Battle of France' from *Fighter Pilot*. Originally published by B. T. Batsford, London 1941. Now published by Leo Cooper. Copyright © The Executors of the late Paul Richey. Reprinted with the permission of Leo Cooper.

'Love in the Blitz' from *The Heat of the Day*. Originally published by Jonathan Cape, London 1949. Now published by Cape (h/b) and Penguin (p/b). Copyright © Elizabeth Bowen 1948, renewed by Spencer Curtis Brown and Graham Watson 1976. Reprinted with the permission of Jonathan Cape on behalf of the Estate of Elizabeth Bowen.

'Lancaster Navigator' from *No Moon Tonight*. Originally published by Angus and Robertson, London 1956. Now published by Goodall/Air Data Publications. Copyright © Don Charlwood 1956. Reprinted with the permission of Air Data Publications Ltd.

'Eighth Air Force' and 'A Front' from *The Complete Poems of Randall Jarrell*. Originally published by Faber and Faber, London 1969. Reprinted with the permission of Faber and Faber.

'The Battle of Athens' from *Going Solo*. Originally published by Jonathan Cape Ltd. Now published by Penguin Books Ltd. Copyright © Roald Dahl 1986. Reprinted by permission of David Higham Associates.

'The Möhne Dam' from *Enemy Coast Ahead*. Originally published by Michael Joseph, London 1946. Now published by Bridge Books (h/b) and Goodall/Air Data Publications (p/b). Copyright © The Royal Air Force Museum, Hendon 1946. Reprinted with the permission of David Higham Associates.

'The Ratio' and 'The Siege of Malta' from *The Collected Poems of John Pudney*. Originally published by Putnam, London 1957. Reprinted with the permission of David Higham Associates.

'Landscape; Open Cockpit; Solitude' from *Flights of Passage*. Originally published by Bloomsbury Publishing PLC, London 1989. Copyright © Samuel Hynes 1989.

'Milo Minderbinder' from *Catch-22*. Originally published by Jonathan

Cape. Now published by Black Swan. Copyright © Joseph Heller 1955, 1961. Reprinted by permission of A. M. Heath and Co. Ltd.

'The Black Widow' originally published in *Collier's Magazine*, January 1945. Subsequently collected in *The Face of War*, first edition published by Rupert Hart-Davis, London 1959. Current edition published by Granta Publications. Copyright © Martha Gellhorn 1945. Reprinted with the permission of Aitken and Stone Ltd.

'The Bermuda Triangle' from *The Bermuda Triangle*. Originally published by Souvenir Press, London 1975. Copyright © Charles Berlitz 1974. Reprinted with the permission of Souvenir Press Ltd.

'Empire Flying Boat' from *Beyond the Blue Horizon*. Originally published by William Heinemann Ltd., London 1986. Now published by Penguin Books. Copyright © Alexander Frater 1986. Reproduced by permission of the author c/o Rogers, Coleridge and White Ltd., 20 Powis Mews, London W11 1JN.

'Howard Hughes and the Spruce Goose' from *Howard Hughes and the Spruce Goose*, first published by TAB Books in 1981. Copyright © TAB Books, Inc. 1981. Reproduced by permission of McGraw-Hill, Inc.

'Breaking the Sound Barrier' from *Yeager*. Originally published by Century, London 1986. Copyright © Chuck Yeager and Leo Janos 1986. Reprinted with the permission of Random House UK Limited.

'The Right Stuff' from *The Right Stuff*, first published by Jonathan Cape in 1980. Now published in paperback by Picador. Reprinted by permission of the Peters, Fraser and Dunlop Group Ltd.

'The Berlin Airlift' from *The Berlin Blockade*, originally published by Hodder and Stoughton, London 1988. Copyright © 1988 by Ann and John Tusa. Reprinted by permission of Hodder and Stoughton.

'The Munich Air Disaster' from *The Munich Air Disaster*. Originally published by Cassirer, 1973. Copyright © Stanley Williamson and Mrs R. V. Thain. Reprinted with the permission of Stanley Williamson.

'Dr Strangelove' from *Dr Strangelove, or How I Learned to Stop Worrying and Love the Bomb*. Originally published by Transworld Publishers, Uxbridge 1963. Copyright © The late Peter George 1963. Reprinted with the permission of A. M. Heath and Company Ltd.

'The General Goes Zapping Charlie Cong' originally published in the *Sunday Times* 5 June 1966. Copyright © Times Newspapers Ltd. 1966.

'The Fall of Saigon' from *Decent Interval*. Originally published by Penguin Books, Harmondsworth 1980. Copyright © 1977 by Frank W. Snepp, III. Reprinted by permission of Random House, Inc.

'Fear of Flying' from *Staring at the Sun*. Originally published by Jonathan Cape, London 1986. Now published by Picador. Copyright © Julian Barnes 1986. Reprinted by permission of Peters, Fraser and Dunlop Group Ltd.

'Flying to Belfast, 1977' from *A Martian Sends a Postcard Home*. Originally published by Oxford University Press, Oxford 1979. Reprinted from *A Martian Sends a Postcard Home* by Craig Raine (1979) by permission of Oxford University Press.

'Concorde at Mach 2' from *Flying Concorde*. Originally published by Airlife Publishing, Shrewsbury 1981. Copyright © Brian Calvert 1981. Reprinted with permission of Airlife Publishing.

'Lockheed SR-71 "Blackbird": The World's Fastest Plane' from *Skunk Works* by Ben Rich and Leo Janos. Originally published by Warner Books, London 1994. Copyright © Ben C. Rich 1994. Reprinted with the permission of Little, Brown and Company (UK).

'Little Bits of Africa on Me' from *A Bend in the River*. Originally published by André Deutsch, London 1979. Now published by Penguin Books. Copyright © V. S. Naipaul 1979. Reprinted by permission of Aitken and Stone Ltd.

'Turin Soccer Charter' from *Among the Thugs*. Originally published by Secker and Warburg, London 1991. Now published by Mandarin. Copyright © Bill Buford 1991. Reprinted with the permission of Reed Books.

'Ventilation Nozzles' from *Room Temperature*. Originally published by Granta Books, Cambridge 1990. Copyright © Nicholson Baker, 1984, 1990. Reproduced by permission of the author c/o Rogers, Coleridge and White Ltd., 20 Powis Mews, London W11 1JN in association with Melanie Jackson Agency, 250 West 57th Street, Suite 1119, New York, NY 10107, USA.